FLORIDA STATE
UNIVERSITY LIBRARIES

SEP 18 2000

TALLAHASSEE, FLORIDA

Central and Southeastern Europe in Transition

Central and Southeastern Europe in Transition

Perspectives on Success and Failure Since 1989

Edited by
Hall Gardner

*With the Assistance of Elinore Schaffer
and Oleg Kobtzeff*

**Westport, Connecticut
London**

Library of Congress Cataloging-in-Publication Data

Central and southeastern Europe in transition : perspectives on success and failure since 1989 / edited by Hall Gardner with the assistance of Elinore Schaffer and Oleg Kobtzeff ; foreword by Lee W. Huebner
    p. cm.
  Includes bibliographical references and index.
  ISBN 0–275–96460–4 (alk. paper)
  1. Europe, Eastern—History—1989– I. Gardner, Hall. II. Schaffer, Elinore. III. Kobtzeff, Oleg.
  DJK51.C453 2000
  947′.009′049—dc21   99–055873

British Library Cataloguing in Publication Data is available.

Copyright © 2000 by Hall Gardner

All rights reserved. No portion of this book may be reproduced, by any process or technique, without the express written consent of the publisher.

Library of Congress Catalog Card Number: 99–055873
ISBN: 0–275–96460–4

First published in 2000

Praeger Publishers, 88 Post Road West, Westport, CT 06881
An imprint of Greenwood Publishing Group, Inc.
www.praeger.com

Printed in the United States of America

The paper used in this book complies with the Permanent Paper Standard issued by the National Information Standards Organization (Z39.48–1984).

10 9 8 7 6 5 4 3 2 1

Contents

Foreword
Lee W. Huebner   vii

Acknowledgments   xi

Introduction
Hall Gardner   1

1. In Search of East-Central Europe: Ten Years After
Jacques Rupnik   5

2. The Balkans: A Distorted, Third World Reflection of Europe
Catherine Durandin   21

3. Rusty Ottoman Keys to the Balkans of Today
Bernard Lory   31

4. The Role of Culture under the Communist and Post-Communist Eras
Antonin Liehm   43

5. The Transformation of the Media in Post-Communist Central Europe
Marcin Frybes   51

6. The Media in Transition in Southern Central Europe
Helen Darbishire   61

7. A Balance of Economic Reforms in Central and Eastern Europe
Nadège Ragaru 75

8. Ulysses and the Lotus Eaters
Michel Koutouzis 97

9. Environmental Security and Civil Society
Oleg Kobtzeff 113

10. The Genesis of NATO Enlargement and of War "over" Kosovo
Hall Gardner 151

Bibliography 187

Name Index 199

Subject Index 203

Contributors and Editors 209

Foreword

Lee W. Huebner

The revolution which has been taking place in Central and Southeastern Europe over the past decade marks an extraordinary and, indeed, an unprecedented passage in human history. Rarely if ever has so large and so diverse a region experienced such fundamental political and economic changes in such a relatively short period of time. The challenge of those changes has been compounded, moreover, by the fact that they have come at a time of unprecedented technological and social change in the rest of the world. If one of the major themes of the 1990s has been the story of formerly communist countries rejoining the non-communist world and its market-oriented democratic systems, then it must also be noted that those systems themselves, simultaneously, were being reshaped in very important ways.

It is a pleasure to welcome the publication of this book, not only because of the insights it brings to bear on the continuing evolution of Central and Southeastern Europe and on the global context in which it is occurring, but also because the process by which this collection has been produced has itself been so interesting.

An unusual set of creative partnerships lies behind the publication of this volume. The essential ingredient at its core, of course, is the talent and experience of an impressive and highly diverse group of experts whose work appears in this volume, along with the commitment and energy of those who, in the Spring of 1998, first assembled and organized these observers into an effective team.

A second indispensable element in the equation has been the Department of International Affairs at the American University of Paris. The faculty and the students of the Department not only created an appropriate and felicitous venue for the course of study at which these papers were initially presented, but also provided a useful sounding board for the ideas which are developed here.

The third party in this partnership helping to link the other two and assisting in the financing of the project, is a relatively new, Paris-based institution called the Center for the Study of International Communications. Working closely with the American University of Paris and other organizations that serve the international community in France, the Center is an independent association, organized under French law. Its objective is to foster a deeper understanding of the communications process and the information media as they operate increasingly across national and cultural boundaries.

Supported by contributions from its members and benefactors, the Center pursues its goal by sponsoring international scholarship students, by hosting delegations of students visiting Europe from other parts of the world, and by organizing a wide variety of lectures, panels, conferences and seminars. These programs are attended by the Center's members and guests from the international community in Paris and by students from the American University of Paris. One of these projects was the Seminar on Central and Southeastern Europe from which this volume has emerged.

The Center's involvement in this project has been a particularly rewarding experience. Those who attended some or all of the seminar sessions welcomed the opportunity to participate in the lively discussions, which characterized these meetings. In addition, it was exciting to see an innovative pedagogical concept come to fruition—a concept, which allowed the research teaching enterprise to unfold in non-traditional ways. It was heartening, at the start, to see an outstanding array of authorities from a wide variety of backgrounds agreeing to participate in such a program. And it was also encouraging to see so many people from the Center and from the American University of Paris community and their own commitment of time and energy to the program's success.

And now the project moves on to another rewarding state, as the ideas generated by the program are shared in these pages with a wider audience. As we welcome a new group of readers to this experience, we do so with the hope that they will also be proactive participants, questioning and challenging the material presented here, comparing and contrasting the variety of perspectives from which these chapters are written, and pondering, too, the long-range implications of these findings.

This book is intended to provide additional raw material for a broad, ongoing conversation concerning the formally communist countries of Central and Southeastern Europe—and the many ways in which they are evolving at the turn of the century, just a decade after the Iron Curtain's fall. In a time of dramatic change in every dimension of life on our planet, the transformation of this region has been one of the most fascinating and consequential dramas of all.

Just how the story will come out is still uncertain—indeed, one of the themes of these essays is that story will undoubtedly come out in different ways in different settings. But another theme is that many of the decisions which will shape those outcomes are still being contemplated—that some basic

Foreword

choices are still being made. We hope that this volume will contribute to a fuller understanding of this complex and critical process—and perhaps in some way, too, to the quality of the decisions that will be taken concerning the region in the months and years ahead.

Acknowledgments

The editors would like to thank the many American University of Paris (AUP) students, Ela Chirileanu, Julian Robert, Onethia Riley, Nick Rimedio, and Patricia Tamaro-Silva, who assisted the production. AUP student Armend Reka in particular provided insights on the Kosovo/Kosova crisis and worked long hours on the final production. Terri Jennings also deserves credit for working to edit this book for Praeger.

Assistant Editor Oleg Kobtzeff would like to thank Doug Weiner of the University of Arizona for his inspiring conversations, and for the book and articles, as well as Alexandra de Miramon of the Organization for Economic Cooperation and Development (OECD), Australian filmmaker-reporter Petra Campbell, and former AUP student, Gabriella Rhebinder. He would also like to thank The American Foundation in Paris and its director, American University of Paris Professor Terence Murphy for his assistance.

Assistant Editor Elinore Schaffer translated chapter 7 by Nadège Ragaru; Oleg Kobtzeff translated chapter 1 by Jacques Rupnik. A very special thanks to Alice Depret for her excellent translations of the chapters of Michel Koutouzis, Bernard Lory, and Antonin Liehm.

Titles for the bibliography were selected by Edith Lhomel, Nadège Ragaru, Elinore Schaffer, and Oleg Kobtzeff.

And last, but not least, Lee and Berna Huebner, Connie Borde, Paul Weinstein, and the Center for the Study of International Communications deserve thanks for their support during and after the excellent lecture series, *Central and Southeastern Europe in Transition: Examining Success and Failure since 1989*, held in the Spring of 1998.

Not to forget the Gardner family who deserve gratitude for putting up with yet another publication—and to the memory of Virginia Gardner.

Except for the editors, the above are not responsible for the final product.

Introduction

Hall Gardner

This book came out of a project conceived by Elinore Schaffer to develop a lecture series entitled *Central and Southeastern Europe in Transition: Examining Success and Failure since 1989* under the auspices of the International Affairs Department of the American University of Paris.

Elinore coordinated the lecture series in liaison with Oleg Kobtzeff, Assistant Professor of the International Affairs department of the American University of Paris, in the spring of 1998. The Center for the Study of International Communication, directed by Lee Huebner, kept the project alive by providing key financial supports that permitted some of the leading eastern European and French scholars and experts in the field to speak.

Not everyone who participated in that timely and informative lecture series contributed to the book, but we have been lucky to obtain some of the very best. A few may be new to English-speaking audiences.

Jacques Rupnik, who introduced the lecture series, likewise introduces the book with a general discussion of the place of central and southeastern Europe in the greater scheme of things in Chapter 1, "In Search of East-Central Europe: Ten Years After." In the process of examining the different historical maps and legacies of the region before and during the Cold War, Rupnik raises very pertinent questions regarding how central and southeastern Europeans view their "new" post-1989 identity, in a situation in which the "map" of the region remains in continuous flux. He argues that how central and southeastern Europeans define their identity will depend upon whether one retains criteria based on culture, religion, or civilization, or if social and economic factors, or purely political factors, are emphasized.

In the second chapter, "The Balkans: A Distorted, Third World Reflection of Europe," Catherine Durandin traces historical west European and Russian attitudes toward the Balkans. She argues that the Balkans region has generally been regarded as a kind of "third world" rather than as part of the European "first world." At the same time, as Russia's ongoing interest in the Balkans makes these a part of Russian history, Russia has regarded itself as both a "European" and a "modernizing" influence in the region—in respect to countering Ottoman rule and in regard to its links with Orthodox and Slavic communities. Here, however, it is not clear whether Russian influence can really be considered as representing European "modernity," or whether it is perhaps better characterized as an even more "distorted third world reflection" of Europe. The fundamental dilemma is that as the past has too often been used as a means to merely legitimize national confrontation in the region, the stereotype of a third world has been difficult to break. This appears particularly true as Balkan peoples have tended to expect Western countries—as well as Russia—to behave as either an umbrella or shelter—resulting in an abdication of local sovereignty.

In the third chapter, "Rusty Ottoman Keys to the Balkans of Today," Bernard Lory examines the largely unexplored effects of the Ottoman empire upon the Balkans. His hypothesis—that ignorance of the Ottoman historical presence in the Balkans is responsible for the West's difficulty in grasping the Balkan problem and that it undermines the possibility of true partnership with this part of Europe—deserves serious academic attention. In particular, he argues that the 1991–95 war in Bosnia has been erroneously cast as a war of religion, when it is perhaps better characterized as a war between rival *millets* forged by former Ottoman rule and then shaped by nationalism.

Antonin Liehm underscores the importance of culture in east-central Europe and the crucial role culture played in undermining both the theory and practice of communism in the fourth chapter, "The Role of Culture under the Communist and Post-Communist Eras." He argues that the era of post-Communism has not driven politics from the public square, but that it has driven culture from it. The fact that politics cannot replace the importance of culture has consequently opened up a moral, if not legal, "vacuum" in east-central European society, which could possibly be filled by the claims of extremist movements. The post-1989 liberty has been characterized by lack of social cohesion, particularly as the new leaderships have failed to formulate cultural agendas.

Issues involving the media are discussed in chapters 5 and 6. In chapter 5, "The Transformation of the Media in Post-Communist Central Europe," Marcin Frybes argues that the process of media liberalization strongly depends upon the evolution of the political situation in each country. The degree of autonomy of the press represents a good test of the democratization process. He raises concerns, however, that the media may not *necessarily* be playing a positive and constructive role in the process of democratization and in the reconstruction of a democratic civil life in these countries.

Helen Darbishire then explicates in chapter 6, "The Media in Transition in Southern Central Europe," the difficulties the media has experienced in the post-Communist period, providing an overview of south-central and southeastern Europe in particular. She discusses the nature of laws dealing with freedom of the press and issues such as defamation. While progress has been made, levels of journalistic professionalism are unfortunately still poorly developed; it is relatively easy for politicians to take the lead in determining the manner in which other groups or nations are portrayed in the media. The latter is in part due to the close relationship between politics and the media that continues to predominate in the region.

In chapter 7, "A Balance of Economic Reforms in Central and Eastern Europe," Nadège Ragaru focuses on the role of finance capital. She argues that the success of the transformation process in central and eastern Europe is largely conditioned upon the ability of these states to anchor new patterns of behavior to totally redefined rules of the game. Moreover, success in this endeavor is heavily influenced by the culture of each country. She argues that there is no alternative to rapid and extensive privatization, and that even after transfer of ownership to the private sector, still more work needs to be done regarding the definition of property rights, corporate governance, and financial restructuring.

Michel Koutouzis provides a very original accounting of global drug wars as they affect the Balkan region in chapter 8, "Ulysses and the Lotus Eaters." He argues that the world of drug trafficking now transcends the former notions of empire, Cold War spheres of interest, and end-of-century capitalism. New developments show a disturbing merger between legal and illicit activities. Koutouzis traces the globalization of drug wars, focusing on drug trafficking in the former Soviet Union, Cyprus, Turkey, Albania, Serbia, and the former Yugoslavia, among other regions. He argues that the illegal drug world has undergone a monumental structural overhaul since the early 1990s.

In chapter 9, "Environmental Security and Civil Society," Oleg Kobtzeff, provides a detailed account of the tragic ecological damage to central and eastern Europe and Russia caused by the ex-Communist system. Kobtzeff makes the significant point that ecological issues helped to undermine socialist and Soviet legitimacy, but that the initial rise of green movements within the former Soviet bloc was followed by the apparent post-1989 decline of green movements within east-central Europe. He proposes a general environmental cleanup through the assistance of international organizations and small ecologically-oriented businesses. On a theoretical level, he questions the new doctrine of the "duty" or "right" to intervene in the affairs of sovereign states in an effort to assist the victims of both natural and man-made catastrophes, if not victims of political repression, even against the will of the leadership of those states. He argues that there has developed a dangerous temptation to militarize a crisis situation and opt for forceful intervention rather than seek political and economic solutions with the concurrence of the state leadership.

In the final chapter, "The Genesis of NATO Enlargement and of War 'over' Kosovo," Hall Gardner examines the complexity of factors that led NATO to enlarge into central Europe (including eastern Germany). The chapter focuses primarily on the often-overlooked German factor as it interacted with the general security interests of the United States, Soviet Union/ Russia, and eastern European states. Gardner argues that NATO's effort to "double contain" a newly unified *federal* Germany (as opposed to a *confederal* state) required NATO to enlarge into areas that would, at least ostensibly, protect German political-economic and security interests, primarily in central and eastern Europe. In detailing the process of enlargement, Gardner argues that NATO was first interested in bringing into membership Poland and the Czech Republic, as these states would provide Germany with a buffer from potential "instability from the East." Hungary, however, was brought in largely as a consequence of its logistical support for NATO in the war in Bosnia. Gardner critiques the argument that NATO needed to "go out of area or out of business" and explores how NATO found itself reluctantly but not-so-accidentally drawn into Bosnia, followed by "humanitarian intervention" in Kosovo. He then analyses NATO's quest for a new legitimacy and argues that NATO's post-1989 mission still involves an ambiguous mix of "collective defense" and "collective security." He questions whether NATO will be able enlarge its membership again in the year 2002 as expected by many states throughout southeastern and northeastern Europe, but without overextending NATO's political consensus, will and resources. And finally, Gardner questions whether NATO will be able to sustain positive relations with Russia and other non-NATO members in the long term (perhaps by bringing Russia into "full" membership). Will NATO be able to work side-by-side the UN and other international regimes in order to establish a new system of "collective security" for central and southeastern Europe—if not for the entire Euro-Atlantic community?

The book concludes with an extensive bibliography that lists of some of the most interesting books and periodicals on the topic of central and southeastern Europe.

Finally transliteration presented the editors with a difficult choice. Should one system be imposed upon all authors? But which system? Should we have followed Library of Congress requirements (e.g., *Gorbachiov*—as pronounced, instead of *Gorbachev*)? Can *Bosniak*—as reporters or economists spell it every day—entirely convey the historic connotations of *Boshnjak* perceived by a historian? Do we speak of Kosovo-Metohia, Kosovo (in Serbian), or Kosova (in Albanian)? In the process of eliminating Kosovo's autonomous status between 1989 and 1991, Serbia added the name of the region, Metohia to Kosovo province, in an effort to further downplay the ethnic Albanian regional identity and demographic majority, and to better "assimilate" the region.

Since one of the purposes of this book is to depict the divergence of perspectives, interpretations, identities, and policy options within central and southeastern Europe (or however that region may be defined), it was decided to let each author use her or his own system, thus accepting a diversity of linguistic choices to reflect the diversity of perceptions of the region and its complexities.

Chapter 1

In Search of East-Central Europe: Ten Years After

Jacques Rupnik

It is difficult to present the new contours of Europe for there does not yet exist a definite map. There is one in the making. There are a certain number of clues, however, as to what Central and Eastern Europe might look in the future. Central Europe, Eastern Europe, East-Central Europe, post-Communist Europe: many different terms have attempted to define the new expanse that appeared after the fall of the Soviet empire.

One thing seems certain: the term "people's democracies" of Eastern Europe, which prevailed for nearly half a century in some countries of Europe, was quite irrelevant at the time, and is even less relevant today.

Therefore, the political and economic geography of that zone must be seriously reconsidered—a task made even more difficult since it is in complete mutation.

Westerners, who had not particularly contributed to it, eventually found it convenient to view this "revolution" as an "event" with a beginning—the fall of the Berlin wall in November 1989—and an end—the demise of the Soviet Union in December 1991. Instead it is a process, and this great geopolitical reconfiguration of the East that began in 1989 is far from being over. It is likely to last, on the contrary, years, even decades! The fall of the Roman Empire or of the Ottoman Empire lasted nearly two centuries. How could the fall of the Soviet empire have lasted only a couple of years?

Behind the label "East of Europe," which designated only countries of the Soviet bloc until 1989, two new zones are beginning to take shape since that year: a Central European area (the "success story" of the transition); a Balkan area (where the national question seems to be the determining factor); and Russia (but what is Russia without an empire?). Each one of these areas possesses very imprecise borders, while the problems that define each one of them are now very different.

Indeed, the notions of Eastern Europe and "post-communism" are hardly relevant any longer. The notion of Eastern Europe could, to a certain extent, be applied to Russia, or eventually, to the Western periphery of the former Soviet Union. But the notion of post-communism is more problematic. For what is there in common between Hungary and Kazakhstan or the Czech Republic and Albania? True, they have shared the experience of living under communism. But these are, and have always been, very different countries. Other factors, other events, even constrasting legacies of communism, differentiate them today.

In fact, the notion of Eastern Europe is a legacy of the Cold War period, associated with Winston Churchill's famous 1946 formula about an "iron curtain" descending upon Europe and dividing it into two parts from the Baltic to the Adriatic. But in fact, it is even more deeply rooted in mentalities.

It dates back to the era of the Enlightenment. Voltaire or Diderot see this area located between Germany and Russia as a zone of instability, backwardness, and "barbary." The latter term was used in opposition to "civilization," which was to finally triumph only by the grace of the Prussian or the Russian enlightened despotism of Frederick II or Catherine the Great. Our philosophers placed their hopes in "civilization" triumphing in this part of Europe in the form of a Prussian and/or Russian version of an almighty state. Further assessment of this experience proved that its results were less than conclusive for the people of the region.

Only Rousseau resisted the illusion—first, when he wrote his project for a Polish constitution, but also, in his remarkable insight: "Russia can conquer Poland, but it will never be able to digest it." All of us have more or less paraphrased this expression in the days of Solidarnosc. This was a profound intuition about Poland, but also, about the nature of that area located between Germany and Russia—endlessly disputed by one enemy or the other, but never willing to be assimilated.

Not only are we confronted by these problems of definition, but so are the inhabitants of all these countries as well. For the Poles, the notion of Central Europe covers the area located between the Russia and Germany and includes the Baltic countries and the Ukraine in particular. Poland has long preserved its privileged ties to Lithuania. A city like L'vov, located today in the Ukraine, has belonged for a long time to Polish territories. It is therefore perfectly comprehensible that the Polish definition of Central Europe is so large.

For a long time, the Czechs had to rely upon a more restrained—somewhat Habsburgian—definition of Central Europe. After the Czech-Slovak divorce the political leaders of the Czech Republic had a tendency to replace Slovakia with Slovenia and held on to a restrictive definition of Central Europe.

In Hungary, when speaking of Central Europe, the "Danubian realm" is what comes to mind most frequently. Again, this corresponds to an area that is defined in a very hazy manner and whose common denominator is not only its location on the banks of the Danube, but also a presence of important Hungarian minorities.

In Search of East-Central Europe: Ten Years After

In the former Yugoslavia, the 1980s were marked by a rediscovery of the theme of Central Europe, particularly in Slovenia and Croatia. But in a way, this was only to draw a line between themselves and Belgrade or Serbia, and to mark a distance from Yugoslavia. This was a sort of a mental prelude to withdrawal from the Yugoslav stage.

Nevertheless, in all these definitions of Central Europe we do find a common denominator: the idea and assertion that one belongs simply to Europe, and that one belongs to the West. Hence, Czech writer Milan Kundera's famous formula about Central Europe as a "kidnapped West."[1] For all these countries, rejecting Sovietism was subordinate to asserting one's belonging to Europe (or to the West). But at the same time, one can sense a desire to mark a distance with territories and neighbors located further east. Thus, the notion of Central Europe conveyed at the same time an aspiration toward European integration, and a mark of differentiation in regard to what was considered as "another" civilization. This is the entire ambiguity in this vocabulary and in the debates in these countries on Europe.

West European misconceptions of Central Europe on the Balkans are the "natives" own misconceptions about Europe. Traveling with leading political figures to the Balkans, as a part of the International Commission on the Balkan, it was striking to contrast ideas on Europe with those of the state governments. For many of the latter, the term "Europe" is not a reference to universal values nor to a system of legal norms (that could eventually be adopted and observed). Europe, in their views, is essentially a divide. Thus, the president of Croatia will treat his hosts with a long speech about the "clash of civilizations." For President Tudjman, Croatia is the rampart of Western and Catholic Europe, as opposed to an Eastern Europe, which is Byzantine and Orthodox. He underlines the importance of historic rifts between different religions and civilizations. At the same time, a parallel argument can be heard on the Serb side: "that is not the real border of Europe. The real border is located between the Christian world and the Turkish-Muslim world."

In the Balkan context, Europe refers frequently to an idea of border, to the idea of a line drawn between different cultures and civilizations. In other words, there are different ways in which two belong to Europe, and one is always somebody else's "barbarian."

What definition of Central Europe on the Balkans can we then propose? Beyond the academic considerations, it is proper to underline that, according to the criteria selected herein, different answers are obtained. If we retain criteria based on culture, religion, or civilization, the definition will not be the same if we emphasize social and economic factors, or purely political factors.

Therefore, if we emphasize the first criteria, that is, the cleavage between Western Christianity and Eastern Christianity, between Catholic and Protestants on one side and Orthodox on the other, we come close to the definition proposed by Kundera: "the tragedy of Central Europe, is that it is culturally in the West, politically in the East, and geographically in the Center of Europe." This was a working definition before 1989. Today, for the first time, that part of Europe (so often rocked between different influences) is placed in front of the historic opportunity to finally harmonize geography and political and cultural affiliation. This interpretation, which insists upon a cultural dividing line between two civilizations, possesses nevertheless explicitly political correlations. For in the end, it is a cleavage that revives questions about the separation between church and state, and about the existence of a civil society and the influence of democratic traditions.

If, on the other hand, one gave priority to social and economic criteria, the accent would be placed on the relative economic backwardness of the Eastern European zone. Indeed, the more one moves further east (or south), the more this backwardness becomes visible and pronounced. This theme of backwardness and of the need to catch up, is one of the themes that dominates political thought in the countries of the region since the nineteenth century with its corollary: an insistence upon the weakness of the indigenous bourgeoisie. This is why the state has often been perceived in these countries as the principal agent of modernization—as the main path toward accessing industrial modernity.

The countries' intelligentsia has traditionally been torn between that concept of the state and the idea according to which the most genuine depositary of national values is the peasantry. The state-oriented heritage of these countries cannot be understood separately from all the ideological debates that prevailed in the nineteenth century. Later, an entire school of thought emphasizing social and economic criteria, pointed to the coincidence (almost too good to be true) between the borders of sixteenth century "second wave" of serfdom and the more recent borders of the Warsaw Pact and "real socialism."

Finally, there exists a third approach that consists in placing more stress upon traditions and political culture. We then obtain an intermediate answer. The Habsburg Empire was certainly not a British-type liberal democracy, but neither was it a Russian-type autocracy. This approach stresses the idea of Rechtstadt, of statehood based on the rule of law. But it also emphasizes the idea of decentralization and autonomous, self-governed regional entities. Such traditions are particularly strong in Hungary. All this amounts to an important legacy of political and legal culture in the Central European area.

Similarly in the last years of the nineteenth century, universal suffrage and democratic and parliamentary institutions have made progress in the lands of the Austro-Hungarian empire, and that later, between the two world wars, democratic constitutions borrowed from the West were adopted almost everywhere. (The Czechs would rather refer to the French model, while Romanians borrowed much from the Belgian Constitution.) What counts is that after World War I there has been an attempt to transplant democracy in all these countries.

The results of this democratic transplant were not always conclusive. From the 1920s onward, and especially in the 1930s, these countries fell one after the other under the sway of different sorts of authoritarianism. Hungary was the first, as early as 1919, with the experience of the Horthy regime. Bulgaria was next in 1923, and then Poland after Marshall Pilsudski's military coup in 1926. The others, mainly in the Baltic countries, succumbed to the power of authoritarian regimes in the early 1930s.

Czechoslovakia was the exception that only confirmed the rule: democracy found itself threatened everywhere. The danger, however, did not come from totalitarianism (whether of the communist or nazi type) but from the semiauthoritarian regimes that permitted nevertheless a large autonomy to society, including to political and labor union activity.

This third criterion, focusing on democratic culture and political traditions, leads to an intermediary answer: Central Europe or East Central Europe constituted itself as an area characterized by political systems that represented a halfway house between Western democracy and Oriental totalitarianism. Let us remember, however, that during the 1930s democracy was not in such good shape anywhere in Europe (certainly not in Germany, Italy, or Spain). Therefore, it is not only East Central Europe that was demonstrating, at the time, any particular weakness or vulnerability. However, these failures paved the way for the establishment of "people's democracies" immediately after the war.

To better understand certain elements characteristic of that area, it is useful to compare three historic maps: Europe in 1914, in 1945, and in 1989. A look at the map of 1914 allows us to observe, first of all, that until World War I, the Central European zone possessed a sort of a geopolitical matrix. It was the Habsburg Empire's significant political and legal legacy. Also, there is a simple way—although too restrictive—to define this Central Europe: it would concern a group of nations that shared and experimented, for centuries, common institutions and a similar legal system making this group very different from the Balkan area and from Russia as well.

Secondly, it is noticeable that the area located in the Southeast of the Habsburg Empire belonged for a long time to the Ottoman Empire and has gathered nations affiliated, in most cases to the Orthodox religion, that is Serbs, Bulgarians, and Romanians. But that does not apply to the Albanians who include a Muslim majority, an important Catholic minority and a small Orthodox minority (not an entirely Greek one, despite what is often said in Athens). This area's strong identification between religious and national affiliations is a legacy of the Ottoman period. In the Ottoman Empire, indeed, religious (millet) and national communities blended and that correlation remains important today.

The former Ottoman zone is also marked by the presence of Turkish and Muslim minorities. This is also one reason why the question of the relations with Turkey remains a concern. Since 1989, Turkey is manifesting great interest toward the Balkans. In one of his speeches in 1990, Turkish President Demirel mentioned that with the end of the Soviet empire, new opportunities were presenting themselves to Turkey in an area spreading from the Balkans to the Chinese border. This was probably a much too ambitious project, but it is evidence, nevertheless, of a rediscovery of an Ottoman space, at least in the mind of Turkish political elites. However, it is necessary to remember that for Turkey, the Balkans remain a secondary preoccupation in comparison to the Caucasus, Central Asia, and the Middle East.

Still, this theme is important for it shows to which point the countries of Central Europe, as well as the nations located in the Balkans, continue to live with the idea that they have been historically confronted by a double menace: the Ottoman Empire and the Turks from one side, and Russia from the other. This idea has profoundly influenced the national and European identity of those nations. We should remember that the major historic trauma, for the Serbs, was the battle of Kosovo in 1389 and their defeat by the Turks. For the Hungarians, it is the battle of Mohacs in 1524. All these countries, until the seventeenth century, had to constantly resist Ottoman pressure. The Turks were finally driven off at the gates of Vienna by the troops of Polish prince Jan Sobieski in 1683.

The third important feature of this map is the German influence—East Prussia—which expanded all the way to the Baltic countries, to Königsberg (today's Kaliningrad, or Krolewiec in Polish, the city of Immanuel Kant). The absence of any German influence would have been surprising today. Since the twelfth to thirteenth centuries, this area has been marked, among other factors, by the presence and modernizing influence German minorities. The influence of eastern Prussia reached as far as Königsberg, with two consequences: a feeling of attraction—for that presence was perceived as a vector of economic and social modernization—but at the same time, a feeling of apprehension (that could even lead to rejection), due to the fears of being dominated because modernization often progressed together with cultural and linguistic German acculturation. The Polish historian Jerry Jedlicki, in a remarkable book originally called *What Civilization do the Poles Need?*[2] shows very well that the apprehension toward industrial modernity in certain regions of Poland was directly linked to the fact that, historically, this modernity had taken the form of Bismarck's Kulturkampf and Germanization. Thus, national identity and modernity were joined in a relationship of even tension and conflict.

In the period between the two world wars, there had been an attempt to construct an East-Central Europe without Germany—the Versailles system in which France played the leading role. It collapsed in Munich in 1938. The period immediately following World War II witnessed the emergence of an Eastern Europe from which not only Germany but also Germans were absent due to the massive displacement of the German populations from territories in Czechoslovakia, Poland, and elsewhere. Then, anti-Germanism also legitimized Sovietization.

Since the end of the Cold War there has been a return of a German presence in East-Central Europe. This can no longer be a presence of the ancient type, since the German populations are no longer inhabiting the area. Neither can it be a presence taking the form of political hegemony. What is really at issue is the predominant role of Germany as an economic partner for most of its neighbors of Central Europe, that is, the weight of the Bundesbank rather than the weight of the Bundeswehr. It is easy to understand why the

German side is preoccupied with the effort to avoid resurrecting the specter of Mitteleuropa, a German definition of Central Europe. In the course of the debate between the presidents of Central European countries in 1994 in Bohemia, then German president Weizsäcker insisted that he even rejected the term Mitteleuropa because for many, it was associated with an idea of German expansion. His preference went to the term Zentraleuropa, Central Europe, free from any particular German connotation. Yet, it is a Central Europe where indeed, Germany has a role to play, for it is part of it in certain regards, as a vector for the rapprochement of Central Europe with the European Union.

The new relations established after 1989 between Germany and these countries demonstrate that there is no uniformity in these matters. As early as the beginning of 1990, the Polish side insisted on the necessity to recognize the Oder-Neisse border before Germany was reunited. The Poles viewed it as a preliminary condition for reunification and wanted it to be included in the "2+4" international negotiations.[3] Memorable are the trips of T. Mazowiecki and W. Jaruzelski to Paris, coming hand-in-hand to obtain support on this issue from François Mitterrand's France. Many at the time said: "these Poles are overreacting." But they obtained what they wanted despite the legal and political reservations of Bonn. Thus for the Poles, most of the specter of German hegemony dissipated, and the relations between Poland and Germany have never been better for two centuries.

The same cannot be said about the Czechs. It is worth recalling president Vaclav Havel's gesture, while visiting Germany in January 1990, when he apologized for the expulsion of the Germans of the Sudeten from Czechoslovakia at the end of World War II. This highly moral gesture had not been reciprocated by German diplomacy. Mainly for reasons of domestic politics, Chancellor Kohl did not consider it useful to respond. Consequently, in the 1992 treaty concluded between Czechoslovakia and Germany, the question of the Sudeten Germans was left aside. Ever since, it has been an issue poisoning Czech-German relations. When such questions miss a historic opportunity to find a resolution, the political price that has to be paid is sometimes very high. Of course, a Czech-German declaration was signed in January 1997 and there is no need to dramatize their differences. Yet, the Czech-Polish contrast reveals the ambiguity and ambivalence of the question of German presence in Central Europe.

The map of Central Europe in 1945 is better as "the Europe of Yalta." It is a result of the greatest military conquest experienced by Europe since the Ottoman Empire—a military and political expansion of Soviet Russia to Berlin, Prague, Vienna, Budapest, Bucharest, and Sofia. Since the nineteenth century, the Russian factor was often perceived in East-Central Europe as a counterweight to German influence. The 1848 Slavic Congress of Prague illustrated that. But it should not be forgotten that autocratic Russia also appeared as an adversary of freedom, especially for the Poles and the Hungarians after the crushing of the Hungarian revolution of 1848 by the Russians and the repeated partition of Poland since the late eighteenth century between Prussia, Austria, and Russia. The latter appeared as a hostile power, a threat not only to national independence but also to liberty.

Even among the Czechs, where the Slavic current had been strong (especially in the last part of the nineteenth century and early twentieth century), the major political thinkers and political leaders, such as Palacky, Havlicek, or Masaryk, all shared the desire to distance themselves from Russia. In 1848, when Palacky addressed the parliament in Frankfurt, he rejected the idea of a democracy associated with an expansion of Germanism because he refused to sacrifice Czech national identity. However, at the same time, he found that protection from a Slavic and autocratic Russia was unacceptable. In this context he declared that "if Austria didn't exist it would have to be invented." In his eyes, Austria had many defects, but in the absence of anything better, in order to escape the pressure of Germany (even if it were a democratic Germany) and the pressure of autocratic Russia (even if it were a counterweight to Germany), it still represented a lesser evil, as long as it could be made more democratic and transformed from the inside. As for Masaryk, he published a book in 1913 with a title—*Russia and Europe*—clearly indicating that in his view, Russia and Europe are two distinct entities.

Russia could be perceived as a counterweight to Germany, especially when the West did not face its responsibilities. Munich 1938 is, of course, the ultimate trauma which, in a certain way, pushed Central Europe into the arms of Russia. Stalin would never have conquered Central Europe if there had not been Munich. It is Munich and Hitler's conquest of Central Europe that allowed the Soviet bloc to constitute itself in the aftermath of World War II.

The Cold War was the partition of Europe in two blocks by a military and ideological iron curtain. However, at times, miniature iron curtains also separated different countries of the Eastern bloc. It first happened between Yugoslavia (ostracized as early as 1948) and the other countries, with Bulgaria and Albania immediately imposing an embargo. Another mini-iron curtain fell between Romania and Hungary. (In the 1980s, it was much easier to travel from Budapest to Vienna, when visas had been abolished between the two countries, than traveling from Budapest to Romania, and particularly to Transylvania where there lived a two million strong Hungarian minority.) Not to mention the ostracism undergone by Poland during the solidarity period, initiated mainly by East Germany and Czechoslovakia whose leaders, fearing contagion, rallied every known anti-Polish prejudice to legitimize such a policy.

These old divisions, even inside Eastern Europe, explain in part why these countries have reservations about cooperating with each other today. Although they have lived through a comparable totalitarian communist experience, they are nevertheless very different. In contrast to Hungary in 1956, to Czechoslovakia in 1968, or to Poland in 1980, 1989 was a chain reaction that wiped out the communist system. The following formula has gained fame: "10 years for Poland, 10 months for Hungary, 10 weeks for the German Democratic Republic, 10 days for Czechoslovakia." A formidable acceleration of history! One could add: 10 hours for Romania or 10 minutes for Albania.

But although the collapse of the communist system had been simultaneous, the situations are different when it comes to elaborating, conceptualizing, and finding the proper transition to democracy.

In 1945 (like in 1918), the victors shifted the borders. For example, Poland was amputated from the territories located in the East and obtained "as compensation" territories in the West previously belonging to Germany. Hence the idea that borders are unstable and movable in accordance with the turnout of forces between the great powers. It is important to remember that the East-Central European borders are no older than the twentieth century and are often more recent than African borders! Because of the recent, fragile, and unstable nature of these borders, East-Central Europe is characterized by a feeling of strong vulnerability, and also the idea that the borders between national identities are fragile, under threat, and likely to change. In the face of such a situation of instability, two attitudes can be observed.

The first one is an attitude of ironic distance, found in all Central European literature—Kafka's entry in his journal, on the eve of the declaration of war in 1914, is typical: "Morning, declaration of war; afternoon, swimming pool." From this point of view, history is ruled by the great powers who, depending on the turnout of their forces, exacerbate the involvement of the countries involved. Hence the famous anecdote about the inhabitant of Czernowitz (the present Chernovtsy), born under the Habsburg rule and who underwent several changes of nationality during his lifetime, without ever changing his residence: from subject of the Empire, to Romanian citizen, or from Soviet to Ukrainian national. Four changes of "national identity" without leaving home, illustrates the fragility of the situation.

The other attitude consists in overcompensating feelings of fragility and insecurity by violently asserting one's attachment to this or that territory, as an authentic "national" territory. Occasions for litigation over land are numerous in all the peripheries, whether among Poland, Lithuania, and the Ukraine or between Romania and Hungary over Transylvania. There often exists "one territory for two dreams"—a territory claimed by two (or more) different nations. Kosovo is an obvious case in point for Serbs and Albanians. Macedonia is claimed by the Macedonians, of course, but also by the Serbs (who have considered it for a long time as "southern Serbia"; by the Bulgarians (who consider Macedonian as a Bulgarian dialect); and by the Greeks (who feel entitled, by Philip and Alexander, to the *copyright* of the very name of Macedonia). In most cases, there isn't an overlap of the ethnic border with the political border, and that becomes a source of tension, particularly in postimperial periods when national states are being constructed.

The national states in Central Europe were constructed in three phases: first of all, multinational empires were formed, whether the Habsburg Empire, the Ottoman Empire or the Russian Empire. Then, immediately following World War I came nations-states that had not been created. But most of these latter new states incorporated national minorities representing a quarter to a third of their population. Finally the third phase developed, directly linked to

World War II and completed after 1989, when nations-states were being constructed with a desire to become ethnically homogeneous. In the aftermath of World War II, Poland, for the first time in its history, became a relatively homogeneous state ethnically. The dream of the nationalistic Polish rightwing came true under communism. The Czech republic is another illustration of the same phenomena: no more Jews, the Germans gone since their expulsion in 1945, and the "Slovak millstone" abandoned to itself after the 1993 separation of Czechoslovakia. Alone at last!

The post-1989 map shows Russia retreating dramatically, although we must guard ourselves against hasty judgments. The Russians are always concerned with the periphery of the former Soviet Union in regard to the question of the limits of their "near abroad." Russian minorities distributed throughout neighboring states, from the Baltic countries to the Ukraine and Central Asia, amount to 20 to 25 million individuals. Besides, no one in Russia today has an answer to the following question: What is Russia without an empire? This is a first element in the Russian apprehension of the idea of Central Europe. This is the origin of the feeling of insecurity that is not shared by the West, especially in France, but which is felt in Central Europe, not only because of the local historic experiences, but also because of the great uncertainty that looms over the very future of post-imperial Russia.

There remains the question: To what extent are Russia's relations with its Western periphery affected by deeper historical-cultural divides between Western Christianity and Eastern Christianity, between Catholics and Protestants in the West and the Orthodox in the East, that do not correspond necessarily to the borders of states? This is just as valid for the Baltic States or Western Ukraine as for the former Yugoslavia.

In the Balkans, we are confronted with the extreme and violent process of what is called "ethnic cleansing," a process used to build a "Greater Serbia", "Greater Croatia" or "Greater Albania." French Senator Baron d'Estournelles de Constant, chairman of the Carnegie Balkan Commission, who in 1913 traveled to the Balkans, wrote in the introduction of the first Carnegie report: "Must we allow these Balkan wars to pass without at least trying to draw some lessons from them, without knowing whether they have been a benefit or an evil, if they should begin again tomorrow and go on forever?" He added that his report could have been appropriately entitled "Divided Europe and Her Demoralizing Actions in the Balkans." Few readers could appreciate his writings in 1914. His words should remain as a motto to describe the whole period we lived through in the 1990s. There are several examples of similarities between present and past conflicts and the manner in which warfare is waged. Hence the temptation to use historical analogies in searching for the origins of the conflicts and treating the Balkan predicament as something separate from Europe. This is what George Kennan has argued in his preface to the 1993 reprint of the first 1913 report, calling the Balkans a "salient of non-European characteristics" including some of those that "fit even less with the world today than they did with the world of eighty years ago." The atrocities penetrated during the Balkan wars of this century would seem to confirm these harsh judgments. But most European states have undergone similar periods of upheaval, horror, and cruelty in a not-so-distant history, yet they have worked their way out of the darkness. In this sense the Balkan predicament remains part of the twentieth-century European predicament.

There is no such thing as a European view of the Balkans. There are only different views derived from different national experiences. This explains the difficulty in finding one common perception and common European policies.

Two main views dominated West European perceptions of the Balkans. First of all, the idea of archaism and anachronism, of ancestral hatreds, focuses on the "return of the past." According to this theory, this region's conflicts find their explanation in historic hatreds between and among people that only the presence of the great powers was able to hold under lock. Today, as the weight of these powers is no longer felt, now that the Ottomans and the Russians are absent, one can see the result! The second main view, on the contrary, views conflict as a belated creation of the nation-state, an unpleasant but necessary process leading to modernity. Indeed the process is at times painful and violent, but these are supposed to be "growing pains," in an effort to catch up, after a certain delay, with the homogeneous nation-states whose construction is supposedly the condition for stability, modernity, and democracy. Both views have been widely expressed.

The first theory is more influential among political elites and in the media. For example Clinton's inaugural speech of January 1993 spoke of the great promises of the post-Cold War era already threatened by the return of "ancestral hatreds." In the House of Commons, John Major used the same concept in the following speech:

The largest single element behind what happened in Bosnia is the collapse of the Soviet Union and of the discipline that is exercised over the ancient hatreds in old Yugoslavia. Once the discipline had disappeared, the ancient hatreds have appeared and we begin to see their consequences when the fighting occurred.

Mitterrand frequently referred to similar terms in explaining what happened in Yugoslavia. One can provide many other similar examples.

The thesis of nationalism in the Balkans as a return of ancient hatreds has many advantages. The first advantage is that ignorance is bliss. When it is hard to understand something new, it is easy to pretend that it is the repetition of something old. Secondly, if you can persuade yourself and others that this is merely the return of the suppressed, then all we have to talk about are the irrational drives shared by Balkan people. Therefore, you can ignore the political nature of the conflict. For late twentieth-century leaders in Western Europe and in the United States it seems very difficult to imagine that it might be a perfectly rational course of action. In the process, fears have been manipulated or hatreds are incited. But, of course, one should distinguish between the use or manipulation of hatreds from their assumed reality. Perhaps the best examples of European thought over these issues was Mitterrand's great conference devoted to nationalism—"L'Europe et les tribus" ("Europe and the tribes"). There, in the very title of the conference, we can detect a way of reading the Balkan conflicts.

On one hand, the European effort for integration appears in a very optimistic light, while the Balkan process of fragmentation appears on the other hand in stark contrast. Thus, the title can be viewed as a plausible attempt at contrasting the Balkans' situation with Europe's. But there is another interpretation of this title. If such a clear-cut separation is drawn between Europe, on one hand, and on the other hand, not Balkan nations but "tribes," then we are talking of two different worlds: Europe marching onward and upward toward the supranational borderless future of Maastricht on one side, and on the other, Balkan tribes reverting to nineteenth-century types of ideologies and conflicts of an irrational nature.

If we are entering the twenty–first century of a borderless liberal free market in Western Europe while "they" are reverting to archaic confrontations centered on ethnic purity and nation building, we are not part of the same history. Moreover, if they are not even nations but only tribes, then they are part of the "Third World." Therefore, if "they" are not part of our history, nor part of our geography, there is no necessity to consider the Balkans or a conflict in the Balkans as a European problem. Consequently, the best course of action when a conflict erupts is just to contain it.

The second prevailing theory, on the contrary, explains the breakup of Yugoslavia not in terms of archaism but in terms of nation-state building. Yugoslavia, in this perception, was merely entering a transition phase between a multinational empire and an allegedly homogeneous nation-state. Incidentally, that argument can be applied to the breakup of the Soviet Union or to the blade breakup of Czechoslovakia. These multinational states or multinational federations are viewed, again, as a transition phase between empire and nation-state. No matter how unpleasant and messy, in this perspective, the difficulties are the growing pains—the cost of achieving modernity.

The idea that ethnic homogeneousness is some sort of prerequisite for political stability is not new in the Balkans. It has been suggested in particular in the immediate aftermath of World War I in the population exchanges that took place between Greece and Turkey.

What is interesting is that such a theory not only has adepts in the Balkans but in the Western foreign policy establishment as well. The problem with this is that the successors of multinational empires were themselves multinational, and that most of the successors to Yugoslavia are also multinational. Therefore, to advocate ethnic homogeneity as a source of modernity and stability or indeed as a prerequisite for democracy is also to invite what a chapter of the 1914 report of the Balkan commission called "extermination, immigration, assimilation"—the most concise definition of what we call today ethnic cleansing.

One of the main problems that has marked the Balkans so far is that the nature of the states is different. Most states in the area have tried to build themselves upon the principle of ethnic nationalism (in a multinational environment). Because they are fragile and vulnerable, they have a tendency to adopt a very central form of government. Thus, a German concept of the nation—defined by language, culture, and religion—is combined with a centralized concept of the state. The Balkan combination of both is more likely to lead to conflict than to democracy and modernity.

What is striking in the two predominant interpretations of conflict in the Balkans—seen as either a resurgence of ancestral hatreds, or, on the contrary, as a stage of modern nation-state building—is that both have similar implications for foreign policy-making, that is non-interference. In both cases, containment appears as sufficient. We know the consequences in Sarajevo, Vukovar and Srebrenica.

To see oneself as guarding borders of a "civilization" encourages a certain form of megolomania. But there are perverse effects in viewing these conflicts "clash of civilizations" or geopolitical forces: if the nature of the conflict is to be seen as a struggle between great foreign powers, local warlords can enhance their stature by pretending to be part of a great international game as if the great powers were interested in them because they are at the crossroads of civilizations and religions. They make it appear that the fate of the world is at stake in their local, sometimes parochial, and ambitious conflicts.

It is a historical legacy for the Balkan nations to overestimate in such a manner the attention devoted by foreign powers to the strategic importance of their region. In truth Sarajevo in 1994 was not the Sarajevo of 1914: Whereas the Balkans suffered from an excessive interest of foreign powers on the eve of the first world war, in the 1990s it was the opposite—they suffered from a lack of interest by the great powers. The area had experienced strategic devaluation, particularly Yugoslavia, which had so skillfully played its game as a maverick between East and West. Therefore, it is not the involvement of Russia, Germany, or Turkey that is behind the conflict (as one often hears frequently in the Balkans), but a certain international environment—the collapse of the Cold War system—that created the opportunity for local protagonists to act.

Finally, there is a last map that was published in the beginning of 1990 by French geographers primarily interested in socioeconomic development.[4] This map focused on industrial fabric, the degree of urbanization, and advantages for communication. These were the three criteria retained for a reflection over the "zones of reconnection" in Europe, immediately following the collapse of the wall.

One of these zones spreads from the Baltic Sea across the larger part of Poland, Silesia, Czechoslovakia, and Hungary, to the Serbo-Croatian border of Yugoslavia. The other "zone of reconnection," located in the north, covers the Baltic countries and mainly Estonia. The geographers were perhaps excessively careful in drafting their map and should have boldly included all three Baltic countries. The main question today is the following: can Kaliningrad become Königsberg again? Doubts arise as I read in the memories of the Countess Dönhoff, publisher of the German weekly *Die Zeit*, a native of Königsberg, she had been displaced from there in 1945. She returned after 1990 and wrote:

"Kaliningrad resembles much more Irkutsk than Königsberg." And part of the answer is there: the city has been destroyed, Soviet-type high-rise apartments have been built to reconstruct it, the population has been expelled, and another population now lives in its place. This is a rather pessimistic answer to questions concerning the restablishment of links with the past, or Germany and the Scandinavian countries serving as vectors, for reconnecting those countries with the West.

But the pessimistic answer provided by Königsberg does not apply to the Baltic countries. And after all, once the results of the economic and political transition of these countries are taken into account, an undeniable kinship with the Central European model can be observed. It is a model that has been successful in regard to both democratic institutions and economic transition. If we recognize that there is a link between that Central European area and the Baltic countries, we obtain something that resembles (to a certain extent—too much, would seem suspicious) the map previously observed and the border between Western Christianity and Eastern Christianity.

The idea of Central Europe isn't being debated now as it had been in the 1980s. It has even become suspicious in the eyes of some (like Vaclav Klaus), at the very moment when a successful Central European model for exiting communism is confirming that idea. Why then such a sudden distrust of the Central European idea and of Central European cooperation? The Visegrad group (constituted by Hungary, Poland, and Czechoslovakia in early 1990) is a good illustration. Some have interpreted this association as a substitute, as a way to postpone the primary objective of these countries, which is simply integration into Europe. It was therefore important for these countries to speak no more of any "Eastern" Europe and even to delete the adjective "Central," while pushing for the acceptance of the idea that "we are simply Europe." The paradox is that they are discovering now that the best way to reach that goal is precisely to stress the relative, yet genuine, success of the Central European model for exiting communism.

The idea of Europe changes in the East as much as in the West. Prior to 1989, Western Europe discussing Europe meant discussing the European Community and Brussels. Dissident intellectuals of Central Europe then replied: "No, Europe is not just a common market or an economic entity! There is also a Central Europe whose culture is in the West, whose politics are in the East and whose geography is in the Center. This is where the idea of Europe based on a culture of values, has been preserved better than in the West, because this is where "it has been most threatened." After 1989, a sort of inversion of roles has been observed. Those who had spoken of a Central Europe and of a "kidnapped West," are saying today: "there is only one Europe which is worth joining, and that is the European Union, the 'common European house' to which we should belong." Followed a polite answer: "But there isn't only the European Community; there is a Europe based on culture, on human rights. Let's build it together as partners. We shall see about EU enlargement later."

The situation of these countries in the 1990s can be summed up as a vicious circle: their main preoccupation is indeed the question of their security. It also appears sometimes as being out of proportion, exaggerated. But it needs to be taken into account. Given the historical experience of these countries, they might have some good reasons to be preoccupied. Without security, the rest is just literature. The experience of ex-Yugoslavia has demonstrated that. The corollary argument would be: "there is nothing better than democracy to guarantee the region's security, for democracies do not go to war with each other." The development of democracy will create favorable conditions for security and for the stability of the region. But how can young and fragile democracies survive without the economic and social foundations of democracy, when the civil societies are weak? The answer depends also upon an economic integration into Europe and into the West. This economic and social integration, this "reconnection" will be possible only if the area becomes an area of security. And so we have come full circle.

Hence, these countries give priority to the question of security within an enlarged NATO, rather than to integration into the European Union. This is understandable for it is easier to enter NATO than the European Union. It is a counterweight not only against Russia, but also (although it is never openly expressed) against Germany. These countries preferred to deal with Russia and with Germany within the framework of NATO, which implies a strong American presence in Europe.

Since 1989, the geopolitical center of gravity of Europe has moved eastward, toward Central Europe. But the institutional center of gravity has moved westward. The Warsaw Pact and ComEcon no longer exist. Only NATO and the European Union remain. This is the tension, or even the contradiction, at the heart of a new European architecture. And it is precisely in Central Europe, where it is experienced in the most acute fashion that will have to be resolved.

NOTES

This chapter was adapted and translated by Oleg Kobtzeff from the lectures by Jacques Rupnick recorded on 28 January and 4 February 1998, and other materials.

1. M. Kundera, "The Tragedy of Central Europe: The Kidnapped West," *New York Review of Books*, February 1994.

2. Jerry Jedlicki, *A Suburb of Europe: XIX Century Polish Approaches to Western Civilization* (Budapest: CEU Press, 1999).

3. The "2+4" agreement was signed in Moscow on 12 September 1990 among the two Germanys and the victors of 1945, reestablishing the full sovereignty of Germany reunited and finalizing the removal of the Soviet troops from the German Democratic Republic.

4. Map by the Observatoire de Geopolitique, University of Lyon.

Chapter 2

The Balkans: A Distorted, Third World Reflection of Europe

Catherine Durandin

The Balkans are but a distorted mirror, a kind of caricature of Europe. The Balkans have been, and continue to be, a "third world of Europe." One of the most convenient references for understanding this assertion is *Balkan Ghosts* by Robert D. Kaplan.[1] Through the data he submits, the author interweaves past and present and stresses how deeply the former dominates the latter. The past is more than just a memory, and is used too often as the means to validate the right of each nation in its confrontation with other nations. History permeates political and international behavior.

Since their early nineteenth-century struggles for a modern national identity, these countries and their élites have continuously expressed their desire to be European, and be regarded as part of the global European destiny. Having now gained their independence, they still want to take part in Europe's history and development. Simultaneously, Russia's ongoing interest in the Balkans makes these a part of Russian history, but of a Russia identifying itself as a Western and modern power—another version of Europe. One should always remember when dealing with Russia that the expansion of power since Peter the Great and especially under the reign of Catherine II was part of a Westernization program. In 1766, Catherine declared: "Russia is a European power."

I will discuss the Balkans as a self-conscious reflection of Europe and as a developing area, in two parts. The first part will be mainly a historical overview. These countries share with all European nations a tragic history. The second part of my discussion will focus on contemporary problems in the post-Communist period, that is, since 1989. These problems involve the West composed of western European countries and the United States, Russia as a weakened but still important military power, and the southeastern European countries.

Historically speaking, what do we mean when we speak of the Balkans as a distorted, "third world" reflection of Europe? From the fourteenth to the seventeenth centuries the Balkan countries—Greece, Moldo-Wallachia, Bulgaria, Serbia, and Croatia—were directly or indirectly under the Ottoman Empire, or the Habsburg rule. There existed a dominant physical Turkish presence in the Balkans, their institutions and influence made the Balkans take a different path from the rest of Europe. For example, the Romanian principalities paid a huge financial tribute to Constantinople and even after 1821 the Romanian princes had to seek the Sultan's consent. In 1866, when he arrived in Moldo-Wallachia, having been sent by Napoleon III and Bismarck, Charles Hohenzollern had to pay a visit to the Sultan in Constantinople as a vassal; as a Prussian Christian aristocrat, he deeply resented this humiliation. After 1699, Croatia began to develop under Habsburg rule, which was to last until the dissolution of the Habsburg Empire in 1918. The centuries of Turkish control cut the Balkans off from the larger events of Europe. They were perceived as a Far East, as oriental. Moreover, this oriental space was not considered as glorious, but essentially as backward.

Then, after 1774, Russian influence in the Balkans becomes important. It was an influence of a complex nature. It can be argued that Russian power was expansionist as soon as it moved toward the Balkans, and toward the Straits and Constantinople. A strong characteristic of past centuries has been the confrontation between Orthodox Christianity—Moscow claiming the title of the Third Rome in the late fifteenth century—and Islam. The other element of Russia's perception of the Balkans is its deep feeling of solidarity and fraternity with its indigenous peoples and other Orthodox people, mainly the Bulgarians whose 1878 independence is due to the Russians. Many historians, including the late Barbara Jelavich, argued that this cultural and religious trend dominates Russian policy toward the Balkans.[2] But there is another, equally important link.

During and after the reign of Peter I, Russia saw itself as a modern, Westernized—a *European*-country. In France, in his correspondence with the empress Catherine II, Voltaire stressed that Russia was a powerful and deeply implicated actor of the Enlightenment. Russia was the country of reason with a Greek inheritance. Russian entry into the Balkans, so criticized by Western European powers after 1815 as a threat to civilization, was viewed by St. Petersburg as an act of modernity being brought to the Balkans. The Balkan elites in the first quarter of the nineteenth century shared these perspectives. One Romanian historian, Vlad Georgescu, has shown through his research (based on letters addressed by Moldovan and Wallachian boyars to the Russian administrator for the Principalities between 1829–1834), that these elites were delighted with the new modern order. The administration of Bessarabia in the 1820s had also been appreciated. In 1829–1834, General Pavel Kiseliov organized the administration of the Principalities and put an end to the Ottoman control of the local economy. Economically speaking, Kiseliov was a liberal. He put an end to the right of preempting local markets enjoyed by the Turks. His decision opened a new era of commercial development especially for the export of grain.[3]

The question remains as to whether or not Russia was a part of Europe or a distorted reflection of it. The question is not a simple one. Romanticism and the French model of 1789–1848 changed the image of Russia as seen from Europe, and partly changed the self-image of Russia. The French Revolution and the Russian mystical counterrevolution that followed the events of 1815 both in Europe and in Russia, raised questions about Russian identity.[4] Secondly, everywhere in nineteenth-century Europe, the most imitated cultural movement is romanticism. The emotional message of romanticism brought the ideas and the ideal of nationality and patriotism to the Balkans. This romanticism did not fit in with the traditional Russian mission. In the middle of the nineteenth century the intellectual elites did not think in such abstract terms as the independence of the state or nation-state. They had no real conception of the state, such as that the French would have. Instead, these elites spent their time pursuing the important work of building a specific identity, and bringing this identity to their countrymen. This romanticism without a true political context was built upon German and French culture as was seen in the work of Herder in Germany, and of the influential scholars Edgar Quinet and Jules Michelet in France. Edgar Quinet had been the discoverer and translator, in 1827, of Herder's book about the destiny of humanity.[5]

The search for a specific identity boiled down to the restoration of the language and of a "historical" memory. Examples usually include a heroic story such as the Kosovo Epic for the Serbs or Father Paisiy's pseudoepic for the Bulgarians. Both told of the people's fight against the Ottoman invaders, or the recovered memory of the Dacians. This is a fully Christian, European memory. Across the centuries of degrading Turkish domination, these Balkan histories serve as a link with the heroic, crusading past of the Serbs, Bulgarians, and Romanians. Where there were no Turks to fight, there was a memory of the former Christian empire in Croatia.

These romantic memories could accept the emancipation brought about by the will and politics of Russia. They could not, however, accept Russian expansionist rule: In 1878, when Russia claimed Bessarabia, the Romanians constructed a deep anti-Russian culture as part of their national identity. So the first step had been a fraternity with the Russians against the Turks, and the second phase was a substantial and systematic anti-Russian attitude with assertions that Russia was a mendacious power. The Romanians embraced the romantic vision of the Marquis de Custine of a deceitful Russia.

Against Russia, these new independent countries sought help and protection from rival great powers, that is, Austria and Germany. The case of Greece also deserves to be examined. Philhellenic romanticism led England and France to support the Greeks in their revolution. Help and support were given to the Greeks from 1821 to 1830 by London, and later, Saint Petersburg. But, at the same time, this romanticism was not supposed to go too fast nor too far. Balkan peoples had to remain within the limits of what seemed reasonable to the great powers, who had their specific vision about their own interests and about the nature of their relationship with the Ottoman Empire. For example, in

1877, Vienna, Saint Petersburg, and Berlin were not favorable to the independence of the Romanian principalities. They agreed at last at the Berlin Congress but imposed conditions. The Balkan countries emerging toward freedom discovered that they were not free of, but depended instead upon, Russia or upon the allies or rivals of Russia. Independence was perceived at the same time with joy and resentment in the Balkan states. In order to gain access to a sublime destiny, it was necessary to stress their exceptional specificity. As their respective forms of nationalism were based on a weak material base, they were pushed toward violence and often chose to respond with terrorism.

THE QUESTION REMAINS: WHY DO THESE COUNTRIES REPRESENT A "THIRD WORLD"?

The Balkans for the better part of the millennium—between 1400 and 1900—were Christian, victims of the Ottomans who in their declining phase after 1600 could be considered as oriental despots.[6] European romantics viewed the Balkan peoples, especially the Greeks, as brothers.[7] But in the clear light of day, after the middle of the nineteenth century, these people were viewed as different, exotic, poor. We know the descriptions left by travelers, English and French alike, such as Saint Marc Girardin, Thouvenel, and later in the 1930s, Rebecca West. The European travelers portrayed the peasants as primitive, naive, cruel, and superstitious. The travelers wrote that the peasants had no fear of death. The military observers during the Russo-Turkish war in 1878 and during the Balkan Wars of 1912–1913 were thrilled by the naive courage of the Balkan soldiers: They danced under the fire of the canons. They fought barefooted. These countries are close yet very remote: The travelers stereotyped the Balkans just like the defense attachés and reporters did during the Russo-Turkish wars of 1877–1878 and later during the Balkan Wars when Trotsky was a journalist. In the beginnings of World War I, John Reed's writings about Serbia portrayed the cruelty of the Serbian fighters.

For all of these foreigners, there was a sense of mystery about the Balkans, particularly as some places remained untouched and almost unknown, like Albania. These travelers and observers knew that geographically they were still in Europe, but they were struck by the exotic nature of the area. And so they emphasized the belief that they had found a different kind of human being—sometimes bizarre—but still, people with a culture that could be understood, one based on classic Greek and Latin roots. Yet, they were not "like us." Between the familiar cultural roots and the completely alien atmosphere of this periphery, there was a contradiction.

At the end of World War I, Western European models, and the direct influence and intrigues of the great European states accompanying the end of the empires, had a mixed influence on the emergence of nation-states everywhere in central and southeastern Europe. The Balkan peoples built their nation-states, but were assigned their frontiers at the Paris peace conferences, and then tried to follow Western models and theories. They also adopted nineteenth-century liberal Western rhetoric. In the 1920s the Kingdom of Slovenes, Serbs, and Croats was established on the basis of a centralized constitution. The Croats were deeply frustrated and during the constitutional elections, they abstained from voting. They felt betrayed. They had fought in the Austro-Hungarian army and the Serbs had fought in the armies close to the Triple Entente. For the Serbs, the victory was a Serbian victory. In 1923, Greater Romania chose a Western constitution, adopted equal rights for all citizens, including the Jewish community, and extended universal suffrage to all males. The Liberal party, which was at the head of the government until 1927, sought to demonstrate its ability to develop alongside with Western Europe. The mirror-image model was supposed to be an accurate map for "progress." The compulsory Western model was viewed as a universal norm.

But, tragically, the Balkans began to follow the European liberal democratic path when this model itself was falling apart in Western Europe. From 1920, the Western liberal model was challenged by the conservative revolution in France, Italy, and Germany, and by the fascists and nazis who argued that democracy had no right to impose itself after World War I. democracy was only the realization of the selfishness of the bourgeoisie. The right wing argued that the bourgeoisie had failed in the West to build justice, rule of law, and equal development for all. Now the time had come for mass movements. The war and its barbaric nature had demonstrated the failure and the hypocrisy of democracy. This argument took on a considerable force in the Balkan countries where the bourgeoisie did not exist, and had never existed as a homogeneous group-even though its rhetoric was being used.[8]

Similar antidemocratic trends developed in the 1920s and 1930s in western, central, and eastern Europe with similar programs also opposed to democratic pluralism, democratic international law, foreigners, and Jews. The same right-wing language was used from Paris to Berlin to Belgrade and to Bucharest. Now nationhood had to be rebuilt upon blood, ethnicity, and historical spirituality. Authoritarian regimes came into power in Belgrade, in Athens, and in Bucharest before World War II.

There were precise links, contacts, friendships among those various right-wing philosophers and political activists. One Romanian student, Florin Turcanu, now lecturer at the University of Bucharest, has studied the link between Charles Maurras and the Romanian right. We also know that some right-wing philosophers in Romania were paid by the German minister of propaganda or minister of foreign affairs. In the 1930s the reflection of Europe in the Balkans was not so distorted. Even then, however, the Balkan nations wanted to be seen as indigenous. They could not bear to be part of a European culture that they did not create or produce.

With such proximity to Berlin, the Balkans remained culturally dependent: the main problem was (and in a way, still is) to rise to the level of Europe. They fought (and fight) to escape their alleged condition of underdevelopment, an exotic subject for foreign travelers. Emil Cioran's book, *Histoire et Utopie,* written in French and published in Paris after World War II illustrates this acute feeling of inferiority. Another work developing this theme is his *The Transfiguration of Romania,* published in Bucharest in 1937 before Cioran left the country: An imprecation mixed with love and hate against Romania—such a poor and oppressed little country. For Cioran, not being a member of a great power, or of a great civilization seems to lead to despair.

These trends—dependence and pretensions of glory—this uncertain game with Russia as a brother and a threat, still remain. As for a *transition* to the contemporary era, Communism, despite all its internationalism, failed to provide a way to gain freedom as an alternative to the *alienation* inherent to Western democracies or fascist Europe. The Communists failed to be truly international. Moscow guided the countries of central and eastern Europe under the law of Big Brother, while Communism, in order to establish itself in different societies in the long term, adapted itself, in the short term, to local forms of nationalism.

The legacy of this distorted view of Europe and underdevelopment is readily visible at the end of this century. In the last decade, the Balkans have been the scene of:

1. A bloody transition in December 1989 and a deep crisis in Romania.
2. A society in Bulgaria more and more dominated by crime and the Mafia.
3. A very difficult democratic transition in Albania, after a violent crisis in 1997.
4. A destabilization in Serbia with the Kosovo, crisis which could spread to Macedonia.
5. A long-running crisis in Bosnia after the Dayton peace agreements.

In every area affected by this situation, Western powers, under the label of Europe or NATO, have been drawn into greater involvement, in order to control, to help, in a way, to rule without knowing when or how this situation will end. And wherever, the government and the public alike feel threatened, like the Albanians did during recent crises, they demand that NATO and the United States demonstrate their military strength. Western countries are expected to behave as either an umbrella or shelter. Hence, an abdication of local sovereignty.

After prolonged Western influence in the Balkans in the nineteenth and twentieth centuries, a new set of Western images has been discovered since 1989. Wherever Communist regimes fell, the right to universal suffrage was declared and experienced by the citizens. Yet, voting did not lead to a real civic democracy in which individuals vote as citizens: Instead, these individuals were to vote as clan groups in Albania, ethnic groups in Kosovo, or as Communist and clientelist groups in Romania in 1990.

Thus the emancipation of the "individual as a citizen" has not occurred. The concept of communal relationship still prevails. So the imitation of liberal democratic institutions is, at best, very superficial.

In the economic life of the Balkans, the IMF, the European programs, and money from foreign investments are the keys to survival. The danger here is that help is granted under certain conditions, including new imposed rules, such as the free market and privatization. "The free market" has become a motto, although in the Balkans, as in Russia, free markets are essentially in the hands of former nomenklatura bosses, or in the hands of local mafias who control drugs, oil, and weapons. Western decision-making often produces unexpected results: the profits reaped by the Romanian oil mafia during the embargo against Serbia only shows how Western choices can be counterproductive. Europe is *very firmly there* if one considers that there is likewise in Europe a crisis of the idea of what politics are supposed to be, and the changing nature of the *social contract*. The populations of the Balkan countries feel excluded much as people without jobs feel excluded in Western Europe. The latter do not understand the meaning of the *social contract*, do not vote any more, or else vote for extremist parties.

The Balkans are, in fact, a "third world" for Europe. Eastern Europe is seen as a place for needing assistance, especially humanitarian assistance. The rate for early death is high and life expectancy is becoming lower: At the same time the birth rate becomes even higher. As this time, the Balkans is a place to invest for profit. And we see significant competition among Europeans and between European and U.S. investors. This competition is significant so far as armaments are concerned.[9]

In the end, the third world is supposed to *progress*, to reach Western standards. Slovenia and Romania are potential candidates for the future expansion of NATO. They have been asked firmly to reach Western standards as far as their behavior—reform in military command and standardization of weapons—are concerned. The high level of military expenses will take an increasing share of the gross national product.

Is Europe back to the point where it was in 1912 on the eve of the Balkan wars, confronted with hypernationalism, underdevelopment, and very modern weapons sold from Western countries? No. In 1912–1914, the great European powers were interested in partitioning the Ottoman Empire. Currently the great powers are not interested in such a partition. THE WEST KNOWS THAT A NEW SET OF BALKAN WARS WILL LEAD TO A REGIONAL CONFLAGRATION. But this is little comfort to the Balkan states, or to the West. The way for a rebuilding of national identity, and even for the restructuring of the Balkans, has not yet been found.

On the eve of World War I, the great Western powers came into conflict over the question of the control of the Balkans. The modern Western states sought, each in its own way, to replace the aging Eastern empires. In 1999, ten years after the overthrow of communism, the West claims to be following the model of universal law, first used to justify its intervention in 1991 against Iraq. But this model is rejected by those who uphold the concept of the sovereign nation-state, such as President Milosevic of the Federal Republic of Yugoslavia.

NATO's intervention in Kosovo at the end of March 1999 brought into sharp focus for the Balkans the basic contradiction between NATO's self-proclaimed pursuit of the lofty imperatives of universal law and the more obvious logic of overwhelming Western power. The people in the Balkans—in Greece, Romania, and Bulgaria—understood, and often rejected, the logic of

NATO power. However, their governments supported NATO and rallied around the notion of universal law against the barbaric activities of the Serbs in Kosovo, without recognizing the subtext of power.

Thus for the Balkans, the balance sheet is a complex one. On one hand, the idealistic Western case for intervention in Kosovo—respect for the rights of the individual, whether Serb or Albanian—has not been generally accepted. On the other hand, the control of the reconstruction of Kosovo by the European Union and NATO is seen as just another manifestation of Western power. The continuation of the embargo against the Federal Republic of Yugoslavia is seen as just another sign of the capacity of the West to impose itself through the logic of overwhelming power, not universal law.

This logic of Western power is opposed by Russia, which is trying to maintain its traditional position of being able to intervene in the affairs of the Balkans. Russia became a member of the Contact Group in 1994, and the Russians entered into Kosovo in June 1999 to again discuss with the West the extent of their role in the Balkans.

Are the Balkans the third world of Europe? In 1999 the region passed under the direct and indirect control by the West, most openly seen in the dominating presence of the International Monetary Fund and the World Bank. Yet, the region remains trapped between the extremes of violent anarchy and the hopes of democracy. And the West itself responds between the extremes of military intervention based on the logic of power and humanitarian programs founded on the demands of universal law—neither of which responds to the basic needs of a region in the process of decomposition. Instead of being dealt with within the logic of its own situation, the Balkans remain buffeted by the rhetorical references to the sovereign nation-state, democracy, and the market economy.

NOTES

1. Robert D. Kaplan, *Balkan Ghosts, Journey Through History* (New York: Vintage Departures Edition, 1994)

2. Barbara Jelavich, *Russia's Balkan Entanglements 1806–1914* (Cambridge: Cambridge University Press, 1991).

3. The documents selected by the Romanian historian Vlad Georgescu, who ended his life with a questionable death in exile in Munich where he worked for RFE, give vivid proof of this, see *Mémoires et projets de réformes dans les Principautés roumaines 1831–1848*, (Paris: Association Internationale d'Etudes du Sud-Est européen, 1972)

4. See Tchaadaiev, *Les Lettres d'un fou.*

5. Johann Gottfried Herder's unfinished 1784–1791 *Ideen zur Philosophie der Geschichte der Menschheit*, were translated by Edgar Quinet (*Idées sur la philosophie de l'histoire de l'humanité*, Paris: Levrault, 1827–1828); on the influence of Herder on Quinet and other contemporaries see Willy Aeschimann: *La pensée d'Edgar Quinet: étude sur la formation de ses idées avec essais de jeunesse et documents inédits* (Paris: Geneva, 1986) See C. Durandin, *Révolution à la française ou à la russe* (Paris: PUF, 1989).

6. This was a popular theme in the eighteenth century; see Voltaire and his letters

to Catherine II; see Charles Hohenzollern writing to his father that the link between Romania and Constantinople was an anachronism, in C. Durandin, *Histoire des Roumains* (Paris: Fayard, 1995),148.

7. Let us remember the way Lord Byron and Victor Hugo saw the Greeks.

8. Zeletin in Romania tried to demonstrate the development of a bourgeois class in the 1920s and thus supported the Liberal Party in his writings in 1927. He was challenged by Manoilescu, who was a supporter of the king and of the extreme right wing and who questioned the existence of a Romanian bourgeoisie.

9. French and American companies have been competing in Romania. In 1998, for example, with a large contract for the sale of ninety–six Cobra helicopters to the Romanian army, the Americans won.

Chapter 3

Rusty Ottoman Keys to the Balkans of Today

Bernard Lory

In the twentieth century, with its repeated Balkan Wars (1912, 1913, 1914–1918, 1940–1945, 1991–1995), the cliché of the Balkan powder keg was coined. But then, as now, this long-standing cliché actually reflects Western Europe's fears as well as its inability to analyze the Balkan dilemma. My hypothesis is that ignorance of the Ottoman historical presence in the Balkans is to a great extent responsible for the West's difficulty in grasping the Balkan problem.

Most histories of Europe devote little space to the continent's southeastern corner, the Balkans. After the fall of Constantinople (1453), this geographic entity usually vanishes, only to pop up again in the nineteenth century with the Serbian uprising (1804–1805), and the Greek War of Independence (1821–1829). Moreover, once the Balkan peoples were conquered by the Ottoman Turks, they disappeared from the annals of European history only to re-materialize after the Congress of Berlin in 1878 when this forgotten periphery suddenly became the focus of intense diplomatic activity.

AN IMMENSE EMPIRE

As with all imperial constructions, the history of the Ottoman Empire can be divided into two phases: (1) conquest and building; and (2) decay and disintegration. The dividing line is usually drawn at the end of the seventeenth century, at which time its territory covered about 15% of the map of Europe, the Near and Middle East to the border of present day Iran, and North Africa as far as Morocco. It included the areas of today's Greece, Albania, Bulgaria, Macedonia, Serbia, Bosnia, and Herzegovina, and half of Croatia. The Sublime Porte also exerted control over what is now Romania,[1] and the southern part of the Ukraine. (Areas that escaped Ottoman rule included Greece's Ionian Islands [Corfu] and the coast of Dalmatia, all under Venetian rule; the small territory of Dubrovnik, an independent state until 1808; and Western Croatia [Zagreb] and Slovenia, both under Habsburg suzerainty. The Ottoman armies reached Vienna twice [in 1529 and 1683] but failed to enter it, and repeatedly sacked western Croatia, Slovenia, and Venice's hinterland. They also briefly occupied Otranto in southern Italy, but failed to take Malta in 1565.)

These lands not only submitted to the same military power, they were governed by the same political system, subject to the same legislation, and viewed as one functional economic unit. It is hard to imagine, as was the case until about 1870, that a traveler could journey from Sarajevo to San'a without crossing a single border.

DURATION

Ottoman domination lasted longer in some places than in others: Budapest was under the control of the Porte for 150 years; Belgrade, for 340 years; Athens, 370 years; Sarajevo, 410 years; Sofia, 500 years; and Skopje, for 520 years. These significant periods can be likened to the short, by comparison, periods of French colonization in Algeria (130 years) or British rule of India (about two centuries) with the attendant impact upon regional populations. It should also be noted that the Ottoman regime was abolished only in 1923 in what became modern Turkey, and it still held sway over Albania, Macedonia, Northern Greece, Kosovo, and southern Bulgaria until 1912. Old people in these areas are still keenly reminiscent of events that took place during the last phase of Ottoman rule.

AN IGNORED HISTORY

Although it is evident that the Ottoman Empire constitutes a "big chunk" of world history both chronologically and geographically, it remains to all but a small circle of scholars very much a *terra incognita*. The historians of different Balkan countries systematically minimize its overall importance. They stress the pre-Ottoman medieval period and then "jump" as quickly as possible to the nineteenth century, devoting minimal attention to the time span of 300 years (fifteenth–eighteenth centuries). Western European historians do no better. They are prone to mention the Ottoman threat to Central Europe, while neglecting its impact on Southeastern Europe. In fact, this portion of the continent and its role in the historic events of the period are viewed as extraneous to European history. Why is it that this big chunk of the past is neglected, rejected, and deemed of such little importance?

WESTERN HISTORIANS

Aside from a general lack of interest on the part of Western scholars on the subject of the Balkans, there are other deep-rooted and half-conscious reasons for neglecting the Ottoman Empire. For centuries, the Turk has been designated as Europe's worst enemy. This has been especially true in German-speaking Central Europe, where tremendous anti-Turkish propaganda was disseminated between the fifteenth and seventeenth centuries by means of the revolutionary printing press. There, the Turk was systematically portrayed as cruel, barbaric, and immoral (a polygamist!). This was understandable at the time, as Christendom (the real unifying agent in Europe) was torn by the wars of religion. The Ottomans were viewed as the practitioners of a strange and unfamiliar religion. Stigmatizing a common enemy was the best way to safeguard some kind of European unity.

Sixteenth-century propaganda reinvigorated the collective representation of the *other*. As a concept, it was never questioned, and today, we still live, albeit unconsciously, with many of the negative cliches that "otherness" generated centuries ago. Most people, even scholars, identify the Ottoman conquest with former invasion patterns like those of the Huns (fifth century), or the Tartars (thirteenth century), because of linguistic affinities with them. They forget that the Ottomans were not nomads (even though they included nomadic tribes in their armies), and that they did not invade Europe through the half-empty steppe route north of the Black Sea. The Turkish-speaking Ottomans migrated west through the most highly civilized territories of Persia and Anatolia, taking from the Abbasids and the Byzantines cultural elements that they incorporated into their own specific civilization.

The image of Turks as the "enemies of civilization," elaborated in the sixteenth century, still lies embedded in European mentality, even though we are ashamed to openly acknowledge the fact. But beginning in 1960, this viewpoint has slowly undergone a subtle shift in that many benefits of reciprocal exchange are now acknowledged. This was primarily due to the presence in Central Europe of hundreds of thousands of Turkish *Gastarbeiter*. A vivid example of the changing attitudes occurred in 1983 during the commemoration of the siege of 1683 of Vienna. For the first time, the accent was not put exclusively on military events, but included such seventeenth-century cultural crossovers as the introduction of coffee into Europe.

The image of Turks as the "enemies of civilization," elaborated in the sixteenth century, still lies embedded in European mentality, even though we are ashamed to openly acknowledge the fact. But beginning in 1960, this viewpoint has slowly undergone a subtle shift in that many benefits of reciprocal exchange are now acknowledged. This was primarily due to the presence in Central Europe of hundreds of thousands of Turkish *Gastarbeiter*. A vivid example of the changing attitudes occurred in 1983 during the commemoration of the siege of 1683 of Vienna. For the first time, the accent was not put exclusively on military events, but included such seventeenth-century cultural crossovers as the introduction of coffee into Europe.

BALKAN HISTORIANS

The picture drawn by Balkan historians is even more Manichaean. After a heroic, but desperate defense against an overwhelming enemy, dark centuries of slavery and exploitation spread over the Balkan peninsula. Flickering embers of national spirit were kept alive in monasteries and amongst freedom-loving bandits. To this day, it is still widely believed that when conditions became favorable, the patriotic flame ignited whole nations in a decisive movement of *national revival*, and it was this surge of popular spirit that caused the demise of the Ottoman Empire, already rife with decay.

However, this historical perspective is a pure product of national romanticism, as those persons purporting the awakening of Balkan nationalism were typical products of the nineteenth-century romantic movement in that they relished dramatic contrasts. By showing the righteous struggle of their nation, they could portray themselves as victims of the vilest of oppressors. The truth is that the Ottoman Empire was in permanent crisis during the entire nineteenth-century, as it was unable to solve its internal socioeconomic shortcomings through meaningful reform (*tanzimat*). Factual evidence paints this rather sorrowful picture.

Once again, the problem is one of historical perspective. When the young Balkan intelligentsia, whether Greek, Serbian, Bulgarian, or Albanian, established a historical discourse, it was one that, more often than not, contrasted sharply with the decadent and agonizing reality at hand. The Ottoman Empire's glory, power, and prosperity (the high-water mark being the fifteenth and sixteenth centuries) were the objects of selective amnesia. The final result has been that Balkan historiography, retroactively, thrust the negative images of the nineteenth century to the forefront, and made them commensurate with the entire period of Ottoman rule. At the same time, these very negative images give legitimacy to the nineteenth–century liberation struggle. Thus viewed, this militant adaptation of history can be compared to an anticolonial discourse in that the Imperial Porte has been systematically shown to be exploiting, violent, oppressive, and so on.

A MODERN APPROACH TO OTTOMAN HISTORY

My purpose is not to condemn Western or Balkan historiography, but to stress the strong influence that the formation of respective historical pasts have exerted upon historians and scholars. Moreover, as this formative past is now obsolete, there is no reason to maintain its mandated vision. A big chunk of Ottoman history should now be seen in a more subtle light, one that notably mitigates the forces of "good" and "bad." Istanbul's legacy should be examined from within and not exclusively on the basis of information garnered by its historical adversaries. This is possible, but not easy.

The Ottoman Empire was run in a very bureaucratic manner, and its many administrations left a vast stock of archives. These documents are written in Ottoman-Turkish, a subtle and difficult language that requires much time and effort to decipher. Since World War II, much has been done to publish these records; so today, an understanding of the huge, complex, Ottoman machine is improving constantly.

It should always be remembered that Ottoman conquest produced an "empire." Making any interpretation, or drawing conclusions from a "national" viewpoint immediately becomes either partisan or anachronistic. To extract from the mass of the Sultan's subjects, only those speaking Greek, Bulgarian, or Albanian is meaningless in the context of an Empire where religion, and not language was the main criteria for group identification. The Greek, Bulgarian, or Albanian populations were diluted within a larger entity, one that must be understood as a whole. Categorizing people by nationality merely hinders such an endeavor.

The empire should also be examined for its own sake and distanced from all ideological controversy. Almost all Balkan historians, consciously or unconsciously, adopt the position of their own nation's propagandists. History is politicized in this part of Europe, and scientific detachment is often put aside in order to advocate what is thought to be a deserving nation's basic rights. But this too is slowly changing.

PRESENT NECESSITY

Why should anyone bother to understand the history of the Ottoman Empire? Does it truly merit the attention of more than a few passionate scholars? The answer is yes to both questions, in so far as the goal is not so much to fathom the workings of the Ottoman Empire as it is to understand the Balkans. The impact of five centuries upon the region deserves a closer examination.

If asked, all Balkan intellectuals would affirm that: (1) very little of the Ottoman impact carries over to influence today's Balkan populations; and (2) all Balkan peoples are Europeans. While the second assertion is true, the first is not. But most interesting is the implicit connection made between the two assertions. Why should the "Europeanness" of the Balkans necessarily be linked to their proclaimed "non-Ottomanness"?

In my opinion, it is evident that Ottoman rule shaped a particular form of European identity. But it does not mean that this inherited identity is inferior in value or dignity to Scandinavian or Iberian European identities. It is simply different. In addition, why should aspects of Ottoman cultural heritage be considered anti-European? Have not historians exposed many Byzantine patterns embedded in the Ottoman ruling and taxation systems? Just as the nineteenth century is dominated by the question of adapting aspects of Western culture into the Ottoman Empire, contacts, trade, and mutual influence came to characterize an exchange that was not based exclusively on warfare.

OTTOMAN HISTORY AS PART OF EUROPEAN HISTORY

Before the term "Balkan peninsula" was popularized in 1808 by a reputed German geographer, the area was referred to as *Turkey in Europe* without any inherent contradictions. (Indeed it would be ludicrous to assume the Balkan countries were excluded from Europe for four or five centuries.) The task put before historians, be they willing or unwilling, is to integrate Ottoman history, or at least parts of it, into a new European narrative. It is imperative that this be done even though scholars may encounter vehement opposition from nationalistic colleagues. But only a few historians are actually conscious of this important challenge.

Furthermore, the most obvious argument against such an endeavor is that a "Muslim" Ottoman state has no place in Western history modeled around Christendom. However, the question remains: How valid is such a point of view at the end of the twentieth century, when millions of European Union citizens practice the Islamic faith? The tragic Bosnian war (1992–1995) showed that 2 million Slavic-speaking Muslims defended their right to live in their European homeland. Ultimately, the debate has less to do with history, than with the current political situation regarding Turkey's admission to the European Community. As an issue, it has aroused heated polemics and sometimes even visceral reactions.

My purpose here however, is not to argue over such a crucial question, but to attempt to integrate Balkan history as a whole into a communal, contemporary narrative and not make five centuries of events disappear without a trace like the magician's rabbit. It is my conviction that ignorance of the Balkan area's historic past, including its many contradictions, undermines the possibility of true partnership with this part of Europe.

THE IMPRINT OF *MILLET* MENTALITY

The Ottoman legacy in the Balkans is not easy to identify. First of all, a truly comprehensive evaluation of the historical period is lacking. Second, Balkan peoples usually deny that such a legacy even exists. Next, I shall try to demonstrate how Ottoman structures shaped one of the area's most striking features, nationalism. In addition, the Balkans' perilous trajectory toward democracy will be considered, by drawing connections (though not always convincing ones) with Ottoman sociopolitical structures.

The political concept of *millet* has no Western equivalent. It has sometimes been compared to the idea of *nation*, but this causes confusion and misunderstanding. It is preferable to stick with the Ottoman connotation of the word, and try to determine its significance in this regard.

The "citizens" of the Ottoman Empire, or rather, the Sultan's subjects, were classified into political, judicial, and fiscal categories according to their religion. The dominant *millet* was that of the Sunni Muslims, who controlled the administration, the army—in sum, all of its bureaucratic structures. Inferior to it were the Jewish *millet*, the Armenian *millet*, the Latin (i.e., Catholic) *millet*, and so on. The Orthodox *millet* or *Rum-millet* was the most important in the Balkans because of its demographic weight. This category included Orthodox Christians speaking various languages including Greek, Serbian, Bulgarian, Romanian, Albanian, Macedonian,[2] and so on.

Every *millet* enjoyed a certain degree of autonomy. It elected its own leaders to manage internal affairs and these officials also served as representatives when dealing with Ottoman authorities. For example, Orthodox Bishops under the auspices of the Patriarch of Constantinople, played the role of *millet-bashi*, a function that gave them important political responsibilities along with their pastoral tasks.

Each *millet* disposed of its own financial resources levied by way of religious taxes, and this revenue was collected separately from taxes demanded by the Sultan. These resources were destined for the community's internal affairs such as the construction of places of worship, teachers' salaries, and so on, but a large percentage of it was given over to the bribing (*bakshish*) of Muslim officials, as the nomination of bishops and patriarchs had to be approved by Ottoman authorities.

In the judicial realm, the *millet* operated mainly in the field of family law (deliberations over marriage contracts, divorces, inheritance, adoption, etc.) and on occasion, it made decisions on the internal workings of the *millet* itself. When conflicts arose between people of different *millets*, it was the Muslim *kadi* or judge who presided.

The *Rum-millet* was also active in the field of education. In the eighteenth century, most schools were located in monasteries. The educational power of the *millet* system became even more important during the nineteenth century when education both developed and channeled national antagonisms. Schools not only aimed to teach reading and writing, but also (or mainly), molded young Greeks, Serbs, Bulgarians, and so on, into patriots.

The *millet* system permeated Balkan social structure. Usually each *millet* had its own quarters (*mahala*) in towns. Only the center of town, or *bazaar*, with its habitual din of commercial and social activity was common to all.

People could not marry outside their *millet*, and if they did, they were repudiated by their group. As the Muslim *millet* was dominant, it attracted many converts. To turn one's back upon one's *millet* was considered the most treasonable offense, and all links were severed between the *millet* members and the defecting apostate.

It should be stressed that the *millet* construct was a social and political system, in which religious belief played little if any role. In the Balkans, where neither the Protestant Reformation, nor the Catholic Counter-Reformation occurred, religion was more a question of group identity than individual conviction.

MILLETS AND NATIONALISM

For centuries, group designation in the Balkans followed the religious *millet* system of identification. However, in the nineteenth century the West introduced a new national identification model. No longer was group affiliation based on adherence to a religious body, but on language, tradition, and history. Because of rapid and (relatively) massive *alphabetization,* the attitude toward language changed radically during this period. The old medieval written tradition, which had served an almost exclusively liturgical purpose, was supplanted by a new approach toward literacy, as now the written language was based on the spoken vernacular. It also proved to be a means of acquiring modern Western knowledge. Schools, which for centuries had only replicated the internal system of each *millet*, became the gateways to Westernization and development.

The educational structure of Balkan Christians was run by the hierarchy of the *Rum-millet*, with the Patriarch of Constantinople at its head.[3] In the nineteenth century, it promoted the spread of Greek language and culture. But a conflict arose between the Greek-speaking clergy and their Slavic-speaking parishioners in Bulgaria and Macedonia, and, by the end of the century, among the Orthodox Albanians as well.

National revivals in the Balkans developed more as internal conflicts inside the *Rum-millets* than as the anti-Turk or anti-Muslim wars of independence so frequently depicted by romantic historiography and Western historians. In fact, the Serbian uprisings and the Greek War of Independence appear to be exceptions rather than the rule.

Western nationalism, introduced into the Balkans in the nineteenth century, did not supplant or abolish the old *millet* categories, but superimposed new categories, of which only some could be adapted to the local standards. Despite an appearance of modernity and a contemporary discourse, the old *millet* patterns continue to be applicable today. This contradictory situation takes many forms.

THE CASE OF BOSNIA-HERZEGOVINA

One language in Europe appearing under various guises has been the object of heated dispute. It was long known as Serbo-Croatian, or Croato-Serbian. Today it is called Serbian, Croatian, Bosnian, and sometimes even Montenegrin. But all these different names cannot hide the fact that it is one linguistic system, with slight variations, mainly in vocabulary.

However, today, three different peoples speaking modestly divergent versions of the same language have identified themselves on the basis of their religion: Orthodox Serbs, Catholic Croats, and Muslim Boshnjaks. The emergence of Boshnjak national awareness has been a long and controversial process. It should be stressed that it has taken place in a post–Ottoman context, from 1878 to the end of the twentieth century, during which time the very logic of the *millet* system should have been recognized as defunct.

Religious practice in Bosnia-Herzegovina during this period was relatively low among the three groups, and probably most of all among the Orthodox. An interpretation of the recent war in Bosnia as a war of religion is an erroneous one. It has been a war between *millets* shaped by nationalism.

THE CASE OF ALBANIA

Albania seems to offer a radically different situation, one that is in contradiction with the *millet*-logic. In Albania, are there not one people, united by language and history, and yet divided into Muslims (about 70%), Orthodox (20%), and Catholics (10%), demonstrating a strict adherence to national patterns in the West?

It must not be forgotten, however, that between 1967 and 1990, all religious practice was outlawed in Albania. No Communist regime in the world had gone so far in executing its atheistic propaganda. Superficial analysts claim that Enver Hoxha's rule was Stalinist in its approach, and exemplified his outrage toward religion. However, the Albanian national feeling was fragile, since Albania was composed of three different *millets*. In order to reinforce national sentiment, the Hoxha regime brutally attempted to wipe out the *millet* differences among Albanians. His anti-religious motives were not Marxist-Leninist at all, but efforts to strengthen Albanian unity.

THE CASES OF ROMANIA AND MACEDONIA

The religious politics under Communist regimes in both countries, though not as radical as that of Albania, did proceed from the same *millet*-driven logic.

In October of 1948, Romania's newly instated Communist government coerced the Greek Catholic (Uniate) Church[4] to unite with the Romanian Orthodox Church. At a time of serious religious persecution, this decision seemed to strengthen the power of the country's principal religious group. But, it should be noted, most religious minorities in Romania were then (and still are) national minorities (Hungarians, Germans, and Jews). The primary exception is the Greek Catholic Church, exclusively composed of ethnic Romanians. It was not so much the fear of foreign intervention from the Holy Papal See in the internal affairs of the country that precipitated the merger. That merger was part of the attempt to reinforce national unity in the post–World War II climate.

In July 1967, a local synod unilaterally proclaimed ecclesiastical self-government (autocephaly) for the Church of Macedonia, which had been until then under the jurisdiction of the Orthodox Serbian Patriarch in Belgrade. The Belgrade Patriarchate strongly condemned this anti-canonical decision. At the present time, the Orthodox Church of Macedonia remains in an unresolved schismatic position.

The Communist authorities in Macedonia, rather than trying to solve a question that disturbed "unity and fraternity" among Yugoslav peoples, upheld the claim of Macedonian hierarchical autonomy. Why was this? The national specificity of the Macedonians was officially recognized late in Yugoslavia's history (1943–1945). Since then, the young Macedonian nation has made many efforts to assert its place among the southern Slavs despite its underdevelopment and lower population numbers. From the viewpoint of Ottoman planning (in terms of designing and finalizing *millet* status), the state structure was not complete without ecclesiastic autonomy, an idea shared by the Communist authorities. With reference to these standards, it could almost be said that the Western definition of nationhood was viewed as incomplete and insufficient.

THE CASE OF GREECE

Greece was probably the Balkan country that paid most dearly for the seriously problematic merging of *millet* and Western patterns of identity. The exchange agreement of 1923 between Greece and Turkey was in appearance, an exchange of national populations, but *millet*-driven in its application. Among the "Greeks" expelled from Asia Minor was an important enclave of Turkish-speaking Christians, the *Karamanlides* (from the region of Kayseri), and among the "Turks" expelled from Northern Greece, were the *Vallahades* (from the region of Grevena), a group of Greek-speaking Muslims.

The interwoven aspects of national and religious elements in Greek identity appeared clearly in 1991–1992 when a quarrel arose between the Athenian government and the European Community. The controversy concerned the mention of religion on Greek passports, an act that was contradictory to the freedom of conscience purported by the European Community. Approximately 95% of Greek citizens are Orthodox and approximately 3% are members of the Muslim community, while only 1% of the population (Greek-speaking Catholics, Jews, Protestants, Jehovah's Witnesses, etc.) poses a questionable identity problem. Members of these small religious groups were openly designated as such on official documents because an implicitly understood *millet*-based principle insinuates that true Greeks are Orthodox. But to the European Community, the procedure suggested religious discrimination.

MILLET MENTALITY AND THE POST-COMMUNIST TRANSITION

By now, it has become clear just how much the *millet* system has exerted its influence on Balkan states throughout the twentieth century and how the Communist system, instead of dismembering it, has used it for its own purposes. And today, the post-Communist system continues to manipulate it to suit its own agenda.

The "minority question" is something of a local specialty in Balkan politics, which, when acute, usually has a religious facet (Hungarians in Romania, Turks in Bulgaria and Greece, Albanians in Serbia, etc.). On the other hand, minorities sharing a dominant religion usually cause few if any problems (Romanians in Serbia, Serbs in Romania, and Arvanits[5] in Greece). The newly restored religious freedom reinforces these old antagonisms, even as new sects imported from the West are denounced most vehemently. Why this reaction? Most likely it is due to the fear of creating potentially threatening new *millets*.

It is important to note that modern urban life has tended to wipe out the frontiers between each of the old *millets*, especially in intellectual circles. This was the case in Sarajevo, where religious differences mattered little before the war. The Bosnian and Herzegovinian countryside, however, retained the old paradigms and the martyred city endured three years of siege because of them. Today in Mostar the system has been reinvigorated to the level of quasi-apartheid.

Western advice aimed at remedying Balkan minority problems often fails to see the complex, overlapping structures and, as a result, is judged as incredibly arrogant to Balkan ears. Perhaps if the West succeeded in solving the divisions in Northern Ireland in a just and orderly manner, it would gain credibility vis-à-vis the Balkans.

OTTOMAN LEGACY AND THE DEMOCRATIC AND ECONOMIC TRANSITION

It would be foolish to expect that an imperial entity like the Ottoman Empire could have prepared its "citizens" for modern democracy. The Balkan people have had to learn self-government on their own. This process began as early as 1830 in Greece, but as late as 1920 in Albania. Therefore, it is difficult to find any regime that can be qualified as a working democracy in the Western sense before the Greek military regime fell in 1974.

A negative picture for the Balkans' future must not be drawn in haste. The Ottoman Empire legated throughout the region a very strange relationship between its bureaucratic core and local autonomy. The enormous empire, as previously seen, was strongly centralized around the Sultan's palace and the Sublime Porte in Constantinople, from whence an elaborate administrative system reached out to different provinces. Yet, when a closer examination of small communities (at village and township levels) takes place, a thriving political life has been found to exist, with assemblies and representatives delegated by the local populations (*knez* in Serbia, *chorbadzhiya* in Bulgaria, *kodzabasis* in Greece). How these two levels of political activity interacted must be studied in detail.

Over time, Balkan populations have been able to settle problems at the local level without outside intervention from what has always been considered a mistrusted and meddlesome state. The principal link between the lower and highest levels of political life has been the necessary reliance on *clientelism* and *bakshish* (bribery and payoffs). Communism, with its initially strong and hierarchical structure, progressively adapted to these older practices, and provincial communities often gained astonishing autonomy under the influence of a local party secretary. In the confused democratic and economic transition of today, *clientelism* has again appeared, as it is the best way to solve local difficulties. A profound wariness of open debate and the belief that important problems are best remedied through unobtrusive bargaining in the corridors of power can also be attributed to the Ottoman experience.

Since 1989, the trend in economic life is once again based on extended family enterprises. Business activity is focused in small trading activities and local services, much like the Greek and Turkish variations of capitalism that have developed outside the Communist sphere. The tiny shops, crowded with heterogeneous products, have appeared everywhere in the Balkans, echoing the old *dukkan* of the Ottoman Bazaar. This is how people have always preferred to buy and sell goods. If one wanted to postulate upon the economic future of the post-Communist Balkan countries, the most probable economic model lies in Turkey, rather than in Western Europe.

CONCLUSION

Historical determinism is a spiteful intellectual attitude. It is not my purpose to assert that because of their Ottoman past, the Balkan people are doomed to remain in a political, economic, or cultural periphery of Europe.

On the other hand, as a historian, I am horrified by the ignorance that regional intelligentsia has shown regarding its proper historical past. I have met very nice, educated, Balkan city dwellers of the former Soviet bloc, who use fashionable Western cliches. Yet, they are unable to analyze the present political and economic situations in their respective countries.

The old maxim "know thyself" holds true here more than ever. It is not by rejecting a major part of their history (the Ottoman centuries) that Balkan people will best find their place in Europe. On the contrary, by understanding and acknowledging this past, they can enlarge and enrich the concept of "Europeanness."

NOTES

1. The Ottomans did not exert direct rule over Romania, but used local vassal princes. This is the main argument to exclude this country from the "Balkan" realm. Endless controversy exists on this topic.

2. And even Turkish! The Christian *Gagauz* of the Black Sea coast were part of the *Rum-millet*. Today, they are an autonomous group within the Moldavian Republic.

3. The Orthodox Church, since the Byzantine period, is divided into several self-governing (or "autocephalous") territorial jurisdictions, administratively independent from one another but considering themselves in full doctrinal and liturgical unity. Almost all were federated by one of the "patriarchs"—the archbishops of Constantinople, Alexandria, Antioch, or Jerusalem (who either presided a collegiate government or ruled with powers, depending on the historical context). The "ecumenical" patriarch of Constantinople enjoys greater prestige and several responsibilities; but there is no central authority in the Orthodox Church. Later, Moscow (in the sixteenth century), then Sofia, Belgrade, Bucarest, and Prague (after World War I), became patriarchates. Since independence, Greek dioceses separated from Constantinople and are regrouped to this day in one autocephalous jurisdiction around the archdiocese of Athens (editor's note).

4. Roman Catholics using the same liturgy and often the same customs (married clergy) as the Orthodox (editor's note).

5. Albanian Christians.

Chapter 4

The Role of Culture under the Communist and Post-Communist Eras

Antonin Liehm

The well-known Hungarian poet Gyula Illyés once wrote, "Each and every time political life is banished from our lands, culture must take its place." In the context of Central Europe, what is the significance of this particular phrase?

To many, it remains an utter mystery how communism, which reigned over the lives of so many people under the label of "collectivism," led in the end to the disintegration of a cowed civil society. But the truth is that Communism hounded each member of the social body into a private refuge where self-styled tactics were adopted in order to survive. Paradoxically, this alienation affected the non-Communist population, by and large the majority, as much as party members, including the *nomenklatura*.

CULTURE AS A POLITICAL SUBSTITUTE

What most characterized an individual's condition in Communist regimes was a feeling of isolation. Yet this feeling only contributed to an enormous need to reestablish minimal links of social communication. That is why people forced themselves to interact outside the exposed public (political) arena, and to reconstruct "horizontal" relations (the Communist hegemony was characterized by its exclusively "vertical" interconnections) in order to recreate the elementary bonds of civil society. It was precisely through culture that people succeeded in forging new social links. Social communication pertaining to cultural matters and independent from the officially structured system was slowly constructed in a covert way without, at the start, drawing attention to the new edifice or its architects.

The movement to make national culture autonomous and try to promote its value had strong historical roots as it had often played a decisive role in regenerating popular cohesion. In nineteenth-century Poland, which had been partitioned amongst the imperial powers of Russia, Prussia, and Austria in the previous century, culture was harnessed to create genuine enthusiasm for the independence movement. At the same time in Bohemia, it was the national intelligentsia who instigated a renewal of the country's political life, filling the vacuum left by a nobility decimated during the religious wars of the seventeenth century.

The Communist system was never an entirely monolithic one. After 1956, a slow unavoidable weakening of its totalitarian characteristics took place in East-Central European regimes. The Communists in power grew less capable of governing and controlling different facets of social life effectively (as had been the case during the Stalinist period).

This trend began soon after Stalin's death in 1953. It started in Hungary, where from 1953 to 1956 the country's cinema broke from the classical Stalinist model. At that time, Hungarian filmmakers adopted Italian neorealism that had been proscribed until then. The liberalization trend spread first to Poland, then to the USSR, not to mention Yugoslavia, which since Tito's break with Stalin in 1948, had enjoyed a special status among Communist countries. The progressive emancipation of culture from Soviet-styled social realism and the loosening grip of Communist ideology would, in the end, contribute to a certain political liberalization vis-à-vis existing Communist regimes, proving that the emancipation of culture from official ideology precedes and anticipates political liberalization.

The pyramidal structure of the Stalinist system rested on a cog-and-wheel mechanical model. Orders, directions, and the official line to follow emanated from the highest level. They were directed downward from top to bottom by means of a complex system of organizations: professional organizations, unions, youth groups, syndicates, as well as parliamentary and regional assemblies. Their principal function was to insure control, working order, and the transmission of directives. Communist leadership favored the creation of unions for writers, cinematographers, artists, as well as other kinds of organizations such as stamp-collecting clubs, and local and regional cultural associations. Every organization was regulated by a structure modeled on that of the party (presidium, central committee, etc.). Militant Communists chosen by party officials were in charge of running them, although party membership was not a prerequisite to join.

The founders of Soviet-styled regimes believed that culture could be used as an effective weapon and an important tool to facilitate the establishment of a future Communist state. That is why, from the beginning, they decided to generously finance the broad spectrum of cultural life. The early years of Communism were not only years of forced and often spectacular industrial development. It was also a time when an important cultural infrastructure was implemented (cultural centers, universities, theaters, film studios, publishing houses, etc.). During this period, many intellectuals and artists were genuine and sincere builders of the new society. In exchange, the regime granted them advantageous material conditions, at least in comparison to the larger population; including relatively decent financial compensation, vacation accommodations, and a system of promotion and reward for those most loyal to those at the top.

Very quickly, however, divergent opinions between the artists and the regime's authorities began to appear, causing conflicts, although at first they were not openly political. Communist leaders were adamant about preserving the Stalinist pyramidal power structure in its monolithic form. No fissures were permitted to show, as the smallest crack could open the way to unauthorized influences, an outcome the system could not tolerate. In the cultural domain, Communist leaders had to forcibly impose a predetermined political and ideological dogma, as well as an aesthetic one, on creative artists. And it was precisely on aesthetic grounds that the first breach of faith occurred. Oddly enough, often at the root of these conflicts were sworn advocates of Communist ideology, both party and non-party members, for example, Vladimir Maiakovski or Serguei Eisenstein. But inevitably personal aesthetic concepts came into conflict not only with the theory but with the practice of the official socialist realism.

Divergent aesthetic opinions became the concern of more and more artists. Protest often involved people who did not necessarily wish to oppose the regime, but only wanted to work independently, an unacceptable position for the Stalinist authorities. But as artistic and creative defections led to cracks in the monolithic structure, the conflicts took on a political dimension.

In the late 1950s and early 1960s after Stalin's death, the hegemonic authority of the Communist party also began to waver when it came to the transmission of orders down the chain of command. Manifestations of an oncoming crisis appeared as contradictory information and the absence of precise strategies led to more autonomy, and cultural and artistic associations were largely responsible. These continued to be administered by the Communists, but as the party itself lost its authority, the members of its "cultural front" became increasingly rebellious, and gained a certain independence.

In 1963, an international conference on the work of Franz Kafka took place in Prague. The main objective of the organizers was to end the long period of censorship regarding his literary achievement. The conference became the battlefield where "orthodox" Marxists confronted "liberal" Marxists. The weekly magazine published by the Union of Czech Writers, *Literarni Noviny* (with a print run of 130,000 issues in a country of 15 million people) published transcripts of all the debates so that a wider reading audience was able to discover a long-forbidden author, and learn that his work bore witness to their own condition under communism. "This is Kafkaesque," subsequently became a familiar rallying cry uttered by people who had never read so much as a page of his work.

During the periodic thaws, culture, and associations connected with it took center stage in Communist societies. Thanks to them, more and more people from all walks of life came out of isolation. Individuals and many groups came to reconstruct new identities and a self-serving web of horizontal communication; they found at the cultural level a space wherein to contemplate the social and political realities in their respective countries. A cultural discourse replaced a dead-letter, political one. In contradiction to widely held beliefs, however, there were in fact more differences between any two Communist countries than between any two capitalist counties. That is why events must be placed in specific political, historical and national contexts.

At the time of each major political crisis in Communist East Central Europe (Poland and Hungary in 1956, Czechoslovakia and Poland in 1968, and Poland in the 1980s) cultural organizations played a pivotal role. In fact, they became the vector of civil society in transition, and the logical environment for all kinds of political opposition. In Poland, the Catholic Church often acted as an ecumenical front behind which political activity burgeoned, and in linguistically isolated Hungary, the government traded a laissez-faire policy for social peace. However, following each challenge from politicized cultural groups, Communist leadership was obliged to provide a period of "normalization," causing serious problems. For example, after the declaration of martial law in Poland in 1981, General Jaruzelski was obliged to dissolve most of the authorized cultural and artistic associations, as their weathered organizers had grown too independent.

Thus, organizations that in theory were supposed to safeguard the cultural domain began to contest party authority openly taking center stage in Communist societies. The phenomenon primarily involved associations of writers, filmmakers, and journalists. Thanks to them, more and more people from all walks of life came out of isolation.

As inner contradictions grew, the situation became more unfathomable to foreign observers: on one hand there was an increased demand for autonomy and, on the other, the Communist officials had no desire to disrupt the steady flow of public subsidies. "How was it possible," outsiders later asked, "that the most well known anti-Communist films could have been made in the Eastern bloc with endorsement and funding coming from Communist authorities?"

CULTURAL CONTRADICTIONS AFTER COMMUNISM

It is intriguing that Western politicians as well as political historians, sociologists, and economists have never focused on the cultural dimension surrounding the fall of communism. In analyzing the dynamics of the post-Communist era it must be recognized that it was not only the ideological and economic aspects of the fiasco, but also the moral aspect that led to its bankruptcy. Trends observed in Communist society such as the dissolution of the social web, alienation, demoralization, and the triumph of egoism and cynicism did not automatically vanish (it was impossible for them to disappear) after the end of communism. On the contrary, the new regimes inherited these social woes.

Communism's demise was a surprise for many. Even the dissidents in these countries never seriously considered what "the end of communism" would eventually imply. Guidelines on questions of social morality, how to recreate social cohesion, or how to rebuild civil society had never been formulated.

Since 1989, huge changes have taken place in East-Central Europe, not only in the shift toward democracy as the restraints of communism broke apart, but also in the creation of an environment conducive to greater freedoms. Right away, all acts forbidden or merely tolerated under the system (on the condition that individuals never questioned the party's policies) became permissible. This sudden new liberty allowed previously repressed social behavior to burst forth. For example, under communism, "He who steals not, takes from his family," had been a popular saying. After the demise of communism, theft in no way disappeared, but metamorphosed into new forms and reached unimaginable levels as a Western-styled legal system was lacking.

Given the fact that social actors were indeed "free," the new public morality was characterized by a total lack of social cohesion. In the absence of either vertical or horizontal social links, society found itself in a moral vacuum, and a partial political and legal vacuum as well.

The use of culture to unite disparate social actors is a recognized fact. However the new political leadership did not pay heed to this area when attempting to bind together post-Communist societies. An examination of the strategies they chose and why they chose them is pertinent.

As there was a resurgence of nationalism, leaders called upon nationalistic sentiment to temper the unexpected, and radical, social changes taking place. The results are only too well known. In certain countries such as Poland, where national feeling was closely associated with Catholicism, it was thought that a stress on religious morality would insure national cohesion. As results were disappointing, the leadership turned to anti-Communist sentiment, but anti-Communism is hardly a viable "ideology" for societies undergoing transition. In addition, as the risks of a return to communism waned, the call for "morality" was soon revealed to lack any positive influence on Polish society's own morale.

There were those, too, who believed that a liberal market economy would by itself be able to regulate the transition toward the new society. But it was quickly observed, notably in Czechoslovakia, that although the market could do many things, it alone could not assure social unity. It was in no way capable of initiating and overseeing the rules of civilized and democratic conduct, nor could it create a social cohesion. However, the new Czech leadership who believed unfalteringly in the power of market forces, went so far as to proclaim that civil society was none other than the "devil's own handiwork" and was thus to be rejected. Accordingly, the only things of importance were individuals and the electoral process, and it followed that social communication had to occur within the framework of a market economy. Society at large paid for this blanket refusal to examine what might have been worth reinventing or preserving.

The headlong rush to adopt market values explains why post-Communist societies and their leaders neglected the importance of culture, leading to its irremediable marginalization. At the beginning of the 1990s, the Czech minister of culture declared that his government lacked a cultural agenda (cultural politics, he said, had been a Communist invention) and he declined even to formulate one. In a country where culture and the arts have always played an important role in politics, the declaration was alarming if in retrospect one considers the role culture could have played in holding together post-Communist societies, in reconstructing civil society, and in acculturating nationalistic trends. Although culture is not in itself fundamentalist, it makes the acculturation of fundamentalism easier. But if culture goes unattended, it will lose its ability to disarm fundamentalist tendencies.

To say that culture must be subordinate to market forces and that it must be self-perpetuating is tantamount to signing the death warrant for numerous cultural activities. Sure enough, this is exactly what happened in Central Europe after 1989. But as subsidies for cultural pursuits were an anathema to the Western economists dictating structural adjustment policies, they were never an important consideration in Eastern European recovery programs.

It remains a fact that the nature of these countries must be taken into consideration. For the most part they are small nations with a limited linguistic outreach and an undeveloped cultural market. But with the euphoric acceptance of liberal market economy and the anti-statist sentiment that succeeded communism, the "American model" has become an indisputable point of reference. However, the American model does not fit the cultural sphere of East-Central Europe. The United States counts close to 300 million people who speak the same language, and along with its dynamic economy, it can call upon an entrenched philanthropic tradition. American culture can also count on a marketable audience of almost a billion English-speaking people around the world. In contrast, success for a contemporary writer in Poland is 2,000 copies sold in a country of 40 million people, and even a very popular and acclaimed Czech film is unable to recover its production costs in a linguistically limited market of 10 million.

The American model thus can not possibly be applied to cultures in small countries like Bulgaria or the Czech Republic. How could these countries possibly create comparable conditions to develop and run their cultural programs? Fascinated with the American model, post-Communist leadership has buried itself in illusions. Nonetheless such aspirations are easy to understand. Leadership only hoped to end the subservience of culture to an all-powerful party apparatus as quickly as possible. That is why they neglected many alternatives used by other non-Communist European nations.

Moreover, Eastern European leaders did not comprehend the basic differences between culture in Europe and culture in the United States. Historically, European culture (especially the arts) has been destined for an elite that has catalyzed cultural development. It took (and still takes) decades, even centuries before European "high culture" reached a wider domestic public, went beyond its national frontiers, and safeguarded its idiosyncratic character. The culture of North America has an entirely different history.

From the beginning, it targeted a population composed of immigrants from the world over who became American by adopting a common language. The American elite was much closer culturally to ordinary folk than its European counterpart. This fact allowed the Americans to develop a unique mass culture, one that has the attention and understanding of a worldwide following.

Today the cultural situation in post-Communist countries gives no cause to rejoice. Although it varies from country to country, generally speaking the "American model" is ubiquitous and damaging. Architectural monuments are made much of and museums are refurbished, not especially because they are major national treasures but because they are tourist-money draws. When the Czech prime minister publicly declared that the image of Bohemia as "a country of art and culture" should be abolished, he was not calling for its complete eradication, only that Bohemia's must create a new national image: that of a country of industry, commerce, and free enterprise.

In the technological world of the present, the production of culture has become very costly. A poet or writer only needs a pencil, while video and filmmakers need considerable funding. It is rare for sponsors in small post-Communist countries to be able to meet these expenses, and it would be a dangerous illusion to think otherwise. The current attitude toward national culture has created a vacuum into which pours a flood of American imports: books, films, television productions, and so on. Even though American popular culture caters to psychological universals—injustice, romance, money, power and a better life—it does not mean that in the distant future, this inundation of foreign, and largely *ahistorical*, entertainment will not create a nationalist-driven backlash. Financial support must come from society, and society must understand the importance of culture for the sake of its own civic and democratic survival. East-Central European leadership has not learned this lesson yet and that is a dangerous failing on the eve of a new audiovisual century. While in other European countries public funding for cultural pursuits is obligatory and substantial, leaders in post-Communist countries remain prisoners of an ideological approach that has severely hampered their efforts. The Polish filmmaker Andrzej Wajda summed up the situation in a simple phrase, "we have struggled for years for a free cinema, and now we have freedom, but no cinema."

To return to Gyula Illyés's quote evoked at the beginning of this text, it can be said that the post-Communist era has not driven politics from the public square, but it has driven culture from it and politics cannot replace the importance of culture.

Chapter 5

The Transformation of the Media in Post-Communist Central Europe

Marcin Frybes

After the "revolution" of 1989, the end of political and ideological controls over the media, and the passage of several new acts of liberal legislation in the field of communication has permitted the progressive establishment of constitutions oriented toward truly free marketplaces of information in all countries of Central and Eastern Europe.

Of course, these new marketplaces are still in a process of construction: there have been many rapid changes and the situation is frequently very unstable. This is a natural consequence of the political and economic instability in all these countries. It is also a consequence of the involvement of several powerful international media groups, which consider this part of the world to be new "territories of colonization" and which, most importantly, control a significant part of these information new markets. At the same time, the growing influence of the international media represents the natural consequence of the quickly changing demands of the public, which is, in turn, a consequence of the important social and cultural changes taking place in all of Central and Eastern Europe.

Today, we can easily say that people in Central and Eastern Europe have access to a large variety of information and pictures of reality, which are not controlled or censored by a central political and ideological power. A real pluralism in the field of mass media exists. This is the most important difference between the communist era and the contemporary situation. But can we also say that the media necessarily plays an important and constructive role in the process of democratization of public life and in the processes of the reconstruction of a democratic civil life in all of these countries? The answer is not so evident.

THE COMMUNIST LEGACY

Only a few years ago, the situation of the media in all these countries was quite the same. Nearly all the media was directed, controlled, and manipulated by communist regimes. The communists possessed a quasi-totalitarian monopoly in this field, strongly reinforced by censorship. In this situation, communist power was able to produce at will stories and pictures about reality that would conform with its ideology. Press, radio, and television in particular were, first and foremost, instruments of official propaganda and manipulation, rather than instruments of information and social communication. The creation of new press titles, their contents and their circulation, rarely depended on social demand but was rather the result of political choices.

In this situation it was difficult, if not quite impossible, to speak about the existence of an autonomous public sector. However, it must be recognized that, in certain countries, a real diversity of official media existed well before 1989 and that not all the media was directly involved in ideological projects. But here, a situation of real diversity is not the same as a pluralistic situation.

In regard to this point, the situation was not the same in all Eastern European countries.[1] In Poland and in Hungary, the diversity of the media supports and of the range of information available became primarily important while the political and ideological control of information became weaker.

In these two countries the press was fairly independent. In the case of Poland, it was mainly a press directly linked to the Catholic Church, which, starting in 1956, gave birth to a real tradition of an independent Catholic press. Titles like *Tygodnik Powszechnyll*, *Wiez*, or *Znak* possessed a certain margin of autonomy. They were often heavily censored but they tried to preserve the traditions of independent and objective journalism. In the case of Hungary, the same happened with some intellectual monthlies like *Alföld* or *Mozgo Vilag*.

This situation cannot only be explained by a certain form of liberalism of the communist regime in Poland and in Hungary, but rather by the existence of relatively strong forces within their civil societies. The questions of liberalization of the media and of freedom of speech were very important points for all the opposition democratic movements that were created in the 1970s and the 1980s to defend. One should also remember the importance of independent publications, of the so-called *Samizdat*, especially in Poland and Hungary.

THE MEDIA: AN IMPORTANT ACTOR OF "DEMOCRATIC TRANSFORMATION"

The First Signs of Liberalization

There were already some signs of liberalization in the sphere of media in certain countries well before 1989, as in the case of Poland and Hungary. In 1988, the communists decided to stop jamming foreign radio stations like Radio-Free Europe, Voice of America, BBC, Deutche Welle, and others. The role of these radio-stations throughout the communist period was very important.[2]

Other signs of liberalization could be seen in the press. In Hungary, the Communist party decided at the beginning of 1988 to dissolve the Department of Propaganda and to abolish the centralized system of press controls. In Poland, since the beginning of the 1980s, the communist authorities were obliged to grant much more autonomy to the press. Martial law, introduced by the end of 1981, could not hold back a general social movement.

Other countries, however, had to wait until the political transformation of 1989 resulted in real liberal changes in the field of social communication and information. This was true even in Czechoslovakia, where some independent movements of the civil society were present in the 1980s. At the same time, the influence of Gorbachev's policy of *glasnost* was evident in a country such as Bulgaria.

The Role of Media in the "Revolution" of 1989

But despite these differences and legacies, the media (and the press in particular) played an important role during the "1989 revolution." This phenomenon concerned new titles (created with the revolutionary process) but it also involved some old newspapers of the *ancien regime*.

A good example of the rapid transformation of an old title is the case of *Svobodne Slovo*, a daily newspaper in the former Czechoslovakia, which played a central role during the "velvet revolution." It was a nonofficial organ of the Civic Forum Movement. The offices of this daily newspaper in Prague were the headquarters for the democratic movement and its circulation by the end of 1989 exceeded half a million copies.

In Hungary, the official press-organ of the Hungarian Patriotic Forum, *Magyar Nemzet'l*, became the major daily newspaper of the liberal opposition by the end of the 1980s, and many of the well-known Hungarian opposition intellectuals published their articles in it.

One example of a new title is the Polish daily *Gazeta Wyborcza*. It is a good example of a new newspaper that very quickly began to play a key political role. It was created in May 1989 (according to the Round Table accords between Communist and Solidarity leaders) by individuals who were involved in the independent press of the Solidarity movement during the 1980s. Its first role was to support the candidates of Solidarity during the first elections in June 1989. Since then, it has been the most important newspaper in Poland (with a circulation of 600,000 copies), and it became a model and a point of reference for many other new independent titles. Directed by Adam Michnik, a well-known intellectual, this Polish newspaper is the most successful experiment in the field of the press in Central and Eastern Europe.[3]

What can help us understand the great success of *Gazeta Wyborcza*? It is the only new daily in Poland that was able to profit from all the different experiences of Polish journalism in regard to the experiences of both the official communist press and the experiences of the clandestine press. The people who created *Gazeta Wyborcza* came from different former communist newspapers (from the weekly *Polityka* for example) but also from the most important unofficial weekly, which was published during the 1980s and played the role of semiofficial organ of the Solidarity's movement, *Tygodnik*

Mazowsze. These facts reveal the capacity to combine different traditions, and different kinds of experiences, and thus help to explain the great success of *Gazeta Wyborcza*.

The Political Role of the Media in the Period of "Transition"

During the entire period of transition, the role of the media (and of the press in particular) was crucial. The latter's role has been influential, especially at the time of different election campaigns. We can say that the press played, and today continues to play, an important pedagogical role that seeks to reinforce and legitimize the principle of democratic elections—a totally new concept for Eastern Europeans. The diversity of the press has helped to develop a democratic culture.

The role of public television (which has still been under governmental control in most of these countries) has been, at the times of different elections, very ambiguous, and in many cases, governmental forces have tried to monopolize public television and to present false images of their political adversaries. This important role of the press is not only limited to the election processes. Certain newspapers have denounced financial scandals, pointing out attacks on civic liberties and other issues that might be dangerous for the development of democratic societies, such as the mafia, racism, nationalism, and so on.

On different occasions, the weekly *Wprost* in Poland (which is another case of a former communist title transformed in 1989); the Slovak daily *Sme* or the private Slovak radio-station *Twist*; and the Czek weekly *Respekt* exhibited great civic courage to disclose certain problems that involved political authorities. Both the post-communist Polish government and the Slovak Meciar government tried to introduce new measures and administrative restrictions against the freedom of the media. Restrictions were successful in Slovakia but not in Poland.

The "Sociocultural" Role of the Media during the Period of "Transition"

The role of the new press is not only a political role. One must also mention its important socialcultural role. The first thing to underscore is the type of "educational" role played by the press. All the changes that happened since 1989 are absolutely new. Very often, vocabulary has yet to be developed to express these changes; this is a real and significant problem for people in Eastern Europe. The average person does not understand the process of transition. The role of the media is then absolutely central. The media (and particularly the press) could be regarded much like the principal "creator" of new categories that could be utilized by people to describe and to understand the new world that was being constructed with the transition process.

The second issue concerns the role of the press in structuring and formulating the new political environments. New political parties and movements have often wanted to demarcate their existence and to define their identity by publishing a daily or a weekly newspaper. This was an important phenomenon during the first years of the transition. Many newspapers were closely identified with a concrete political option. For example, the Slovak daily *Verejnost* played the role of official daily of the movement "Public against violence"; the Hungarian daily *Magyar Forum* was linked with the party of Prime Minister Jozef Antall; and many other titles played similar roles, especially in Bulgaria and Romania. In many cases, these new projects failed after a year or two; but this political press was absolutely crucial in helping to establish a pluralistic system of political parties. Today, this kind of press exists only in Bulgaria and Romania, but their circulation is not very substantial.

THE MAIN TRENDS AND CHARACTERISTICS IN THE CONSTITUTION OF NEW MARKETPLACES OF INFORMATION

The process leading to the liberalization of the media strongly depends on the evolution of the political situation in each country. These two things can be analyzed in common. It is thus possible to consider the degree of autonomy of the press as a good test of the democratization process. There were, however, many common tendencies within each of the states.

In the first place, the political changes, which occurred in 1989, permitted the new democratic governments to abolish censorship and other administrative restrictions and to adopt new laws, which, theoretically at least, gave a guarantee of freedom and pluralism.

In the beginning of the 1990s, with the end of all these old restrictions, there was an important explosion of freedom of speech. Within only a few months, the global number of press titles increased in a spectacular way. In Bulgaria, the total number of titles was 250 in 1989; in 1991 there were 1,500 titles. In Hungary there were 1,800 titles in 1988 and 3,000 titles two years later. In Romania, in 1991 there were 1,500 titles while in 1989 there were only 500. In Czechoslovakia and Poland, the dynamic was similar.

The same phenomenon took place in the case of radio stations. Before 1989, there were only three or four channels of the state radio; and after 1989, the total number of new stations increased very quickly. In the field of television, there were also a lot of new projects but the politics of new governments ensured that these projects would not really succeed.

The increase of new titles led, in certain cases, to higher circulations. For example, in Romania, the daily *Romania Libera* and *Adevarul*—the former official communist daily—had a circulation of about 1 million copies in the beginning of the 1990s. At the same time, the weekly *Zig-Zag* or *Express* had a circulation of about 400,000 copies and other "difficult" and "intellectual" titles, like the magazine *122* or *Dilemna* ran about 100,000 copies. Then, the circulation decreased (a consequence of the high prices of paper and of overall production).[4] This marked the beginning of a general trend in these countries—the press and particularly the daily newspapers—have become less popular. Therefore, the public audience of the press has decreased.

The explosion of the free of speech movement can be divided into three different levels, which correspond to three different dynamics.

1. The creation of new titles and of new media generally.
2. The transformation of the former communist media and linked with it, the process of privatization.
3. The strategies of investment of important mass-media international groups (such as Bertelsmann, Murdoch, Hersant, Orkla Press).

The first dynamic (the creation of new titles) was particularly strong at the beginning of the transition process. But the first stage of euphoria—which came from the new freedom—lasted only a few months. New problems concerning the introduction of the mechanisms of the market economy became a real problem. The end of public subsidies, the rise of the general costs of newspaper production, the aggressive competitiveness, and, last but not least, the arrival of important foreign mass-media groups, changed this initial situation, which was a bit too idealistic and romantic.

The development of new media outlets encountered serious barriers largely due to the lack of financial resources and of capital funds, which were indispensable for modernization and for further development. In this situation, a lot of new publications (and generally a lot of new projects in the area of the media) failed.

The Privatization of the Press

The process of privatization of the former communist press took place in a very wild manner and opened the door to many scandals, even in Poland, where the first government created a special parliamentary commission to supervise and control the privatization process. The former empires of the communist press had been quite important. For example the Polish communist empire, *RSW Prasa,* was an enterprise that had employed 35,000 persons, and published 250 titles.

The process of privatization of the former communist press was characterized by many irregularities. In Hungary, the privatization began prior to the first democratic elections of May 1990 with an important scandal, once the Communist party decided to sell seven of the most important regional daily newspapers to the group of Axel Springer. One of the conditions of this operation was that the new owner would maintain the old management in all these daily newspapers.[5]

The Privatization of the Press: The Growing Involvement of International and National Mass-Media Groups

Foreign investors played a central role in the process of privatization of the press in Central and Eastern Europe. This was quite natural because, at the beginning of the transition period, there were no national capital funds capable of investment. During the first period of transition, foreign groups (such as Axel Springer, Rupert Murdoch, Robert Hersant, Robert Maxwell, Bertelsmann) bought the great majority of the press in Hungary (80% of the

Hungarian press). In Poland and former Czechoslovakia, it was the same process, which had provoked significant national reactions against it. In 1992 a group of Czech intellectuals and journalists created a special association whose main objective was to preserve the "national character of the press" and to change the existing laws. They wanted to limit the foreign participation in the media to 30% of total capital. The same phenomenon occurred in Poland one year later.

In Slovakia, Romania, and Bulgaria, the involvement of foreign investors was much more limited. The principal reason was the great instability of the political situation and the continuing influence of post-communist groups.

It must be noted that besides foreign investors, some national mass-media empires have also appeared. Most of these had a "communist" origin and there are evident links between these new empires and political parties (especially those political parties that are a natural continuation of the old communist parties). In Romania the principal post-communist media-groups were: *Barricada*, *GIP*, *Topaz*, and *Express*; and in Bulgaria, *Media Holding*, *168 Hour*, *Express*, *Tron*.

However, it must be noted that besides international groups and "post-communist" empires, some new national "press-groups," which belong to prominent locals, have also emerged. The latter are often old émigrés. It is the case of Wojciech Fibak group in Poland, of Fidelis Schlee and Josef Kudlaczek in the Czeck Republic and of Andrew Sarlos in Hungary.

The quasi-total privatization of the press-market has become something very inconvenient for the new national governments. Prior to 1989, the state controlled—in a direct or indirect way—the entire press. After 1989, governments found themselves in a situation where they had to create their own titles and support them; moreover they had to explain their political actions in these newspapers. The Hungarian government then created the daily *Uj Magyaarorszag* in 1991; the Slovak government, the daily *Nova Smena Mladych* in 1996; and the Polish post-communist government, the weekly *Fakty* in 1996.

The Main Characteristics of the New Media Markets

In creating new marketplaces for the press, a central role is played by foreign investors. The influence of foreign and international media groups in different countries is not the same but its presence is very important. (These groups control much more than a half of the market and in certain countries as much as 80% of the market of the daily press.) The latter is the case of Bulgaria after the German group WAZ bought the two principal dailies: *Trud* and *24 Hours* in 1997, which formerly belonged to a post-communist media group. In all these countries, the titles that belong to foreign investors have become a reference point for the national press. This is particularly evident with the women's magazines and the magazines for young people.

Even strong titles, which have been very proud of their independence, and which possess a real tradition from the period of independent and illegal press (like the Czek daily *Lidove Novinyl* and the Polish daily *Gazeta Wyborcza*) were obliged to open themselves to foreign investors. The Ringier group from Zurich bought 51% of the capital of *Lidove Novinyl* and an American group, Cox, invested 12% of the stock of *Gazeta Wyborcza*. In the second case this decision did not possess any great ramifications but in the case of *Lidove Novinyl*, it transformed the character of the daily newspaper.

In the creation of new marketplaces for television, a central role has been played by the state and also, in some countries, by foreign investors. But the process of privatization and liberalization of television is not yet finished. New laws for television have not been adopted as fast as the new regulations in the field of the press. The political influence of television is much more important and the new governments after 1989 had decided not to lose this option as a means to defend their policies.

The first law on radio and television was adopted in Czechoslovakia in 1991. It clarified the situation of the new private radio stations, where development had been quite illegal. It also accorded the first authorization to a private television channel, *TV Nova*. The latter belonged to an American media group (Central European Media Enterprise Group), created by two former American diplomats in Central Europe. This group is also present in new private televisions in others countries: *Pro TV* in Romania, *TV Markiza* in Slovakia, and *TVN* in Poland.

In all Eastern European countries, new laws on radio and television have been adopted. But this does not mean the end of problems. The adoption of these new laws has not permitted the depoliticalization of the debates about the future and the social role of state television. In all countries (with the exception of Hungary, where public radio and television is controlled by three independent social foundations), the members of boards of directors have been nominated for explicitly political reasons. This favors a situation where "Opposition parties loudly condemn government manipulation of public broadcasters but in fact, they wait only to get into power to do the same."

A situation in which control of television plays an important role in political struggles does not help the process of modernization and the necessary restructuration of public TV channels, which have given positions of advantage to all private television stations and the cable networks. The latter· have only recently begun to develop and their success is very impressive. In Poland, the private channel *Polsat* or in Czech Republik, the channel *TV Nova* are now the most important television channels, with a public audience greater than the old channels of public television.

As a prisoner of state bureaucracy (which is a direct legacy of the communist period), and since it depends much more on public subsidies than on publicity campaigns, public television has had many problems in resisting the competition of new private stations. This is true because private channels emphasize the entertainment programs (like games, quiz shows, and serial stories) that correspond better to the public demands.

Contrary to the marketplace of the press, it is American capital that plays the dominant role in the field of television. For example, the most important foreign mass-media investor in Poland is the American company Date Chase Enterprise, which controls the Polish Cable television network with an investment of 100 million dollars.

CONCLUSION

New laws, which could create the solid foundations for the construction of new media marketplaces, cannot guarantee media independence alone. These laws must be accompanied by a new political culture and by the existence of strong civil societies. These two forces (political culture and strong civil societies) were practically destroyed during the communist period. And it is now clear that the process of their progressive reconstruction will be longer and much more complicated than the simple passing of a few new laws.

In most cases, the example above is not only the consequence of the communist system. In most Eastern European countries, the pre-communist traditions in these areas are not very important and deep. Before World War II, only Czechoslovakia had a real democratic experience. All the other countries were dominated by a premodern agricultural culture, and thus it is rather difficult to speak about a strong tradition of civil society and democratic culture. This is an aspect of the process of transition that is very often forgotten.

The transition is not merely a change that moves from communist authoritarianism to democracy, and that represents a process of "emerging from communism." It is rather an experience of much deeper change, which represents a movement from situations without a strong democratic tradition to an entirely new situation, where democracy becomes the main objective. The problem is not only the communist legacy, but rather the pre-communist one.

Even the question of implementing new laws is not so evident. The governments and legislators have faced a lot of important questions when they have tried to establish new legislative norms in the field of communication.

First, in determining the nature of legislation to be passed, governments of legislation have to decide if they want to apply a particular foreign model, or apply some foreign standards. To try to apply some external solution (which is good for stable modern societies) is the easiest alternative (and a great temptation). But foreign models can be automatically transposed for societies that are living a process of radical transformation.

Second, they have to adapt new media legislation to the already existing legislation in the field of economy. The media is a profitable business. During the entire communist period, and even in the first years of the transition, no one thought in these terms regarding the media. Now, it is quite natural but it still requires the adaptation and transformation of some of the initial laws and regulations.

The question of new laws is important but does not represent everything. That is why the central question remains: What is really the role played by the new free media in establishing new democratic political culture and in reinforcing civil societies? The answer is not evident.

We must even say that a very rapid implementation of new marketplaces for media has not been favorable to the consolidation of civil societies. In many cases, the rules of market economy and the spirit of competition have contributed to the destruction of some of the elements of civil societies that had begun to emerge during the 1980s. In competition with great international media-groups, smaller local initiatives were often inexperienced and poor and could not resist. Some old, ambitious and intellectual publications have totally disappeared from the market, and other publications have lost their initial purpose because they had to take into account their readers' needs.

At the beginning of transition, media was seen as an important element of cultural and not political life—an important cultural good. Journalists then tried to reconstruct a new culture of information and to develop new ways of social communication. The principal question was to present information as thoroughly as possible and to develop critical views for the public.

Today, in a market economy, the media are seen as an economic product. The work of journalists is not very important. What is central, however, is the capacity to earn money, to sell more copies, and to reach a greater public.

I lived this experience when I was a correspondent for the daily newspaper *Gazeta Wyborcza* in Paris. During my four years there, I saw its evolution. At the beginning we were all idealistic. We thought that the Polish public was interested in all the important discussions and changes that had happened in France and in Western Europe. But quickly we discovered that it was not true. Thus, I was obliged to write articles about more peripheral issues, because it was more important to develop a headline or uncover a scoop rather than explain what was really happening in France.

NOTES

1. Cf. Jacques Semelin, *La liberté au bout des ondes* (Paris: Belfond, 1997).

2. This is well described in the book of Tristan Mattelard who speaks about these media as "l'audio-visual Trojan horse." Cf. Tristan Mattelard, *Le cheval de Troie audiovisuel—le rideau de fer à l'épreuve des radios et télévisions transfrontalières* (Grenoble: Presses Universitaires de Grenoble, 1995).

3. Pawel Smolenski, *Gazeta Wyborcza* (Paris: Noir sur Blanc, 1991).

4. Cf. Marcin Frybes and Anne Nivat, "Le nouveau paysage médiatique à l'Est," *L'Autre Europe* no. 28/29 (1995).

5. Henry F. Carey, *From Big Lie to Small Lies: State Mass Media Dominance in Post-Communist Romania*, EEPS 10, no. 1 (1995), 16–45.

6. Edith Oltay, "Hungary," *RFE/RL Research Report* Vol.1 no. 39, October 1992, p. 41.

7. Karol Jakubowicz, "Politicians Endanger Independence of Polish Public TV," in *Transition* no. 8, vol. 2, (1996), pp. 28–30.

Chapter 6

The Media in Transition in Southern Central Europe

Helen Darbishire

THE *INDIPENDENT* NEWSPAPER
In April of 1997, in the midst of the crisis and chaos that swept Albania, a group of about thirty young journalists formed a new newspaper called the *Indipendent*. They founded this newspaper with their own money—each contributing what they could, ranging from ten dollars to a couple of thousand dollars, and getting a proportionate number of shares in return. The total amounted only to a few thousand dollars, but it was enough to get started.

During the campaign running up to the June 1997 elections, the newspaper practiced some reasonably high-quality journalism—as good as anything Albania has ever seen—and even had some scoops—such as publishing transcripts of taped telephone conversations between the Italian ambassador and senior figures in President Berisha's government. This led to the Italian government withdrawing its ambassador. The paper's circulation was only a few thousand, but increased steadily.

However, by August the paper was in serious financial difficulties, with cash-flow problems caused by slow returns of money from vendors, low advertising revenue in Albania's stricken economy, and Albania's generally high tax-burden for the printed media. In addition, the editors were experiencing the difficulties in running a paper in which every shareholder, that is, every journalist, felt they had the right to make editorial decisions: The disputes about what the front-page story should be were, at times, farcical.

So talk started about selling out. Possible investors or buyers were consulted. The paper received some support from international donors, amounting to a few thousand dollars, and although more was promised, it did not come in time. The *Indipendent* was eventually bought out by Albania's leading newspaper, *Koha Jonë* to which it represented serious competition, and was closed down. *Koha Jonë*, which means "Our Time," is also independent, but run along rather less democratic lines, with many journalists not having proper contracts, let alone shares. And it is a newspaper that sells well because it often engages in sensationalism. Nevertheless, it too struggles to survive economically. It should be noted that, thus far, Albania is the only country in Central and Eastern Europe in which there is no investment in the press by foreign companies.

The story of the *Indipendent* is one that is familiar in many of the ex-Communist countries further north, but something that occurred more often between, say, 1990 and 1992 rather than today. Now in places like Poland, Hungary, and the Czech Republic the market for the print media has in some ways stabilized, even if the electronic media sphere is still in a developmental phase. However, in Southern-Central Europe, the whole media environment is still much more in flux, for a variety of reasons that I will try to outline here.

SLOW REVOLUTIONS

It is now often said that the revolutions in Central and Eastern Europe didn't really happen in 1989 or 1990, or at least they by no means fully happened. We can all say with hindsight how naive it was at the time to think that totalitarian ideologies were done with in 1989 and that "history was finished." In fact, the transition away from communism is proving to be a much slower process. Some analysts commented that the November 1996 elections in Romania were the final phase in the anti-Communist revolution. In Albania one commentator saw the last year's mass hysteria and firing of Kalachnikov's into the air as part of the rejection of fear and oppression that Albania is still struggling to make.

It seems clear that the so-called transitional process is moving at different speeds in different countries, according to a whole mix of political, economic, social and cultural criteria. In early April 1998 in Brussels there were discussions on the first ex-Communist countries to be admitted to the European Union (EU). Poland, Hungary, the Czech Republic, Slovenia, and Estonia look likely to make the grade in the not-too-distant future. As for the rest I suspect that they are a long way off. Or some of them certainly should be if democratic developments and human rights are to be the yardstick.

We talk about "the transition" as if it is a process that has only one direction—forward. But in the Balkans I sometimes think that it is very hard to judge what stage the "transition" is in and that it is easier to see it as a general mess, without clear definitions of direction, forward or backward. As one Albanian said to me recently "You know, Helen, we started off on the road towards Europe but we seem to have found our way to Latin America."

For the media in this southern region, the process is very similar to the overall political and economic one largely because the media are so dependent on these two factors. There is too little ideological crusading journalism and too much political journalism for it to be otherwise. Whereas media elsewhere are coping with the realities of the transition to the market economy and foreign investors, in the Balkans it is still domestic political influence that holds sway, including in its relationship to economic factors.

Defamation and Tolerance of Criticism

Under the old system, journalists knew what could and could not be said, and the system of state control of information functioned mainly through self-censorship. There were areas where some diversity of opinion was allowed, but most journalists knew where the limits lay—even though these limits would shift from time to time. These were not limits defined in law, but in the structures of the totalitarian system. The ruling elites of the one-party states enforced a monopoly over the mass media with the help of loyal *apparatchiks*, self-censorship, and material incentives.

So dissidents knew what they were risking if they went too far, but it was not a question of knowing the law, and it did not really matter if the laws were good or bad. Thus, for example, there is the Czechoslovak Press Law of 1966 that, in a democratic society, could be seen as a good model for promoting a free press. Of course, it didn't achieve that result before 1989, because, in general, it was not the legal system that placed limits on the free flow of information.

One exception to this was the former Yugoslavia, which had the most diverse press of the former Communist countries. There was a space for expressing opinions, although as the media became increasingly organized at the level of each of the six republics during the 1980s, what could be said in one republic might be taboo in another. It was therefore more necessary to have the limits on the media defined in law. The 1974 Constitution defined freedom of expression and the press (Article 166) with vague limits (Article 203) that are not so far from the European Convention on Human Rights. However, the Federal Criminal Code, Article 133, contained detailed restrictions and imposed prison sentences. Such offenses as inciting the overthrow of the socialist system of self-management, advocating resistance to government decisions, and disseminating malicious and untruthful information (at home or abroad), carried possible prison sentences of up to ten years.

This chapter was invoked by many of the high-profile prosecutions of dissidents in the 1970s and 1980s, for example, those of Franjo Tudjman in Croatia and Alija Izetbegovic in Bosnia. The first human rights petition in Yugoslavia to gather more than 100 signatories called for the abolition of Article 133—this was back in the autumn of 1980.

During the 1990s, freedom of expression was a major and leading element in the changes across Central and Eastern Europe. The media, particularly the print media, was suddenly free to say whatever it wanted. At first the challenge was to move away from the mind-set of the totalitarian regimes, and that meant that journalists needed to find a new understanding of their "role" within society. A plethora of experts from Western Europe and America descended to train journalists on ethics and fair and balanced reporting. Some confusion arose because of the different models they proposed. In the Anglo-Saxon tradition there is a clear distinction between information and commentary. The reporter's task is to deliver pure information, free from emotion and opinion. Opinion pieces are placed elsewhere in the paper and clearly identified as such. Reporters are not there to play a "role." On the other hand, the European model grew out of a different tradition: a newspaper was formed as the instrument of a political party or sociopolitical cause. If a newspaper was an organ of the left, it would fiercely attack all that was right-wing or conservative, and vice versa. This one-sidedness obliterated the line between information and commentary. The aim was not simply to inform, but also to support a given argument. It should be noticed that there is now some blurring of this distinction, with, for example, French newspapers increasingly separating news and comment, and standards of professionalism and objectivity are, of course, high.

However, given the nature of the changes in Eastern Europe, the tendency has been toward the second model, the old European model: to be against something—communism, totalitarianism—and to be for something—democracy, the market economy. This is a factor that in my view has hampered the development of professional journalism, particularly in the Balkans where many newspapers and now electronic media are linked to political parties, even if these are parties claiming to promote—or are genuinely promoting—democratic principles. It has also interfered with the development of an understanding of the natural tension that always exists, and should exist, between media and government. Particularly from the perspective of politicians who have been heard to make complaints along the lines of: "You are for democracy, we are a democratically elected government, how can you dare to criticize us?!"

So, while the media have been finding their place in society, the political classes, still often dominated by those whose mind-sets had been formed under communism, have been finding it increasingly difficult to tolerate the criticisms fired at them from the media. This has led to numerous laws, proposed and in some cases introduced, that restrict freedom of expression. The two most important types of laws are defamation laws and press laws. I am going to take a little time to look at these because I believe that they have played, and continue to play, a very significant role in the development of the media in Southern-Central Europe.

Defamation laws are laws that cover offenses that in the Anglo-Saxon tradition are known as libel (written insults or untruths) or slander (spoken offenses). In Central and Eastern Europe these are contained either in Civil Codes, where the penalty is a fine, or in Criminal Codes, where a prison sentence is possible. Many of the new Criminal Codes in the transitional democracies contain provisions on insult and defamation and many of these provide extremely high penalties, including long prison sentences. I should note at this stage that in Western Europe in the past fifteen years and more, no journalist has been sent to prison for defamation and even if laws that would permit this still exist on the statute books in many countries, they have become "dead letters."

Another principle of defamation legislation in Western Europe and the United States, and something that has been vigorously supported by the European Court of Human Rights in Strasbourg, is that public figures, especially politicians, have to tolerate a much greater level of criticism and intrusion into their public lives than do private individuals. Furthermore, to win a defamation suit, which will normally be a civil case, the individual has to prove that the information was false, and that it caused some kind of damages—either material or moral, depending on the country. In the United States, public figures also have to prove some malicious intent in an allegedly defamatory article, and this is a principle increasingly followed elsewhere.

However, the laws in Eastern Europe turn all of this on its head. Public figures are more protected than private individuals, most protected are senior government officials such as the prime minister or president. Often the honor of the nation, the state, and its emblems, such as the flag or anthem, are also protected. In many cases not only fines but also prison sentences are possible, in some cases prison sentences are mandatory.

It should be stressed that the existence of these laws in itself is enough to have a chilling effect on the practice of journalism; their enforcement greatly increases the tendency toward self-censorship. Journalists I have interviewed in the countries where these laws have recently been enforced—such as Romania, Croatia, Slovakia, Albania, and Montenegro—have no doubt that they raise overall levels of self-censorship within the profession.

Croatia

One of the most notorious cases from the past couple of years has been the trial against the satirical weekly, *Feral Tribune*, in Croatia. Two journalists from *Feral Tribune* were prosecuted for criminal defamation and criminal insult for two articles and a compound picture that essentially described President Tudjman as a fascist and follower of General Franco of Spain. The charges carried possible total prison terms of up to twelve years each. The charges were brought using a mechanism in the criminal code that provides special protection for what are known in Croatia as the five "sacred cows": the president, the leader of the Parliament, the prime minister, the head of the Constitutional Court and the head of the Supreme Court. This is a provision that was introduced in 1996.

There was much international pressure in reaction to this case and in September 1996 the journalists were acquitted of the charges. However, after some political maneuverings, the charges were reintroduced and further trial hearings have followed, the latest being in December 1997. At this hearing the judge decided that in order to come to a fair verdict the Croatian authorities needed to get in touch with the Spanish minister of justice to gather additional information on Franco's doctrine. Since it is unsure whether or when there will be a response from Spain, it is possible that the two journalists will have the prosecution hanging over them for the next year or two before the matter is settled.

In the meantime the case has had two notable effects in Croatia. On one hand it is reported to have had a very chilling effect on the local media, which is already under tremendous political pressure. On the other it is reported to

Romania

In Romania the crime of insult under Article 205 of the penal code carries a possible two-year prison sentence. This and the crime of defamation (Article 206), which can result in up to three years in prison, are regularly used against journalists. For example, in July 1996 two journalists from the *Telegraf* newspaper from the Black Sea port of Constanta were found guilty of insult and sentenced to seven month's imprisonment. In addition they were fined and banned from working as journalists for one year. Their alleged crime was to have accused two local officials of corruption, which was deemed to be insulting even though a local inquiry had found that the officials had indeed been involved in malpractice. The journalists immediately filed a complaint with the European Court of Human Rights in Strasbourg, which resulted in the general prosecutor suspending the jail sentences. They were later pardoned by the outgoing President Iliescu, in part perhaps because of the international pressure that had resulted from the case.

Slovenia

Similarly, in Slovenia a journalist who described the behavior of the local mayor as schizophrenic, in a satirical article that pointed out contradictions in the mayor's behavior, was found guilty of criminal insult and sentenced to one year in prison. The case is still being appealed and may go the Strasbourg court. But in the meantime the journalist, Bernard Nezmah, told me that the whole process was a serious interference with his working life as a journalist. In this way, even if a journalist is eventually cleared by the courts, the whole process of a defamation charge is some kind of a punishment in itself, and will be likely to make him or her more wary about what he or she says or writes in the future.

Slovakia

In Slovakia, people's reputations are protected under the civil code, which at least does not entail prison sentences, but, as the following case shows, the fines can be disproportionately high.

In May 1996, eighteen members of the Slovak cabinet brought a case against the newspaper *Sme,* which had published a statement by a journalist that a policeman who had been killed in suspicious circumstances was "the first victim of a political Cold War made by the Government against all citizens of Slovakia."

The members of the cabinet claimed to have suffered "mental trauma" as a result of this allegation. In November 1996 the court found the newspaper *Sme* guilty and fined it a total of US $ 250,000—certainly enough to put the newspaper out of business. The case is still being appealed.

What is particularly worrying about this case is that none of the individuals in the cabinet had actually been named in the article. Furthermore the court required neither proof of the mental trauma that they claimed to have suffered, nor the impact they claimed this had had on the members of their families. Some cynics commented that if the mental trauma had been so great, perhaps the eighteen should not have continued in their government posts!

PRESS LAWS

Another hotly debated legal topic in Eastern Europe has been the vexed question of Press Laws—laws that define and regulate the place of the print media in a society. The American model is not to have such legislation, preferring to regulate the print media through general laws. On continental Europe press laws are much more common and have a long history—the French law dates back to 1881.

In some of the transitional democracies, the impetus for a press law comes from the journalists themselves, who feel that they need to have their new-found freedoms defined in law. Such is the case in Romania, where the government is resisting the introduction of such a law. The Romanian minister of justice recently stated that the danger in such a law would be that journalists would use it to violate other rights, such as the right to privacy, by using freedom of the press as a pretext.

On the other hand, in Georgia I have heard U.S.-trained government lawyers urging journalists not to push for a law because it might curtail their freedoms.

However, in many of the transitional democracies the debate is not whether or not there should be a press law—there is a driving force from all sides to have one—but rather what it should or should not contain.

Such is the case in Slovakia, where there have been over fifteen drafts that have been proposed to replace the old Czechoslovak 1966 law. The journalists want to protect their rights; the government, it seems, wants to curtail them. Certainly the government versions of the draft have contained some extremely dangerous provisions.[1] Similarly last year's draft media law in Serbia contained some very anti-democratic provisions, including ones clearly designed at curtailing foreign support for the independent media (some independent media in Serbia have only survived on donations from NGOs and IGOs, such as UNESCO and the EU).

Albania now has what many people, particularly Americans, see as one of the best press laws in Eastern Europe. It consists of only two articles:

1. The press is free
2. The press may only be regulated by law.

This was introduced in September 1997 to replace a previous law (dating from October 1993) that had had a number of provisions that had been used by Berisha's government against journalists, such as a provision that the press shall tell the truth. This was used, for example, in 1995 to prosecute a journalist who had quoted a member of parliament, speaking in parliament, alleging corruption of another MP. Because the journalist could not prove that the allegations were true, he was fined $2,000. After an international outcry the journalist was pardoned by the president.

What is interesting about the 1993 Albanian press law is that it was taken almost wholesale from the German Land of North Rhine-Westphalia. However, what Albania lacked were the democratic traditions and legal framework, which in Germany make the law one that promotes freedom of expression, including relevant jurisprudence that gives definitions to some rather more vague articles, such as revealing state secrets. This shows the danger in taking Western European legislation unquestioningly and thinking that it will necessarily help media freedom in Eastern Europe.

It should be noted that those in Albania are actually unhappy with their current press law and they are looking to add a few articles. Some are positive, such as the right of journalists to protect confidential sources of information, a right which was lost when the old law was abolished.

It should also be noted that the debate about press laws—to have or not to have—is a lively topic in Western Europe as well. In the United Kingdom recent debates about press ethics, or the lack thereof, have led to proposals for specific press legislation. The press has staved off such legislation through new self-regulatory mechanisms. However, in Southern-Central Europe there has been a severe failure of journalists to promote professional ethics and to set up mechanisms for self-regulation, which has become another motivating factor for calls from politicians and the public at large for press-specific legislation.

ECONOMIC PRESSURES

From 1990 onward there was an explosion in the printed media in all the post-Communist countries with tens and even hundreds of new titles appearing, often quite disproportionate to what the market could really sustain. Many of these publications were short lived, but for a while they did exist. In the Balkans I would say that there is still a disproportionately high number of publications. At one point Albania had more newspapers per capita than anywhere else in Europe. In Bosnia today, taking all the entities together, there are about 130 publications for a population that in Western Europe would be considered well served if they had one-tenth of that number.

This situation means that newspapers in the Balkans are often struggling to survive. Unlike countries such as Hungary and Poland, there has not been a rush of foreign investors. The instability of the Balkans, the war, the lack of democratic development in countries like Slovakia, the poor economies of Macedonia and Albania, all have discouraged outside investment. The result is that both newspapers as entities and journalists as individuals are more easily susceptible to pressure from political or other outside sources.

The pressure comes in various forms. In Slovakia and in Serbia, there have been government maneuvers to control print and electronic media by facilitating buyouts by companies supportive of the government. Controlling of the placement of advertising by companies run by or close to the state is another classic form of keeping papers from being too critical. Private advertising can have the same effect: in Albania the independent press did not write articles exposing the pyramid investment schemes whose collapse led to last year's chaos because they were dependent on advertising from the companies running these schemes.

Another government mechanism is the control of taxes, which newspapers pay. In Albania the tax burden for the media was raised in 1993 and 1994 to such an extent that—with a combination of import taxes on paper, advertising taxes, a new circulation tax, a news-vendors tax, value-added tax, and employer's taxes on salaries—some publishers complained that 100% of the cover price went to taxes alone. There is also a profit tax, but very few newspapers find themselves in a position to have to pay that! There were of course complaints that pro-governmental papers were not paying these taxes, whereas the financial police regularly visited opposition papers. Recently, however, the new government reached an agreement to grant newspapers a three-year tax-holiday on the condition that all profits are reinvested in the media enterprises.

In Slovakia, the government of Prime Minister Vladimir Meciar has repeatedly threatened to increase the value-added tax (VAT) paid by newspapers, from 6% to 25%. The most recent threat came in October 1997. Some newspapers complain that this increase could put them out of business.

One interesting thing about the Slovak proposal was that it included a distinction between "commercial" or sensationalist press and "noncommercial" or quality press. Observers saw this as a way of targeting press critical of the government. As Meciar himself put it: *"Please write the truth . . . the other possibility [is to] divide the media into the 'vulgar press' and the 'serious press.' We can then differentiate your incomes according to the tax code."* What Meciar means by "the truth" is, of course, open to interpretation.

The problems of surviving in a fragile economic environment clearly make the media more susceptible to political pressure. It also has a negative impact on journalistic professionalism. First, journalists may be more likely to take bribes, although in my estimation this problem is not so widespread in the Balkans as it is in, say, Russia. Whatever the case, low-paid journalists under pressure to produce large amounts of copy don't have either the time or motivation to carry out real investigative journalism. Then, economic problems push newspapers toward sensationalism because they need to sell as many copies as possible. The overall quality of journalism remains low, and professional ethics are not adequately promoted or respected. There are some notable exceptions of course, but this does describe the general environment in which the media operate.

In some countries economics also affects the type of people who go into journalism. In Moldova, for example, journalism is poorly paid and not seen as a prestigious profession, so well-educated young people will opt instead for jobs with foreign companies or in the banking sector, which is relatively well-developed. The result is that journalists are either of the old school and mind-set, or are poorly qualified. Similarly the brain drain that has been experienced in the former Yugoslavia during the war has undoubtedly had some negative impact on journalism.

ACCESS TO INFORMATION

There is no real access to information legislation in the Balkan region. In Romania there has been a sustained campaign for this but none of the proposed drafts have yet made much progress in parliament. On the other hand state secrets are either very broadly defined in criminal codes (e.g., Albania), or defined in great and wide-ranging detail in specific legislation (e.g., Slovakia). In Slovakia each ministry has a list of which documents are secret, but journalists have not been able to get copies of these lists, so they do not know what information they are permitted to ask for! Furthermore, the transitional process in which the climate of government secrecy is replaced with one of openness is very ill-advanced in Southern-Central Europe. This has a negative effect on the media, but also other sectors of civil society, such as NGOs. There needs to be greater cooperation between the media and NGOs in pushing for access to information. This has started to happen in Slovakia, for example, where journalists and lawyers have done some work with environmental NGOs to look at proposing possible legislation.

Lack of government transparency has a number of effects on the way journalists function. It can make journalists much more dependent on government contacts for information, and therefore less likely to criticize. Or the journalist does a favor or possibly even pays for information, which starts off a spiral of influence and corruption. Or the journalist gets lazy and writes articles that are based on rumor and gossip rather than hard facts. In every way, professionalism suffers. If a journalist is really trying to be professional, he or she needs to be very dedicated to the required legwork. One example of such persistence comes from the news agency Beta in Belgrade, which, in 1995, was regularly being denied information from government ministries. The journalists set up a rota to call the spokespersons in each ministry at the same time each day to ask for information. Upon refusal, they'd be very polite and say they'd call back the next day. Although this strategy wasn't totally successful, the journalists reported that they had started to get press releases and even more detailed information from some ministries.

HATE SPEECH

It would be impossible to complete an overview of media in the Balkans without looking at the so-called problem of hate speech. Much has been said and written about the role the media played in inciting the conflict in the former Yugoslavia. It is undoubtedly true that the manipulation of the media by politicians prepared the way for the war. Even the so-called independent media were caught up in it to a certain extent, although it was on state-controlled television that the most gross abuses occurred. It can be argued that there are some journalists and information ministers who should also be on the list for the Hague War Crimes Tribunal.

The media war that preceded the war, and then the problems of survival and identity that the ex-Yugoslav media had during the war, clearly interfered with any kind of normal transition process that we have seen elsewhere in Eastern Europe. Indeed, it is only now that the media in places like Bosnia are really beginning that process. There is a double challenge facing journalists: moving on from war journalism and getting on with the interrupted transition process.

But it is not only in former Yugoslavia that the media have engaged in speech that is intolerant and inciteful of hatred and violence, particularly toward either national minorities or neighboring nations. This is a problem that has been documented in Romania, Bulgaria, Slovakia, Greece, Macedonia, and Albania as well. There have been a number of research projects on this problem, and the clear conclusion is that levels of hate speech are determined above all by politicians and the kinds of messages that they are putting out. This is not only true of state-controlled media but also independent media. It seems that with levels of professionalism still ill-developed and with the close relationship between politics and the media that still operates in the region, politicians can relatively easily take the lead in determining the way other groups or nations are portrayed in the media.

In this way, the media can be used more effectively as an early warning tool to identify problems and the build-up of ethnic tensions. But it would be wrong to advocate prosecution of the media for hate speech, as this would just suppress the signaling mechanism. Rather, such media should be monitored to identify problems that need to be addressed. Too few of the lessons of the former Yugoslavia and its wars have been learned; this is another one that would be stupid not to ignore.

INTERNATIONAL COMMUNITY

There has been a great deal of activity by the so-called international community in Central and Eastern Europe and it is important to consider the impact which this has had on the development of the media.

Both NGOs and IGOs have been very active in the media field in a number of areas. One aim of this activity has been to promote professionalism. There have been many short seminars that discuss media issues but most people are now tired of these and are looking for longer, hands-on training, both in and out of country, which address issues in greater depth and ensure a real transfer of skills.

When it comes to defending journalists' rights, an early mistake was to focus training on journalists themselves, without looking at other elements of the society that are influential on media freedom. NGOs soon recognized the need to widen their training programs to include lawyers, judges, prosecutors, and government officials. One of the most satisfying seminars that I have done was a three-day workshop with journalists and judges in Slovakia on the problem of defamation. Even though this seminar was held in 1997, it was the first time these two groups had come together to discuss such an issue and we had to do a lot of work behind the scenes to build up trust. But in the end it was very successful and there was clearly an increased understanding between the two sides of the issues involved and of the way in which, in a democratic society, balances can be struck between freedom of expression and the right to protect one's reputation.

Financial support for the independent media has also been an important element in trying to get a pluralistic media environment established, often in the face of a government's desire to keep control over the media. Aid has come in the form of direct cash contributions and equipment, ranging from computers to complete printing presses. Now the support is also aimed toward the electronic media, building radio and television networks in Bosnia and Serbia, for example. And sometimes help is needed to get new media started. I have recently been working on a project with UNESCO to support a new independent television station in Albania with funds to buy a transmitter and other equipment as well as to train the journalists who have proved their independence in the print media and now want to transfer these skills to electronic media.

Such financial support has proved invaluable in helping the independent media to survive. UNESCO's persistent lobbying, which in 1994 succeeded in getting assistance to the media included in the list of sanctions-exempt humanitarian assistance in former Yugoslavia, was a very important development, and one that has established a principle for other zones of conflict around the world.

An interesting initiative being practiced by one NGO in the Balkans is to provide small sums of financial assistance to journalists who want to write investigative pieces. The journalist presents an idea and an estimation of the time the work will take, and then gets paid a small sum, from about $50 to $150, to research and write the article. This encourages the journalist to take time, research facts, push on doors, and so on. Of course, there is a risk that journalists will be accused of being paid by "foreign agents" to write the stories, but the project organizers are avoiding this by encouraging articles not just on political issues, but also on social issues, health, education, women, and so on, on which there is often far too little quality information in the press in much of the Balkan region.

Certainly mistakes have been made in the way money has been given, and the sustainability of projects has not always been ensured. One recent report blamed the international community for creating the artificial media market in Bosnia with its incredibly high number of newspapers. The report also suggested that by spreading good journalists so thinly over so many publications, the overall quality of the papers was brought down. This warning was heeded at a recent donor conference in Albania, at which it was agreed to try to channel investment to the better-quality media, and those that look as if they will survive economically on their own in the long term.

However, the most serious mistakes by the international community have been at the political level. Perhaps the most glaring example is that of Croatia, which, in my view, should not have been admitted to the Council of Europe with its law and practice on media freedom as it was at the time, and as it still is. Media freedom is a barometer of other freedoms in a society, and a healthy media is an indicator of the development of a civil society. In Croatia the space for alternative opinions is very limited indeed. The *Feral Tribune* trial, which I mentioned above, brought some international pressure but more from NGOs than IGOs.

Of course, one must not be naive and one must recognize other political realities, such as the implementation of the Dayton peace accords for Bosnia. But nevertheless Croatia's application for membership in the Council of Europe could and should have been used with more force to secure at least some legislative changes before it was granted. Similarly, such bodies should be more prepared to use sanctions—threats of suspension, withdrawal of economic privileges—when media freedom is violated.

Another country that gives human rights activists great cause for concern is Slovakia. At the economic level Slovakia might have been in the first batch of countries for EU membership, if it were not for the clearly anti-democratic tendencies of Prime Minister Vladimir Meciar, which are becoming more apparent every day.

This leads to another important point: when monitoring elections and when judging whether or not they have been free and fair, a greater account must be taken of the role the media has played, particularly the state-controlled media. There should also be a more sophisticated consideration of the media environment. Much of the monitoring that is done only focuses on allocation of election spots to parties or candidates during the official campaign period, without sufficiently assessing the overall media environment and the way the flows of information are controlled within the society. It is the latter that has an important influence on how people form their judgement of the political environment.

CONCLUSION

In Southern-Central Europe, in the Balkans, the media is still developing, and the progress of the whole media environment is dependent on political, legal and economic developments. The independent media in these countries is often in a particularly precarious position because it is also under political pressure. And equally in those countries in which journalists are working to transform state-funded electronic media to public service media a combination of economic hardships and political pressures are hindering the process. It is therefore clear that external support is still required. This support should continue at the level of professional and technical expertise, economic aid, and assistance with the drafting and reform of legislation. Equally important is political pressure to protect media freedom and the rights of journalists in which is still, at best, a very fragile transition toward democracy.

NOTES

1. In April 1998, a draft of the proposed new Slovak election law was made public. It was a potentially incredibly repressive document for freedom of information.

The worst provisions were that only the state media may carry campaign information; private media are prohibited from doing so. No information relevant to the campaign may be carried by other media. No opinion polls may be published during the month before the elections, nor may exit polls or other surveys be published until the final official election results have been announced. In this way the state has complete control of all information relating to the elections. This was still only a draft, but if adopted, it would totally remove the possibility of a free and fair election in Slovakia in September.

Editor's Note: The above draft was based on the 16 March 1990 law. The new draft did come into effect on 20 May 1998.

Chapter 7

A Balance of Economic Reforms in Central and Eastern Europe

Nadège Ragaru

In 1997, Central Europe confirmed the signs of economic recovery observed since 1995. At the same time, however, the spectacular economic crisis in Bulgaria during the winter and the political instability in Albania provided ample reminders that transitions to a market economy could easily derail. Against this background, a "balance sheet" of reforms in Eastern Europe, a decade after they were first launched, appears all the more challenging, because the rapid internal differences within the former communist zone might soon outweigh sweeping analyses and broad-based remedies.[1]

Rather than review the latest developments on a state-by-state basis we will concentrate on basic themes, illustrated by concrete examples from one or two countries. Emphasis will be on Romania and Bulgaria, two states that tend to be under-researched. The purpose here is to give flesh to often all-too-dry economic analyses. Instead of distributing pluses and minuses, we will focus on the "human face" of change.[2]

During the first years of transition, special (at times exclusive) attention was devoted to macroeconomic performances and ruling elites. Predicated upon the ultraliberal credence of Eastern European reformers, the exclusion of bottom-up approaches made it difficult to perceive social responses to transition beyond considerations on increased poverty and deteriorating welfare. In particular, most analysts failed to investigate how societies made sense of emerging systems, borrowing from communist and pre-communist heritages as much as from Western-dominated market ideals. Such considerations appeared more clearly when there occurred a move away from the initial phase (macroeconomic stabilization and liberalization) and toward the application of structural reforms.[3] It then became obvious that the success of transformations would be conditioned upon anchoring new patterns of behavior to totally redefined rules of the game, and that success would be heavily influenced by the culture of each country.

What did we know or believed we knew at the onset of economic transformations? What were the basic dilemmas, and to what extent have they been overcome? Eastern Europe's specific path was marked by simultaneous political and economic changes in contrast to the transformations experienced earlier in former Latin American authoritarian regimes. The shift to a market democracy followed the assumption that politics (ultra liberalism) would prevail. Interaction between politics and economics was envisioned as one-sided. At stake was the political feasibility of changes, meaning the ability of societies under stress to bear the social costs of painful reforms. Hence, fears related mostly to potential backlash. The extent to which economic dynamics might influence the political process as well as the need to redefine the state's ability to restructure obsolete enterprises were left aside. In this respect, a near decade of reforms has had a sobering effect. First, no one would advocate the mere withering away of the state. Questions now relate to ways in which weak states can be reformed so as to limit market instability and enforce new laws and rules. Second, reforms are often understood as a highly political event, whose outcome depends on the collusion between a variety of social, economic, and political actors in each unique Central and Eastern European (CEE) state.

Drawing attention to the nature of the social and economic systems that are now emerging might give some new life to past debates on gradualism and shock therapy. It seems to have been forgotten that beyond the sequencing and speed of reforms, the social fabric of the future was at stake. Advocates of gradualism favored a mixed economy that would retain the social concern inherited from socialism while adjusting to the requirements of the free market. Gradualism was soon discarded as those economies that delayed the necessary reforms fared much worse than those submitting to "shock therapy," because economic stabilization was hampered by the lack of structural reforms. It might now be time to shed new light on reform achievements in societies where distrust of political elites, disparities between "new rich" and "new poor," and marginalization of large segments of the population, have become widespread.

In order to address these issues, four major challenges to reformers in CEE must be considered: privatization and the redefinition of property rights, the development of a sustainable financial system, agricultural policies, and, finally, sound policies of regional development. Each of them brings to the fore the role of the state, as well as new patterns of interaction among diverse social interests. These challenges underscore the absence of ready-made solutions to current hurdles and the need for national debates on still embryonic development. (This chapter will focus on issues involving privatization and the redefinition of property rights as well as the development of a sustainable financial system.)

PRIVATIZATION: LONGER THAN EXPECTED?

Privatization has long been acclaimed as a central pillar of transition from centrally planned to market economies.[4] There is an ideological argument behind this statement, since private property is often heralded as *the* basic axiom of capitalism. This might explain why privatization originally tended to be narrowly defined as a shift of property rights from state to private hands, and equated with *de-etatization* (the radical withdrawal of the state from former command economies). As if endowed with some magic quality, private ownership of the means of production was expected to guarantee optimal allocation and efficiency. Typically, relative achievement in terms of the liquidation of state assets was used as a primary criterion for measuring the overall progress of reform. Now that the process is well advanced in most of Eastern Europe (Poland and Hungary in particular), analysts and decision-makers realize that transfer of ownership was only the first in many steps toward the free market and that other questions needed to be answered. Did restructuring of industrial conglomerates "in the red" follow their privatization? What kind of relationship is being developed between newly privatized companies and financial institutions? In cases where property is dispersed between insiders (managers, employees) and shareholders (both private and public), what kind of mechanisms assure operational harmony between potentially conflicting goals and methods?

Before addressing the questions listed above, it might help to step back and analyze the complex interaction between objectives and methods that emerged from the privatizations across the region. Above all, one needs to emphasize the diversity of methods tried (public tender/auction, direct sales, voucher programs, restitution, etc.). Most reforming governments opted for a multitrack approach whose major goals fluctuated depending on electoral politics and social contexts. In most cases, many amendments to the laws on privatization were passed before private ownership was securely established. Hundreds of companies had to go through two or three (at times piecemeal) sales before they found a final owner. In Bulgaria, for instance, two successive laws on restitution (February 1992, November 1997—the so-called Lutshnikov law) broadened the original scope of restitution but led to the cancellation of several sales in 1998. In other words, there is no clear-cut dividing line between "before" and "after" state withdrawal. Rather, privatization has been a trial and error process that yields hybrid results.

Retrospectively, it looks as if privatization has become overburdened with a variety of emotionally laden expectations. Hopes, nostalgia, and conflicting interests have converged to make the reintroduction of private property an explosive issue. From the very beginning, privatization schemes had to reconcile conflicting goals. Some were ethical, aimed at compensating victims stripped of their assets at the end of the 1940s (restitution or so-called reprivatization). Others were related to egalitarian political philosophies, often in tune with the beliefs of populations subjected to Marxist propaganda for several decades. Others were more strategic. Eager to achieve public support for market reforms at a time when austerity sent tremendous shock waves through wide sectors of the population, some political leaders advocated broad-based and low-cost redistribution of public assets. One must not underestimate the symbolic dimensions of the process. Thanks to privatization, CEE would at last take revenge on the past—by meeting the structural requirements for the development of stable democracies and creating a middle class of small owners "from scratch." Finally, although short-lived, for a while privatization was also seen as a means to end the Communist party's stronghold on economic assets so as to curtail its overall influence on the transition process.[5] One advantage of the voucher system of small holdings was to prevent property from being concentrated in just a few "red" hands.

Contradictory economic objectives added to the confusion and nourished public skepticism about privatization. What was to be de-étatized? At what speed? What kind of property structure would ensue? Was the restructuring of socialist firms supposed.to precede or follow ownership reform? Thus the two core dilemmas: efficiency versus fairness; speed versus *ex ante* (no prior) restructuring. Others should not be overlooked. At stake here were governmental priorities. Was privatization supposed to help the state reduce its internal debt burden by maximizing sales proceeds? Or would it induce obsolete conglomerates to modernize by injecting fresh capital and technological transfers? Accordingly, privatization schemes differed in the degree of centralization and in the role of market forces in sales and citizen participation. Regardless of the policy adopted, the outcomes were often unexpected.[6]

PRIVATIZATION METHODS: A BALANCE SHEET

Among the many privatization methods, three will be examined here: vouchers, manager-employee buyouts, and direct sales.[7] The voucher mechanism, whereby employees receive company vouchers, is exemplified by the Czech program. Among its major advantages is the speed with which it permits transfer of state property into private hands (24% in the first wave, 43% in the second). By 1996, 80% of the former state companies had been taken over by private agents (66% in Hungary, 50% in Poland, and 50% in the Slovak Republic).[9] Bonds, as well as vouchers, allow for extensive participation of the population and spread ownership of shares broadly throughout society. However, dispersion of property deprives small shareholders of the ways and means to exert their new rights effectively (appoint and dismiss mangers, receive dividends, or dispose of their assets). In addition, as one analyst puts it, "the voucher system gives some illusion of ownership by the public, and may contribute to productivity improvement, but does not bring capital, technologies, or know-how needed to turn companies around."[10]

Bulgaria mirrors these drawbacks. There, a mass-privatization scheme was adopted in 1995, after the market technique favored until then had proved inadequate.[11] Bonds aroused little interest among average Bulgarians who lacked information and were reluctant to invest in the debt-ridden enterprises listed for mass-privatization. Between 12% and 15% of the assets of 1,063 firms were privatized during the first wave launched in 1996.[12] The second wave, initially scheduled for the summer of 1998, has failed to arouse greater interest.

Manager-employee buyouts have been the method favored in Poland and Hungary.[13] Its value resides in the speed with which it can buy up state assets and muster workers' support for change. However, allowing employees too much influence may slow down enterprise restructuring in cases where reforms would entail large-scale job dismissals or low wages.[14] More importantly, since financing the purchase itself usually exhausts the borrowing capacity of the new owners, further investment in the companies is likely to be minimal, thereby hindering technological and managerial modernization. Finally, employee-management buyouts may benefit managers who dispose of greater expertise, greater bank confidence, and may use disparity of information to boost their own investment. In such cases, buyouts become management-led, and restructuring is conditional to managers' willingness to introduce new practices. One major variable is the relationship between insiders (managers and employees) and outsiders (shareholders) in terms of operational and strategic decision-making. Distinctive features vary greatly across countries, branches, and according to the size of the enterprise.

Direct sales usually avoid the problems of privatization discussed above.[15] Resorting to strategic investors is likely to encourage in-depth restructuring of companies when major concern is profit, especially when deals include obligations regarding future investment and financial reform. This method was prominent in Hungary until 1994–1995, when it stalled owing in part to lack of political will. With a revised privatization law in May 1995, Budapest opted for an accelerated pace by putting major public utilities companies on the privatization list (telecommunications, electricity, etc.). Even when there is commitment by the authorities, tenders and public auctions are liable to be slow and can only be selectively applied to particular branches or groups of firms. In Bulgaria, for instance, despite renewed emphasis on quick privatization following the election of a reformist majority in April 1997, the search for strategic investors has proved fruitless. According to the National Statistical Institute, in the first five months of 1998 no single privatization deal of this type was concluded.[16]

Two lessons from the privatizations over the past years stand out. First, there is no alternative to rapid and extensive privatization. Second, after transfer of ownership to the private sector, most of the work still remains to be done, notably and imperatively: the definition of property rights, corporate governance, and financial restructuring.[17]

POST-PRIVATIZATION REFORM: DEFINING PROPERTY RIGHTS AND CORPORATE GOVERNANCE

In cases where transfer to the private sector is delayed, parasitic behavior patterns tend to become institutionalized as a substitute for actual market mechanisms, preventing further economic transformation. In the reform process, semi-legal and illegal practices *do* contribute to the survival of highly indebted firms. As these informal codes become routine, however, they prevent successful adoption of market-type rules. This point was forcefully made in Russia's case.[18] Against the background of institutional void and deep-seated structural distortions, "good policies" based on near-exclusive reliance on the regulatory virtues of the market failed to bring about anything beyond a low-level equilibrium. With restructuring stalled, few economic agents could return to the production assets they once had in the market place. These underutilized "factors of production," first and foremost, comprised human resources, so economic agents were left to seek gains by extra-market means, or to resort to subsistence production.[19] Moving toward equilibrium would notably require reviewing preferences (production vs. trade). But there is no active reformist constituency to pressure managers and politicians into renouncing guaranteed income.

In Bulgaria's case,[20] positions on boards of directors of major public corporations have become an increasingly coveted "commodity" because of prestigious "perks" they provide (mobile telephones, cars, vacations, etc.). For politicians defeated in the last legislative elections, membership in the supervisory organs of state companies provides a temporary haven until they go back into politics. Meanwhile, those currently in office abuse their access to information to obtain government subsidies, debt relief, tax breaks, licenses, or concessions for the firms they "represent." So long as state control over the economy affords political leaders a golden opportunity to divert economic resources for private purposes, there is little reason for the ruling elite to alter the status quo. The Union of Democratic Forces was voted in (April 1997) on the promise that it would sever ties between the Mafia and the political elite and speed up mass privatization. Despite pressure from the International Monetary Fund (IMF), Bulgarian Prime Minister Ivan Kostov has not put an end to clientelism. Paradoxically, his reformist government is faced with the same problem that provoked Zhan Videnov's downfall (Kostov's socialist predecessor) in December 1996. In Bulgaria, delays in privatization have thus encouraged a corrupt political system where competing economic groups use members of parliament as lobbyists to the disadvantage of the general public and to the detriment of reforms.

Likewise in Romania, obstacles to rapid privatization came from a coalition between the ruling political class, the bureaucracy and former managers.[21] The sheer number of institutions dealing with mass privatization created highly counterproductive conditions. Agents appointed to supervise the process had no interest in being overzealous, since their new mission provided them with good salaries and status. In that context, one needs to go beyond the usual dichotomy between insiders (managers and employees) and outsiders (shareholders). In theory, problems of corporate governance in newly privatized companies have been attributed to the dominance of insiders over outsiders. The outsiders are expected to compel private firms to adopt economic rationality and modern management as in the West. In actual fact, collusion has not disappeared between some members of the political elite, bankers, and managers (stemming from solidarity formed when they worked for the state security or the party). In December 1996, a new reformist government, headed by Ciorbea, tried to give new impetus to the privatization process. After failure a year later (April 1998), the Ciorbea cabinet was forced to resign.

A second problem related to post-privatization reform involves the definition of property rights. As noted, changes in ownership structures do not automatically lead to effective transfer of property *rights* (understood as the right to select managers and members of the board of directors, share in the residual income, or make use of physical assets). CEE states are practically devoid of adequate legal mechanisms and institutions that would guarantee the full exercise of these rights. The relationship between the pension or investment funds to which vouchers have been entrusted and the individual participants in the mass-privatization scheme remain blurred, which raises the question of the funds' ability to represent their shareholders. Beyond these considerations lies a potentially more sensitive issue. What does private property mean to people who were accustomed to collectivism and who regarded (state) property as something from which one was implicitly entitled to "help oneself" (products, material, equipment, etc.)? What happens when the state is understood as a provider and an arbiter of last resort and enterprises are partially privatized, with the state retaining a significant fraction?

A Bulgarian case illustrates the confusion that results from ill-defined roles and responsibilities in state divestiture. In 1996, a tobacco company (Dzhebel Service 4U in the Rhodopes mountains) was privatized. Shares were divided among a German publishing firm (around 40%), a local tobacco producers' association, and the state, which retained 33% of the business. At the beginning of 1998, the new German owners owed the Dzhebel producers approximately 3 billion levs for the 1997 harvest. The local producers' association raised the problem before the municipal council (two members of the town council were on the firm's corporate board). Following disclaimers of responsibility, they protested to the minister of agriculture and asked for state arbitrage. In Dzhebel, local producers complained that they could not contact the German owners. At the same time, governmental officials argued that they could not help, since the company was no longer state-owned. On May 19, 1998, during a town celebration, people booed the local party leadership (Movement for Rights and Freedom) representing the Turkish minority, and tension was on the rise, yielding a crisis of trust in local and central elites. This highlights two elements. First, in cases where property is being divided among several state and non-state owners, local actors (shareholders) are unable to determine who is in charge and should be held accountable. Second, this problem is aggravated by the fact that average citizens still expect the state to intervene and settle pending problems.

Few authors have attempted to consider what the retrieval (or restitution) of property might mean for the new owners. What is property? Is it a symbolic gain, a source of social prestige, an asset for investment or sale, something that should be held for the children? Before tackling issues pertaining to the full exercise of property rights, related problems of entitlement (ownership), accountability, or responsibility must be investigated. More importantly, property represents a particular form of societal relationship that requires an analysis of "the total system of social, cultural and political relations."[22]

FOREIGN INVESTMENTS: A PANACEA?

Reform is often said to move ahead faster when foreign investments materialize.[23] In states that lack domestic savings and well-developed financial markets, foreign direct investments (FDI) indeed play an essential role in upgrading obsolete industries. On the whole, CEE governments were prompt in removing obstacles to foreign activity. While they have adopted differing legislation, most of them include a mix of fiscal advantages (tax holidays) and untrammeled repatriation of profits. They also provide for the establishment of free trade zones. Differences mostly concern the acquisition of agricultural land and minimal thresholds for capital investment or foreign equity (shares).[24]

As a result, foreign investment in the former communist bloc grew from 1% in 1989 to 5% in 1995.[25] However, disparities across countries are striking. Between 1989 and 1995, Visegrad countries (Hungary, Poland, Czech Republic, Slovak Republic) attracted between 70% and 90% of all regional foreign investment.[26] In 1997, the United States injected $17 billion into Eastern Europe (the former USSR included),[27] but most funding continued to be channeled toward Central Europe (mainly Hungary and Poland). Bulgaria and Romania, following renewed government commitment to structural reforms, have made timid headway. In 1997, Bulgaria managed to collect more than $510 million, for a total of $1.25 billion between 1989 and 1997. As for Romania, over the 1990–1997 period it attracted a relatively modest $1.5 billion.[28] Differences in per capita FDI are even more striking. Between 1989 and 1996, only $52 per capita was invested in Romania, $130 per capita in Hungary, and $140 per capita in Poland.[29] The persistence of regional imbalances remains disturbing, as it builds upon and further consolidates internal differences in the former communist countries. Moreover, foreign investment favors specific sectors such as manufacturing, although services are slowly being put on privatization lists, as are banking systems.

Common knowledge views foreign investments as a blessing for a variety of reasons. First, they provide badly needed capital for restructuring at a time when local intermediaries are still underdeveloped. Second, FDI promotes microeconomic restructuring, notably through transfers of technology and management skills. Adoption of Western norms of quality control, development of new marketing techniques, and research and development strategies are expected to foster modern entrepreneurial cultures. Third, FDI is supposed to help create a competitive environment that pressures domestic firms into modernizing their own structures. A "spillover" effect is expected to attain both the suppliers and the clients of newly privatized companies. Finally, standardization of production lines and managerial practices may accelerate integration into the European market and, later, into the European Union itself. From this perspective, studies of foreign investments typically focus on the conditions required for a suitable business climate and for investors'

A Balance of Economic Reforms in Central and Eastern Europe 83

confidence. Qualitative surveys assess Western perceptions of the various recipient countries, and policy directives pinpoint public relations strategies that are most likely to attract FDI. What really happens following the signature of the longed-for investment contracts is overlooked. Innumerable questions need to be addressed. Do most foreign investments contribute to the dynamic restructuring of distressed economic sectors? To what extent are promises of future capital investments kept and, if this is not the case, do CEE states have the means to enforce contracts? Do the new private owners abide by local labor codes and what role can trade unions play in newly privatized companies?

Foreign investments differ greatly depending on the companies they target, the form they take, the amount of capital invested, as well as investors' objectives. To begin with, enhanced competition does not automatically ensue from the influx of foreign investments. Profiting from low entry costs, some multinational companies might invest so as to achieve a monopoly in the national market before local competitors catch up with Western standards. Witness developments in the Hungarian food-processing sector, to mention but one example.[30] During privatization, so-called strategic investors could also buy firms and preempt other Western companies from expanding their activities in a given branch. Similarly, the takeover of former state-owned firms is not necessarily driven by a wish to turn them into efficient partners, but a way of making sure that they will not stand on their own feet and, thereby, sever existing trade links. Foreign participation may well precipitate rather than prevent the decay of local industries. This risk is all the more meaningful as these states are still redefining their role in industrial policies. Finally, one should not too quickly equate the recovery of individual enterprises with the development of open and growth-oriented economies. This requires diversified production and strategic balance between branches.

A fair assessment of the advantages and drawbacks of FDI calls for more in-depth study of the motives and strategies of foreign investors—how CEE fits into their scheme of development and competition as well as what kind of returns they expect. For instance, should CEE be considered a target in itself or should it be a springboard for export to the East (the former Soviet Union, the Near East) or the West (the European Union). One analysis of international firms' strategies in Bulgaria explains that deciding whether or not to invest in a given market does not solely depend on the merits of the chosen site itself.[31] Investment decisions also take account of other variables, such as opportunities to improve a firm's relative position in its national market by opting for a strategy of internationalization.[32] In such circumstances, immediate returns will not rank first among investors' priorities.

A similar analysis might hold with regard to foreign *capital* inflow (private bank loans, securities, etc.). The speculative movements against the ruble during the summer of 1998 might yield mixed conclusions about the interaction between actual structural reforms and high levels of short-term foreign lending. To address this issue, a review of developments in CEE financial markets is in order.

BANKING SYSTEMS AND FINANCIAL MARKETS: A PENDING CHALLENGE

While attention was focused on stabilization, liberalization, and reform of ownership structures, building stable financial markets was long underestimated by CEE reformers. It was not until bank failures and a system-wide banking crisis hit the region that the need for sound finance became a core concern and stress was laid on institution-building. The Russian devaluation in August 1998 and regional contagion demonstrated how macroeconomic stabilizations could regress. Hence, the nature of bank and stock-market structures will play a central role in determining the fate and the sustainability of current growth. The shift to a market economy requires a stable regulatory framework to allow for efficient mobilization of domestic capital and popular trust in the financial system. Considerations of political stability also come into play. The collapse of financial pyramids, which caused the destabilization of Albania in 1997, revealed the potentially dramatic repercussions of financial crises on democratic change.

The first years of transition were dominated by active promotion of competition by introducing new players into the financial game. De-monopolization was the key word. Unfortunately, it was not always accompanied by legal requirements and supervision mechanisms to prevent the spread of speculative and corrupt practices at the expense of average citizens. To advance transition, contracts must be enforced and depositors protected from bank defaults. As a result, transitions have now entered a new stage; initial transformations are becoming progressively domestic. An analysis of developments in the financial systems will make this point clear. First, we will trace transformations in the banking structure, with the emergence of private banks and the restructuring of debt-ridden state-owned banks. Second, the still timid development of stock markets and the conditions for devising stable financial arrangements will be reviewed.

Communist Legacies and the Bad Loans Issue

Banking reform is a central component of CEE transformation for at least three sets of interrelated reasons.[33] First, modifications in the banking system are tightly connected to enterprise restructuring, notably through hard budget constraints. Only when banks are compelled to take responsibility for their debts can firms be expected to do likewise. One can thus expect dynamic changes as soon as creditors take decisive action to recover their loans. Second, laying the basis for sustainable growth requires the creation of financial intermediaries that can mobilize domestic savings effectively so as to finance the development of small and medium-sized businesses. This is all the more important in a context where financial markets are still in their infancy and where non-bank financial intermediaries remain underdeveloped. Finally, delayed bank reform affects the *real sector* (wages, prices, income, purchasing power). Given the central role of commercial banks in allocating financial resources, the impact of bank failure can resound throughout the economy. Financial instability can ruin otherwise sound economic policy.

A Balance of Economic Reforms in Central and Eastern Europe

Here, communism left an especially damaging legacy. In a centrally planned economy, the banking system revolved around a national bank, which operated as both a central and a commercial bank, and a few specialized banks (for foreign trade, domestic savings etc.). There was no clear division of roles. Savings and loans were dealt with separately. Loans depended on decisions made by the ministry of finance under the requirements of the plan. Banks were little more than centrally administered cash dispensaries. An intermediary role was outside their competence. Building a sound financial system thus requires that independent central banks be created alongside a network of smooth-functioning commercial structures with clearly defined regulations.

At the beginning of transition, stress was laid on liberalization. Most CEE countries established Western-type, two-tiered structures and devised a legal framework to establish new private banks whose number quickly soared. Despite the reformers' commitment to competition, significant imbalances remained between the former oligarchic communist structures and new private institutions. In 1993, for instance, state-banks controlled 78.9% of all deposits in the Czech Republic, and 87.2% in Poland.[34] More importantly, the new commercial banks were often small, undercapitalized and lacked experienced managers.

After 1992, banking crises multiplied throughout the region, starting in Hungary and Estonia. They paved the way for a significant departure from previous banking policies. Thus in the next phase, impetus was given to introducing regulatory mechanisms and active state involvement in bank restructuring.

In part, the rapid deterioration of the banking sector's solvency stemmed from the accumulation, under communist centralized administration, of nonperforming loans disguised as subsidies to state-owned enterprises. In command economies, national banks exercised direct and administrative control over capital investments. Notions of assets and liabilities were purely conventional. Investments were primarily determined by the objectives of the plan, and loans were granted with no consideration for investment return or profit. When the transition began, the credit, which had been extended to state enterprises, was transformed into formal loans. Following the collapse of East bloc trade, the shift to the market and ensuing restrictive monetary policies with high interest rates provoked severe economic dislocations. For bankers and governments, the problem was the following: If banks acknowledged that past loans would never be repaid and subtracted them from the asset column of their accounts, their net worth was likely to become negative. Many would face insolvency and possible bankruptcy. Hence, at stake was the viability of the entire new banking system.

For fear of unleashing a system-wide crisis, CEE governments did not compel banks to carefully report their nonperforming loans. In order to prove that loans were good, banks needed to show *debt service* meaning that interest payments on these loans was being made. Since state enterprises lacked necessary resources to face ever-increasing installments (due to high interest rates), new credit was extended with no guarantee of future reimbursement. In many cases, complementary loans were also required so as to provide for employees' salaries and deter imminent factory closures. Here again, these governments viewed bad debts as a lesser evil than the brutal dismissal of thousands of workers, so central banks were extensively used as lenders of last resort. Sooner or later, this spiral was bound to blow up in the face of speculative movements.

That is exactly what happened in Bulgaria in the spring of 1996. The case is worth relating as an example of the tremendous upheaval that can result from unclear rules of the game and weak supervisory institutions. In 1990, a two-tiered banking system was created, consisting of the Bulgarian National Bank (BNB), and commercial banks formed from sector-specific state banks and the fifty-nine BNB branches. A banks and credit law passed in 1992 gave the BNB authority to grant and revoke licenses for conducting banking operations, and provided for inspections of the commercial banks. It also gave the second tier (including the state-owned banks) considerable autonomy. In addition, the law required banks to set aside at least 20% of their profit after taxes as a reserve fund, representing 1.25% of their total assets. Finally, a Bank Consolidation Company was set up to bring about mergers between small banks, strengthen their capital base and prepare them for privatization.

As in other Eastern European states, Bulgarian banks were beset with bad loans.[35] A first attempt to address the issue in 1991 by limited conversion into public debt of 25% of the bad loans made before 1990 brought only temporary relief. In December 1993, a second attempt to settle these bad loans was made by the National Assembly when it adopted a Loan Settlement Law. However, the program failed to speed up the banking sector's rehabilitation due to the absence of incentives for firms and banks to enact change. The new law only bailed out troubled financial institutions and did not include preventive measures against new nonperforming loans. In 1994, when two banks (Mineralbank and Economic Bank) that held most of the junk bonds issued as part of the restructuring mechanism faced a liquidity crisis, the BNB refinanced them to such an extent that it endangered its own monetary base. This action provoked expectations that the state would forgive new debts in the future. The inability to accelerate state-owned sector reform and impose strict supervision on financial institutions favored the spread of corrupt and speculative practices.[36]

A crisis in 1996 resulted from the convergence of several negative trends.[37] First, successive bank bail-outs sharply increased domestic debt. Repayment not only crowded out private investment but also led to growing state deficits. Second, the continued appearance of bad debts undermined the banking system. Toward the end of 1995, it had fostered a crisis of public confidence that turned into a massive run on deposits in 1996. Measures to insure deposits (March 1996) came too late. The spiral was accelerated by a simultaneous speculative assault on the *lev*. The currency crisis, third component of the 1996 collapse, was not unprecedented in Bulgaria's transition. In 1994, similar speculative movements had been stopped thanks to an International Monetary Fund (IMF) agreement. Repayment, after rescheduling Bulgaria's foreign debt in November 1994, represented a heavy drain for a country that lacked capital, especially foreign investments. Bulgarian authorities started relying on short-term funds between two IMF agreements. IMF refusal to renew support in 1995, coupled with lack of confidence in the banking system guaranteed that the 1996 currency crisis would spread to the entire economic system.

In May 1996 at least seven of the forty-seven banks operating in Bulgaria were in severe trouble (including Mineralbank, Economic Bank, Balkanbank, TS bank, First Investment Bank, and Biochim). A new bankruptcy law was subsequently adopted which gave the BNB power to request the opening of bankruptcy procedures against ailing banks. Meanwhile, the IMF made its help conditional upon the liquidation of sixty-four debt-ridden state-owned companies. Against the backdrop of contradictory macroeconomic policies and weak government legitimacy, the IMF (November 1996) suggested the introduction of a currency board. The proposal was only adopted after popular protests in January 1997 put an end to Zhan Videnov's socialist government and brought a reformist government (Union of Democratic Forces) to power. The *lev* was pegged to the German mark (July 1997) at a rate of 100 *levs* for 1 DM. Since then, macroeconomic stability has returned to Bulgaria. Banking regulations were significantly altered by two new laws (spring of 1997) on the BNB and on commercial banks. Moreover, the placement of eighteen banks under conservatorship (tutelage) and the launching of several bankruptcy procedures opened the way for progressive consolidation of the financial system. Most state-owned banks now provide coverage for a large part of their nonperforming (bad) debts. The fact that under the currency board the BNB cannot act as a lender of last resort has forced financial institutions to revise their lending practices.

Several issues remain pending. Following discussions with the IMF and the European Bank for Reconstruction and Development (EBRD), the Bulgarian government announced its intention to privatize several insolvent banks (First Private Bank, First Investment Bank, Bank for Agricultural Credit, United Bulgarian Bank, Expressbank, Biochimbank, Bulgarian Postbank, and Hebrosbank). In August 1998, a consortium of international investors acquired 78% of Postbank, but as of 1997 state-owned banks still held 66% of total banking assets. In addition, delays in mass-privatization weigh upon the state budget and hamper financial discipline. Collusion between political and economic interests are still the rule in a country where power is perceived as a path toward private enrichment.

Other Eastern European countries were faced with largely similar, though often less dramatic, banking problems. In order to address them, they have resorted to a great variety of restructuring strategies with often mixed results.

Restructuring the Banking System: Centralized and Decentralized Approaches

Two types of approaches (centralized and decentralized) were adopted to restructure banks throughout the region.[38] In the first option, debts are placed in a central agency for collection and liquidation (the Slovenian variant) or bad debts are deducted before recapitalization (the Czech case). The second strategy allows individual banks to initiate financial restructuring and loan recovery. Poland and Hungary, leaders in bank reform, successfully opted for the second approach.

In 1993, Poland adopted a comprehensive Enterprise and Bank Restructuring Program aimed at preparing the privatization of seven of the nine commercial banks that had been created from the National Bank in 1989. Banks were given a key role in supervising the consolidation of heavily indebted enterprises.[39] The entire program was based upon the recognition of the interconnectedness of enterprise and bank restructuring as the basis for a decisive upgrading of the economy. By March 1994, approximately 600 had reached agreement with their creditors. As a result, bad loans have dropped from 29% in 1994 to 10% in 1997.[40] Among CEE countries, Hungary is the second success story. True, Budapest started with better initial conditions, since bad loans were only 6% of Gross Domestic Product (GDP)—9% of bank loans and 20% of loans to enterprises in 1991 (against 21%, 29%, and 36% in Czechoslovakia).[41] In three years, however, problem loans had risen to 26% of total loans (September 1994). In part, this reflected better accounting standards; it also showed a deterioration of bank portfolios. A consolidation program failed to curb the trend in 1993–1994 (due to weak governance and lack of a time-bound privatization plan). In 1995, the Hungarian government changed its strategy. Instead of new expensive recapitalization, it accelerated privatization and opened banks to foreign investment. (OTP was partially privatized and received $140 million in fresh capital, while Budapest Bank was bought by General Electric and the EBRD.) This innovative policy resulted in a significant improvement in capital requirement ratios and returns on capital.

Despite Hungary's and Poland's success, the rest of the region remains loath to privatize financial institutions, or even force state-owned banks to face the same competition that CEE governments have unleashed on trade and manufacturing. Even after the real sector started recovering, reformers still saw state-controlled banks as a strategic link to the economy. Czech Republic authorities, for instance, pursued a centralized approach that mostly revolved around the deduction of $4 billion in debts. Banks had initially been included in the massive voucher privatization and shares distributed among several hundred investment funds. The funds then consolidated their stake by buying new equity from individual shareholders and from the state. Privatization, however, was only partial, the role of the funds unclear, and changes in banking operations did not follow. By 1996–1997, the Czech government was compelled to launch a stabilization program targeting small banks, under which they had to liquidate part of their problem loans and submit commercial and financial plans to the Czech National Bank. Two banks lost their license and six were placed under conservatorship. By mid-1998, nonperforming credit still represented 29% of the total, most of it concentrated among four of the country's largest (state-controlled) banks. Privatization is expected to speed up at last, following the government's decision to sell three banks.

A Balance of Economic Reforms in Central and Eastern Europe 89

Throughout the region most state banks have engaged in portfolio restructuring with differing fortunes. Among the relative achievements are the introduction of better accounting techniques and stricter criteria for evaluating loan quality. Step by step, regulations are being put in place, as are capital-asset ratios, loan classification, and provisioning rules. Bank managers have learned to set aside loan-loss reserves and pay greater attention to loan quality and their capital base. Finally, most CEE states have designed deposit insurance schemes. Yet, emerging banking systems remain very fragile and sensitive to external shocks, as seen by the Russian devaluation in August 1998. Though the crisis did not directly affect CEE banking institutions, it hit countries that suffered from weak macroeconomic fundamentals. Slovakia, whose financial sector is burdened by bad credit and low capital requirements, was forced to abandon its fixed exchange rate in October 1998. At the end of 1997, the country's third largest bank (IRB) had been placed under central bank administration and recapitalized, underscoring the instability of the banking system. Romania was also unable to withstand the Russian shock wave. In a country where bad loans made up 57% of total loans in 1997 (as opposed to 19% in 1991), Moscow's crisis exacerbated the problem.

CEE banking systems still face several daunting challenges. First, central banks are unable to reconcile their various missions; in particular, managing monetary policy and supervising commercial banks. Thus, while monetary policy might require that interest rates remain high, lower rates would likely promote consolidation of the banking system. In addition, independence of the central banks is far from guaranteed. "Everywhere political influence is paramount, with the result that priorities are shifting according to economic and political circumstances."[42] Second, proper banking procedures appear difficult to implement. Changes often remain on paper, while attitudes (behavior) lag behind. Everywhere, central banks lack management skills, time, and reliable information to effect change.

More important, alongside a few foreign banks and several new private ones, CEE banking systems are still characterized by a few dominant banks, most of them inherited from communist monopolist structures. This leaves extensive room for anticompetitive practices. Collusion between state banks and governmental officials allows for preferential lending to cronies' firms and negatively affects relations between banks and business. On average, private banks appear more efficient and more profitable. They are nonetheless not immune to bad debts, and often lack the capacity to compete with dominant state structures that do not hesitate to impose lower deposit rates. The German model, a logical choice in the absence of efficient capital markets, has been adopted everywhere. This system, however, permits excessive concentration, causing rapid spillover of financial crises. Finding a balance between competition and concentration remains one of the basic dilemmas confronting banks. On the one hand, competition can increase efficiency and decrease service costs. On the other hand, dispersed ownership structures can jeopardize effective corporate governance. Hence, strict entry conditions (through licensing) are essential to assure that newly established private banks meet necessary capital requirements and enjoy a solid financial base.

Most Eastern European states have opened up their banking systems to foreign participation. (In 1997, seven of the 28 Bulgarian banks had foreign owners, 11 out of 33 in Romania, 30 out of 41 in Hungary, 15 banks in the Czech Republic.)[43] However, with the notable exception of Hungary where foreign-owned bank assets stand at more than 40%, foreign banks weigh little in transition economies. Foreign assets range between 10% to 15% in Central Europe (Poland, Slovakia, the Czech Republic) and fall below 10% in Bulgaria and Romania.[44] Acclaimed as a major vehicle for increased competitiveness and improved management, foreign banks can access capital at lower cost in their home country and likely employ Western-trained personnel. Local banks, liable to enjoy less confidence, are often unable to compete on an equal footing. This selection process could lead to the elimination of newly founded private banks before they evolve into efficient intermediaries. In order to resist foreign competition, private banks, for instance, might be compelled to opt for short-term profits at the expense of effective mobilization of domestic savings and enterprise restructuring.

Finally, the quality and diversification of financial services offered by CEE banks remain under question. For the most part, banks limit themselves to taking deposits and extending loans. Even the basic role of intermediaries remains rudimentary. To contain risk, those who have managed to overcome their problem loans have become exceedingly cautious in lending to firms. They often prefer to concentrate on fee-generating services. In countries where governments have large financing requirements, private investment is systematically crowded out. Short-term loans are favored over long-term financing that would support small and medium-sized business modernization. In addition, the amount of credit extended by CEE banks remains far below Western Europe (the Czech and the Slovak cases possibly excepted). Finally, difference between deposit and lending rates are significantly higher than in Western economies.

Effective mechanisms to channel savings toward investment activities are still lacking. The situation is further complicated by the absence of strong capital markets, the impact of the Asian crisis in 1997 and the Russian collapse in 1998.

Capital Markets in Their Infancy

As shown above, CEE financial systems remain mostly bank-based. Capital markets are just beginning to take shape and are of limited importance compared to bank intermediaries.[45] In 1997, the ratio of stock-market capitalization to GDP was above 30% only in two countries: Hungary (up from 4.2% in 1994 to 36.2%) and the Czech Republic (down from 30.9% in 1994 to 30%). Elsewhere in transition economies, this ratio did not exceed 15%. All in all, the volume of transactions on CEE stock markets remains low. Developing nonbank financial intermediaries would provide alternative means of pooling risks and, by supporting private sector expansion, would fill an important void. As private corporations, their survival would depend on making good investment decisions, and greater efficiency could ensue.

Since the beginning of economic transformation, development in the stock markets and the banking system have gone hand in hand. Countries that have managed to consolidate their banking systems are also those where stock market securities are most widespread. The explanation is that comprehensive privatization is a basic precondition for strengthening capital markets. However, depending on the methods adopted (voucher schemes vs. sales to strategic investors), stock-market capitalization and *turnover* (transactions) vary greatly. For instance, voucher privatization typically yields high turnover since it initially underestimates enterprise assets.

Hungary, Poland, and the Czech Republic have best integrated into international financial markets. The Budapest Stock Exchange boasts the most developed capital market among CEE states. In 1997, market capitalization in dollars was multiplied by three as a result of listing ten new companies coupled with a simultaneous rise in share prices. Second after Budapest, the Czech stock market for a long time suffered from lack of transparency and weak protection of minority shareholders. To solve these problems, a Securities and Exchange Commission (SEC) was set up in April 1998, which, although funded by the government, has the power to revoke licenses and to discipline trades and capital transfers. In addition, the technical operation of the stock market has improved. Poland launched a stock exchange as early as April 1991. Warsaw's market underwent a sudden (and mostly speculative) expansion in 1993–1994 with an exponential increase in share prices and a significant inflow of foreign capital. This development came to a brutal stop a year later, impelled by the withdrawal of Western speculative capital along with small shareholders attracted by unrealistic, high turnover. Compared to Prague, Warsaw trading is limited, but the market stands out as liquid and benefits from a well-developed regulatory framework. In 1997, daily transactions averaged $43 million per day.[47]

In contrast, the Bulgarian stock exchange, which began operating in October 1997, is embryonic. Despite the Bulgarian authorities' announcement that some companies might be privatized by public offers on the stock exchange, to this day only one firm (Elkabel, specialized in electric equipment) went public by stock offers in May 1998. The Romanian stock exchange is slightly more advanced. Starting from a stock market capitalization of 1.3% of GDP in 1996, it reached 6.8% in 1997. Thanks to its role in the privatization process, the stock exchange is likely to develop further in the coming years. Government securities nonetheless remain scanty.

To differing degrees, these stock markets have benefited from the growing interest of initially reluctant Western investors. In 1997, for instance, they were responsible for 70% of the market capitalization in Hungary and 35% in Poland. In the Czech Republic, Western investors accounted for 50% of the daily transactions in 1996. A sharp increase of private capital flow in 1996–1997 reflected the progressive integration of Central European economies into the international market. Most were short-term commitments attracted by high interest rates and huge governmental financial needs. Interestingly enough, countries where structural reforms lagged behind received the bulk of short-term capital. Growing dependence on foreign investors also meant sharp trend reversals if investors lost confidence in the stock markets. Risks became obvious in the wake of Russian financial turmoil. The August 1998 crisis also revealed increasing internal differences within the former communist bloc and unequal vulnerability to financial shocks.

Following the Russian devaluation, stock indexes collapsed throughout the region, share prices fell, international reserves were depleted, and local currencies came under pressure. In countries with a floating exchange rate, substantial depreciation was registered (the Polish zloty and the Czech koruna lost about 10% of their value in a week). Confronted with speculative attacks on its currency, Slovakia had to abandon its fixed exchange rate in October 1998. Portfolio preferences shifted to more stable stock markets. Most sensitive to Western investors' withdrawal were the states that had accumulated short-term liabilities and that presented large budget and current account deficits. Romania and the Slovak Republic financial markets were the most destabilized. Already in the first half of 1998, the Slovak stock index had decreased by 41% and the stock exchange had come to a standstill as a result of poor market liquidity and severe financial imbalances. Against this background, Russia's crisis precipitated a resource outflow.

One can only hope that lessons will be drawn from the Russian crisis and, in particular, that CEE authorities will think about their debt structure and reduce dependency on foreign bank lending to local financial institutions. Western capital is highly volatile and may withdraw brutally. Aside from these considerations, in order for Eastern European capital markets to achieve balanced and stable growth, several measures should be implemented. First, CEE stock exchanges need to do away with low transparency and violations of minority shareholders' rights. Second, contracts and information need to be improved. Finally, it remains to be seen whether and under what conditions bank involvement in the capital markets should be encouraged. Actually, tight interaction between banking and securities markets may favor a rapid spread of financial crises to the real sector. In 1998, firms were partially protected from market instability by their weak ties to the stock exchanges. There is no doubt that the effects of the Russian devaluation and foreign capital flight would have been more dreadful if banks and stock markets had been more closely intertwined.

NOTES

1. For further information, see Transitions économiques à l'Est (1989–1995), Etudes de la documentation française: Paris, La Documentation française, 1996.

2. See the illuminating Dezsö Kovacs and Sally Ward Maggard, "The Human Face of Political, Economic, and Social Change in Eastern Europe," *East European Quarterly*, 27(3), Sept. 1993, pp. 317–345.

3. Recent investigations into the dynamics of institution-building have similarly emphasized the role microeconomic practices play in embedding "abstract" laws and rules in a given society. This is one among many insights that can be derived from the

excellent Joan M. Nelson, Charles Tilly, and Lee Walker (eds.), *Transforming Post-Communist Political Economies* (Washington, DC: National Academy Press, 1997).

4. For further evidence on early debates on privatization, see D. Lipton and J. Sachs, "Privatization in Eastern Europe: The Case of Poland," *Brookings Papers on Economic Activity*, 2, 1990, pp. 293–341; O.J. Blanchard and R. Layard, "How to Privatize?" LSE Centre for Economic Performance Discussion Paper, 50, August 1991; Z. Sadowski, "Privatization in Eastern Europe: Goals, Problems and Implications," *Oxford Review of Economic Policy*, 7(4), 1991, pp. 43-69; B. Adam and G. Schwartz, "Privatization: Reflections on the Eastern European Experience," MOCT-MOST, 3, 1992, pp. 17–24; J. Machacek, "Privatization: More Than an Economic Goal," *East European Reporter*, 5(1), 1992, pp. 55–58; and "Diversité des privatisations en Europe centrale et en Russie" *Le Courrier des pays de l'est*, 390, June/July 1994, special issue.

5. In countries like Poland and Hungary, though, from the very onset of change privatization was conceived of as a major vehicle for the economic reconversion of former communist *nomenklaturas*. For an analysis of this process, see Georges Mink and Jean-Charles Szurek, "L'ancienne élite communiste en Europe Centrale: stratégies, ressources et reconstructions identitaires," *Revue française de sciences politiques*, 48(1), février 1998, pp. 3–41.

6. For a good presentation of initial privatization programs, see Roman Frydman, Andrzej Rapaczynski, and John S. Earle (eds.), *The Privatization Process in Eastern Europe* (Budapest: Central European University Press, 1993). A comparative analysis of advancement in reforms can be found in Michael Borish and Michel Noël, "Privatisation in the Visegrad Countries: A Comparative Assessment," *World Economy*, 20(2), March 1997, pp. 199–219. The case of Bulgaria is reviewed in S. Keremidtchiev, "Les privatisations en Bulgarie: mécanismes et intérêts," *Revue française d'administration publique*, 74, April/June 1995, pp. 211–215 and Zoya Mladenova and James Angresano, "Privatization in Bulgaria," *East European Quarterly*, 30(4), January 1997, pp. 495–515. On Romania, see among others, Daniel Labaronne, "Les lenteurs de la privatisation en Roumanie: Une analyse du comportement des acteurs publics," *Revue d'études comparatives est-ouest*, 2, 1997, pp. 101–128.

7. The so-called "small-privatization" process, which was rather swiftly implemented in most Eastern European economies, is left aside here. Reprivatization through restitution (notably of lands) is also left aside.

8. See, among others, J. Kotrba and J. Svejnar, "Rapid and Multifaceted Privatization: Experience of the Czech and Slovak Republics," MOCT-MOST, 4, 1994, pp. 147–185; S. van Wijnbergen and A. Marcincin, "Voucher Privatization, Corporate Control and the Cost of Capital: An Analysis of the Czech Privatization Program," *CEPR Discussion Papers*, 1215, 1995; and J. Mladek and I. Hashi, "Voucher Privatization, Investment Funds and Corporate Governance in Czechoslovakia," *British Review of Economic Issues*, 15(37), October 1993, pp. 67–96. An assessment of vouchers as a privatization mechanism can be found in J. Svejnar and M. Singer, "Using Voucher to Privatize an Economy," *Economics of Transition*, 2, 1994, pp. 43–69.

9. Quoted in Michael Borish and Michel Noël, "Privatisation in the Visegrad Countries: A Comparative Assessment," *World Economy*, 20(2), March 1997, p. 215.

10. See Wojciech Nasierowski, "Emerging Patterns of Reform in Central Europe: The Czech Republic, Hungary, and Poland," *Journal of East-West Studies*, 2(1/2), 1996, p. 153.

11. On the Bulgarian mass privatization program see Zoya Mladenova and James Angresano, "Privatization in Bulgaria," *East European Quarterly*, 30(4), January 1997, pp. 495-515.

12. Quoted in "Bulgarie. La deuxième phase de privatisation lancée," *La Tribune*, 21-07-1998.

13. For more information, see notably Igor Filatochev, Irena Grosfeld et al., "Buyouts in Hungary, Poland and Russia: Governance and Finance Issues," *Economics of Transition*, 4(1), 1996, pp. 67–88. A broader presentation of buyouts is available in M. Wright, I. Filatotchoev, T. Buck, and K. Robbie (eds.), *Management and Employee Buy-outs in Central and Eastern Europe*, European Bank/CEEPN, London, 1993. The Hungarian Case was studied in greater detail in J. Kornai and M. Wright, "Accountability, Governance and Finance in Hungarian Buy-outs," *Europe-Asia Studies*, 46(6), 1994, pp. 997–1016.

14. Similar preoccupations were voiced by Tomasz Mickiewicz in an article on employee control over decision-making in state enterprises in Poland. See Tomasz Mickiewicz, "The State Sector during Transformation: Employment, Wages and Investment," *Communist Economies and Economic Transformation*, 8(3), 1996, pp. 393–410.

15. On the Hungarian privatization program till mid-1995, see Peter Mihalyi, "Privatization in Hungary: Now Comes the 'Hard Core,'" *Communist Economies and Economic Transformation*, 8(2), 1996, pp. 205–216.

16. *Economic Analysis and Forecasting*, Sofia, pp. 23.

17. On the issue of corporate governance, one might refer to the comprehensive and insightful Roman Frydman, Cheryl W. Gray, and Andrzej Rapaczynski (eds.), *Corporate Governance in Central Europe and Russia*, Budapest, Central European University Press, 1996, vols. 1 and 2. See also I. Filatotchev, M. Wright, T. Buck, I. Grosfeld, and J. Karsai, "Governance, Finance and Buy-outs in Russia, Poland and Hungary," *The Economics of Transition*, 4, 1996, pp. 567–588.

18. See Leonid Polishchuk, "Missed Markets: Implications for Economic Behavior and Institutional Change," in Joan M. Nelson, Charles Tilly, and Lee Walker (eds.), *Transforming Post-Communist Political Economies* (Washington, DC: National Academy Press, 1997), pp. 80–101.

19. See Polishchuk, "Missed Markets," p. 82.

20. The question of distribution of political goods in the form of management posts has been studied in Andrei Shleifer and Robert W. Vishny, "Politicians and Firms," *Quarterly Journal of Economics*, November 1994, pp. 995–1025.

21. See Daniel Labaronne, "Les lenteurs de la privatisation en Roumanie. Une analyse du comportement des acteurs publics," *Revue d'études comparatives Est-Ouest*, 2, 1997, pp. 101–128.

22. See Katherine Verdery, "Fuzzy Property: Rights, Power, and Identity in Transylvania's Decollectivization," in Joan M. Nelson, Charles Tilly, and Lee Walker (eds.), *Transforming Post-Communist Political Economies*, (Washington, DC: National Academy Press, 1997), p. 103.

23. For a good introduction to this issue, see Saul Estrin, Kirsty S. Hughes, and Sarah Todd, *Foreign Direct Investment in Central and Eastern Europe: Multinationals in Transition* (London: Pinter, Royal Institute of International Affairs, 1997).

24. On the legislative framework for foreign investments, see Mariana Gheciu, "The Legal Framework of the Foreign Investment in Central and East-European Countries," *Journal of East-West Business*, 2 (3/4), 1996, pp. 125–141.

25. Quoted in Franck Moulins, "Une analyse dynamique du rôle de l'investissement étranger dans les restructurations industrielles des pays d'Europe centrale et orientale," *Revue d'études comparatives est-ouest*, 2, June 1997, p. 5.

26. Ibid., p.6.

27. ERBD, *Transition Report*, London, 1998, p. 79.

28. Romanian Agency for Development, Bucarest, 1998.

29. "Europe centrale et orientale, Communauté des Etats indépendants en 1997:

acquis et disparités économiques," *Le Courrier des pays de l'est*, pp. 428–429, March/April/May 1998.

30. For more details, see Edith Lhomel, "Industries agro-alimentaires et investissements occidentaux en Europe centrale et orientale," *Le Courrier des pays de l'est*, 377, March 1993, pp. 18–23.

31. See Leonidas Maroudas and Yorgos Rizopoulos, "La Bulgarie dans les stratégies d'internationalisation des firmes occidentales," *Revue d'études comparatives est-ouest*, 1, March 1995, pp. 115–138.

32. This holds especially true for the automobile sector. On FMN strategies, see Jaroslav Blaha, "L'industrie automobile en Europe centrale: la grande vague des investissements étrangers," *Le Courrier des pays de l'est*, 433, Octobre 1998, pp. 3–25.

33. Several recent publications provide a very comprehensive overview of developments in the banking sector. See, among others, Ronald W. Anderson and Chantal Kegels, *Transition Banking*, (Oxford: Clarendon Press, 1998) and John Bonin, Kalmal Mizei, Istvan Szekely, and Paul Watchel, *Banking in Transition Economies* (Cheltenham: Edward Elgar, 1998.)

34. Quoted in Céline Gondat Larralde et Laëtitia Lepetit, "Relation entre structures de marché et performance dans l'industrie bancaire. Analyse empirique des marchés bancaires d'Europe centrale et orientale," August 1998, mimeo, p. 5.

35. For further details, see Hristin Vutscheva, "Bad Credits: Institutional and Financial Aspects," Sofia, Center for the Study of Democracy, September 1994, mimeo.

36. On corruption in the Bulgarian banking system, see the unyielding report written by the then undersecretary of the Parliamentary Commission against Corruption, Edvin Sugarev, "White Book of the Bank Bankruptcy," Sofia, 1996, mimeo.

37. A good summary of the 1996 banking crisis can be found in *Economic Survey of Europe in 1996–1997* (Geneva: United Nations, Economic Commission for Europe), p. 75–84. For further details, see "Bulgarie," *Etudes économiques de l'OCDE* (Paris: OCDE, March 1997), esp. chapter 3 "Le secteur bancaire," p. 72–111.

38. For a general overview of bank-restructuring programs, see Michael Borish, M. Long, and Michel Noël, "Restructuring Banks and Enterprises: Recent Lessons from Transition Economies," *World Bank Discussion Paper*, 279, 1995. See also D. Begg and R. Portes, "Enterprise Debt and Financial Restructuring in Central and Eastern Europe," *European Economic Review*, 1993.

39. On the Polish case, see Cheryl W. Gray and Arnold Holle, "Bank-led Restructuring in Poland (II): Bankruptcy and Its Alternatives," *Economics of Transition*, 5(1), 1997, pp. 25–44 as well as Fernando Montes-Negret and Luca Papi, "The Polish Experience in Bank and Enterprise Restructuring," *MOCT-MOST*, 7, 1997, pp. 79–104.

40. Quoted in *Transition Report* (London: EBRD 1998), p. 133.

41. Quoted in Michael S. Borish, Wei Ding, and Michel Noël, "A Review of Bank Performance During Transition in Central Europe," *Communist Economies and Economic Transformation*, 9(3), 1997, p. 339.

42. See Alfred Steinherr, "Banking Reforms in Eastern European Countries," *Oxford Review of Economic Policy*, 13(2), 1997, p. 108.

43. See *Transition Report*, (London: EBRD 1998), pp. 158–190.

44. Ibid., p. 95.

45. For an introduction to the question of financial markets in Eastern Europe, see Daniel Hantson, "Les marchés financiers en Europe centrale et orientale," *Le Courrier des pays de l'est*, 420, July 1997, pp. 3–12 and Christain de Boissieu, Alain Henriot Dan Sandrine Rol, "Les marchés de capitaux émergents: une vue perspective," *ACCOMEX*, Chambre de commerce et d'industrie de Paris, 13, January/February 1997, pp. 6–24.

46. See *Transition Report* (London: EBRD 1998), 96.

47. Statistics quoted in Hantson, pp. 10–11.

48. On the repercussions of the Russian devaluation, see "From Asia to Russia—Contagion and Transition," in *Transition Report* (London: EBRD 1998), pp. 71–76.

Chapter 8

Ulysses and the Lotus Eaters
Michel Koutouzis

Today, the world of drug trafficking transcends the former notions of Empire, cold war spheres of interest, and end-of-century capitalism. It is rather a composite of workable elements from these three historic models joined together in a netherworld where the rules and regulations of everyday life are taken for granted. In this gray zone, licit and illicit merchandise cross paths; criminal networks have usurped the trade routes of antiquity, the highways of pilgrimage, and the byways of tourism; clandestine swapping of goods has become the substitute for interstate trade; embargoes suddenly add zeros to the price of sought-after merchandise; time and money are worth their weight in gold; and the kings and courtiers meet on islands surrounded by water so blue it makes a person wince.

THE CHANGING FACE OF THE DRUG BUSINESS

Until the 1980s, drug refining, export, and distribution was largely in the hands of large criminal organizations, which had with foresight invested in various pipeline activities (plantation, transportation, and transformation of raw materials; transportation of semi-refined/refined products, distribution; and money laundering, etc.) during the previous decade.

The main players operating on a global scale were considered to be Italian organized crime, Turkish *maffyas*, Chinese triads, Colombian cartels, Southeast Asian warlords, and the Japanese *Yacusa*. Each group held a monopoly over a geographic area. But it was not at all unusual for one or more groups to join forces in a mutually beneficial venture. Beginning in the early 1990s, however, the illegal drug market underwent a monumental structural overhaul.

A number of factors were responsible for this transformation, the first one being the upbeat efforts and growing success of national law enforcement agencies, which had begun to coordinate their efforts on an international scale. Very often the excesses caused by smuggling a single product, the conspicuous consumption of its ringleaders, or the obvious nature of banking transactions had attracted suspicion or made some henchman somewhere an easy target of international law enforcement. The closure of one or more nerve centers along the pipeline was usually enough to throw the whole chain of command into chaos. Very quickly, the leaders and managers of various criminal organizations realized that smaller, more diverse activities were safer and a decentralized structure was less vulnerable to discovery and dismantlement. They initiated their own downsizing like any other contemporary business venture.

PRODUCTION EXPLOSION

The colossal growth of landmass under drug cultivation has made for an increased availability of narcotics, particularly in the vast Russian expanse and its "near abroad." Spurred by human initiative, it has also triggered the migration of plants from one ecological niche to another. For example, opium poppies *Papaver somniferum*, which are indigenous to central Asia, but will grow well in northern latitudes from Scandinavia to the equator, now cover large areas of Central and South America. The coca shrub, *Erythroxylon coca*, cultivated in the Andean highlands, has made its appearance in the Georgian Republic (Abkazia). In addition, plots and fields that once only supplied local markets now produce cash crops for export. The stringent programs of structural adjustment imposed on developing countries by international financial organizations have pushed subsistence farmers the world over into cannabis, opium poppy, and coca production as a means of supplementing flagging state aid. This occurs despite the United Nations Drug Control Program's (UNDCP) attempt to replace drug-producing plants with agricultural products, for the obvious reason that people make more money supplying drug networks.

Fabrication of synthetic drugs has also grown to keep up with a dramatic surge in demand. At $15 to $20, in Paris, a tablet of ecstasy is five to six times less expensive than a gram of cocaine. Over the last several years, this "recreational" drug has become the number one best-seller among the synthetic or chemically manufactured drugs ever since the central ingredient ephedrine, extracted from the medicinal herb *Ephedra vulgaris,* was synthesized in its industrial form ephedrone.[1]

Globalization has also been responsible for bringing startlingly diverse cultural mores, consumption habits, and existential philosophies into direct contact with very different or incompatible beliefs. By making certain practices glamorous or enviable in film or print, these practices are sampled and adopted with trendy enthusiasm. Cocaine has found eager users in Japan. Laotian heroin has found a massive regional South Asian market. Methamphetamines have penetrated Africa and Asia even as medical prescriptions for antidepressants and appetite suppressants have skyrocketed in developed countries. Like any other market at the end of the twentieth century, this one is determined by supply and demand, dumping, exchange value, strategic timing, and consumer profiles.

SMALL WARS AND INSURGENCIES

A third factor responsible for the upsurge in drugs is the growing number of low-intensity conflicts on all continents. In the past ten years, Europeans have been confronted with various violent paroxysms resulting from the Soviet Union's collapse,[2] the closest one being the bloody unraveling of the former Yugoslavia at its back door.

The nuclear powers, particularly the United States and the Soviet Union, kept each other in check and fortified themselves with proxy clientele states. Yet far from ending small localized wars, the end of the cold war divested people within many of these states of their ideological motives and instead freed up "worthy" ethnic, religious, and nationalistic reasons for killing.

Deprived of logistical support from one or the other superpower ally, soldiers and guerrillas on the ground are today forced to find alternative methods to finance their struggles. Smuggling contraband and drugs has turned out to be relatively simple and as gainful as everything that can be had: opium, oil, Kalashnikovs, fissile material, nuclear weapons, and human beings can be sold.

SYNTHETIC DRUGS AND THE POTENTIAL OF EASTERN EUROPE AND EURASIA

The mid-1990s has only confirmed the energetic drug market entry of countries once tied to the Soviet bloc. Just a few years ago drug traffickers there had small ambitions, that is to say delivering their limited surplus to Western Europe. Today, however, markets in North America, South Africa, and Australia have become enticing prospects, and polydrug production has increased.

Criminal organizations in the former Soviet bloc, given the right climatic conditions, may choose to cultivate drug-yielding plants. But they also have the option to convert disabled chemical factories, pharmaceutical plants, or even disaffected military sites impervious to outside interference, into state-of-the-art production centers for synthetic drugs or chemical precursors.[3] The conversion incentive contains a number of favorable aspects. First of all, there are plenty of qualified and underpaid chemists and pharmacists in Eastern Europe and Central Asia willing to supplement their incomes. Secondly, not having been exposed to huge quantities of free-flowing drugs over the past decades, citizens there are like a captive audience willing to accept almost anything that is fashionably done in the West. The polydrug market has unlimited potential.

THE RUSSIAN MODEL

In 1991–1992, criminal structures springing from the nomenklatura began pillaging the state in the first phases of privatization. During this period, bloody politico-mafia wars took their toll, dissuading any major interest in the drug trade. This zealous bloodletting allowed the small-time narco-trafficking gangs of Central Asia to commercialize their locally grown heroin and additional stocks imported from Afghanistan. On the same small scale, Ukrainians exported poppy straw[4] and Georgians and Azeris built clandestine chemical laboratories and rudimentary pipelines. Members of the Russian Jewish Diaspora also consolidated pipeline connections between Israel and major urban centers in the Commonwealth of Independent States (CIS) and Central Asia.

Indications of a muscled takeover of the drug business by regional political figures became apparent with a steady rise in murders and assassinations in the mid-1990s. The bombing death of "Aliocha the hunchback" in Tadjikistan is a prime example. (In 1995, the Russian Business Roundtable, an association of high-ranking business leaders, also lost nine of its top thirty members to assassins.) However, by the end of the privatization period, just when the "new rich" were adopting protective security measures against kidnapping, extortion, and murder, the drug business was taken over by highly adept professionals.

In 1996 the different services of the Russian Ministry of the Interior registered 97,800 drug-related crimes, a 21% rise over the preceding year. The highest number came from Krasnodar (5,991) situated in the transit zone between Central Asia and the Caucuses, both regions of conflicts. Saint Petersburg (with 5,656) came in second position. In Russia as a whole, 20,000 crimes consisting of "illegal preparation of narcotics, transport, stocking and sale" grew 74.3% over the year before. But confiscation by law enforcement officials fell off sharply. Oddly enough, in 1996 police only seized 18,743.4 kg of "narcotic" substances, 10.5% less than in 1995. Seizures coming from illicit cultivation for the same year were only 2,709 kg, or 65% less than 1995. These figures did not corroborate at all with the noticeable rise in polydrug consumption. When questioned, the authorities pointed to a certain lassitude in drug enforcement. But the falling figures really indicated widespread and well-coordinated schemes of police corruption organized by people in high places.

For over three-quarters of a century, the Soviet Union's institutionalized Communist party bureaucracy oversaw the country's civic and industrial functions and that of its satellites with an iron hand. In order to accomplish this feat, it relied on two hermetic structures: The Red army and the KGB. After 1991, the Russian military became a disorganized and demoralized institution that carried little prestige, and the KGB broke up into several organizations.

Along with the *apparatchik*-turned-entrepreneur, many ranking members from both state institutions are suspected of association with regional mafia groups and actors in Russia's unorthodox capitalism. (In 1994, it was estimated that over 3,500 mafia groups existed, and at least 10% of them operated abroad.) Their former status still allows them access to information and information permits the maintenance of monopolistic positions, access to easy capital, and, by way of underworld connections, the ability to destroy competition or people who threaten to interfere (as the November 1998 murder of Russian parliamentarian Galina Starovoitova proved). People of this caliber have almost exclusively fashioned Russia's recently discredited "Kremlin Capitalism." In the farther reaches of the Commonwealth of Independent States and in ex-satellite countries, the same kind of shrewd strongmen have transformed themselves into regional bosses or kingpin rulers who reign greedily over their own self-styled satrapies. And many of them have earned the reputation of being able to design successful companies out of almost nothing in highly inaccessible places, since they always seem to have the liquid assets to prove it.

A FISCAL PARADISE IN THE EASTERN MEDITERRANEAN

Cyprus's affiliation with the nonaligned movement made it an attractive destination for the transfer of money from the Eastern bloc. At the onset of the Lebanese Civil War in 1975, part of Beirut's banking establishment was relocated on the island. As its reputation of discretion and efficiency grew, Cyprus became attractive to Soviet businessmen with hot money looking to outmaneuver exchange controls, and for a place to establish holding companies without intrusive audits. Considerable funds from Serbia have also been funneled from Belgrade into secret accounts in this fiscal paradise.

In the process of Russian privatization (1991–1995) millions of rubles disappeared from circulation to end up in offshore banking centers, primarily in the southern Republic of Cyprus. It was relatively easy to skim money off the top of international loans and foreign investment in joint ventures, as it was next to impossible in many instances to determine precisely who owned firms in Russia. Rules to compel disclosure of corporate ownership did not exist or were simply ignored.

The incredible rise of offshore businesses in the southern portion of divided Nicosia, the Island's Greek-speaking half (approximately 25,000 in 1996, contributing over $400 million to the local economy and 10% of them were in Russian hands) has made it an Eastern Mediterranean's banking center. The financial success of the Republic of Cyprus has led the Turks to establish the First Merchant Bank in the Turkish Republic of North Cyprus (Turks represent 20% of the island's population), which, along with new luxury gambling facilities, such as the *Jasmin Casino*, provide easy money-laundering access. Considered a strategic outpost for the military defense of Anatolia by Ankara, it has become a vital transshipment area for Turkey's maritime "Balkan Route." One among numerous heroin routes branching outward from Turkey like a many-headed Hydra, it has attachments to an extreme right-wing group, the Gray Wolves, linked to the Turkish army.

The proposal that Cyprus join the European Union in the near future has prompted Nicosia to cooperate with antinarcotics squads (of Syria, Egypt, and Israel) and regulatory financial institutions. The island's legislation has had to conform with UN recommendations and the European Convention on Money Laundering (Law 18–III). The enmity that has governed Greco-Turkish relations on Cyprus since 1974 and the mutual distrust Athens and Ankara have for each other has been exacerbated by the war in the former Yugoslavia and the ongoing expansion of the Turkish drug trade.

THE TURKISH CONNECTIONS

Since the 1960s, Turkey has been the primary transit route for Golden Crescent heroin making its way to Western Europe. However, beginning ten to fifteen years ago, South Asian countries, notably India, began to reduce the manufacture and distribution of precursor chemicals in response to pressure from New Delhi and international drug enforcement agencies. Previously large quantities of chemicals (acetic anhydride and others) had been smuggled into Afghanistan and Pakistan in order to monopolize the treatment of morphine base in close proximity to the highland poppy fields. As the sources of precursor chemicals dwindled, Turkish drug lords took over the operation, increasing internal poppy cultivation. In addition, the UN sanctions placed on Iraq after the 1991 Gulf War deprived Turkey of oil and an export market for manufactured goods. Lacking a petroleum source of its own, it made the choice to concentrate efforts in the enlargement of internal heroin production at a time when the Turkish army's counterinsurgency action against the Kurdistan Workers Party (PKK) was draining the state coffers.[5] Rough drug-profit estimates were $25 billion in 1995, and $37.5 billion in 1996. Only networks working in close association with the army and police could account for such high figures.

Evidence for the shift in production strategy was confirmed in annual seizures. During 1994–1995, Iranian authorities seized hundreds of tons of opium and morphine base crossing the country's eastern frontier, but less than a ton of refined heroin. That same year, 2.7 tons of morphine base were seized inside Turkey, while 1.6 tons were confiscated in shipments going out. Then suddenly in 1996 close to 4 tons of pure heroin were confiscated inside the country along with a record-breaking single seizure of 21 tons of precursor chemicals. Explanations for this dramatic rise directly implicated the Turkish government.

In 1984, seeking self-determination for Turkey's 15 million Kurds, the PKK launched its guerrilla war against Ankara, attacking police garrisons and army posts throughout the country. The movement had numerous Kurdish sympathizers, including expatriates and "businessmen" who were believed to funnel profits from drug trafficking back to the PKK.

The Turkish army retaliated with a purely reactive strategy until 1993, when it began a campaign of terror, seeking out and destroying guerrilla strongholds in urban areas, silencing pro-Kurdish activists, and depopulating Anatolian villages thought to be supporting the rebels. Three of the army's strategic ploys were (1) the selection and training of mercenaries drawn from the Turkish Intelligence Organization (MIT), (2) the establishment of special police teams made up of Kurdish guerrillas turned informers, and (3) the formation of a progovernment corps of village guardians to act as spies. In 1994–1995, a ruthless crackdown on the PKK drove the guerrillas into retreat. Rapidly, however, branches of the progovernment mercenary units degenerated into corrupt gangs driven by greed to take over the drug trafficking and money laundering schemes that had generated the enormous Kurdish revenue. Fighting over the spoils, these special units soon began a vicious internecine struggle.

On the night of 3 November 1996, a Mercedes Benz on its way from Kusadasi overturned in a traffic accident on the Susurluk Highway. The driver, Huseyin Kocadag, a former Istanbul deputy police chief known to have organized anti-Kurdish repression was killed along with a female passenger. Sedet Bucak, a pro-government Kurdish village chieftain and right-wing DYP (True Path party) parliamentarian survived. Another passenger who did not survive was a certain Abdullah Catli, a wanted drug smuggler with *maffya* connections known for his role in suppressing left-wing activists throughout the decade following the military coup in 1980, and suspected to have been involved in the 1981 plot to assassinate Pope Jean-Paul II. At that time Catli had been second in command of the Gray Wolves, the youth arm of the far-right National Action Party (MHP) led by Cyprus-born Alpaslan Turkes (d. April 1997). Given the quantity of automatic weapons in the car and the profile of its occupants, it was surmised that they had been on a gangland mission to assassinate members of a rival organization.

Among the documents in Catli's possession was a diplomatic passport, six identity cards bearing various aliases and a license to carry arms signed by Interior Minister Mehmet Agar, chief of the county's 120,000-member police force and a close collaborator of Turkey's Deputy Prime Minister Tansu Ciller. In the wake of the scandal, Agar was forced to resign.

Along with linking the Ciller regime with the Gray Wolves, the Susurluk incident also drew attention to the government's involvement in a plot to destabilize the Aliev regime in Azerbaijan over rival interests in the future Caspian Sea oil pipeline. In addition, an ongoing investigation has only confirmed long-term suspicions: that successive Turkish governments have assisted drug traffickers, protected terrorists, and financed gangs of killers to eliminate Turkish dissidents and Kurdish rebels. Furthermore, anonymous members of the Turkish military machine and former officers of the MIT have "unofficially" corroborated the fact that over the past two years hundreds of kilos of heroin, confiscated from the PKK, but never appearing in recorded statistics, have been funneled back into the Gray Wolves' channels only to be shipped westward.

Turkish drugs entering Europe via the maritime "Balkan Route" through the former Yugoslavia are handled by Mafia middlemen of various nationalities including Italians, Central Europeans, and Albanians, as well as individuals eager to supplement their incomes. Summer tourism is a perfect foil for couriers who are paid roughly $15,000 to transport a kilo of refined heroin into Western Europe at a minimum risk to the grower-producer. The Turks have also adopted alternative routes via Bulgaria and Macedonia. To this end, laboratories have been set up in remote hillside farms near Edirne and Kirklareli in Turkish Thrace and some of them are even equipped with hidden garages holding a variety of transport vehicles including buses, passenger cars, and freight trucks specially designed to carry hidden stashes of drugs. Given that a kilo of heroin in a bulk delivery goes for $20,000 at the Turkish end of the pipeline and will be sold at a mark-up price of $60,000 in a Western European city, incentive is high. As Greek borders have come under surveillance, it is not unusual for drug-laden vehicles to follow the Black Sea coast to Batumi or Poti, where containers are then shipped to Varna, Bulgaria's main port, or on to Odessa in the Ukraine.

BALKAN CHAOS

After the push for a "Greater Serbia" ended in disaster, the Federal Republic of Yugoslavia (FRY), comprised of Serbia and Montenegro,[6] came under the UN sanctions imposed in June 1992. The well-used drug channels that had been so audaciously used until then, were rerouted northward (Bulgaria, Romania, Hungary) or southward (Greece, Macedonia, Albania). As a result, criminal organizations associated with drug running were severely jeopardized during the early period of the conflict. However, the alternative routes tapped into unexploited territory and, in the long term, proved to be a drug-trafficking windfall. When the sanctions were finally lifted with the signing of the Dayton accords in 1995, the old pipeline was reactivated even as the newer ones continued to thrive. As a direct consequence, polydrug use increased sharply in Central Europe, and marijuana consumption everywhere was seen as a banal social practice. "Smoking marijuana is like drinking whiskey here," said drug counselor Dr. Jiri Presl,[7] on the subject of Europe's burgeoning drug market.

At the onset of hostilities in Yugoslavia, the Serbian secret service agencies operating out of Belgrade had the serious task of finding the means to finance and supply the escalating war effort of the Yugoslav People's Army's (JNA) under Serbian control. They turned to sympathetic networks with an international scope and to fluvial, rail, and trucking firms serving Central and Western Europe. For example, as UN sanctions blocked the Danube River traffic inside Serbia, cargo-carrying trucks on barges unloaded their containers when reaching the monitored border and caught up with the containers further downstream along the Romanian and Bulgarian frontiers. The scheme worked for both incoming and outgoing goods.

Serbian president Slobodan Milosevic had become head of the Beobanka several years before getting involved in politics. It is suspected that he received considerable help from Beobank insider Borka Vucic in setting up a number of front companies and bank accounts, which she personally attended to from Cyprus, enabling payments to be secretly conducted to and from creditor countries supplying arms, oil, and other items in defiance of UN sanctions. When the sanctions ended in 1995, Mrs. Vucic returned from Cyprus and became director of Beogradsk Banka, the holding company that now owns Milosevic's former employer, Beobanka. Cyprus's promise to regulate unlawful transactions in view of European Union membership may have caused Serbian hidden accounts to be transferred elsewhere.

During the war, narco-trafficking and politics were closely entwined in Serbia's capital, to such a point that members of the political and military establishment, war profiteers, embargo-jumpers, and business leaders were often murdered when they attempted to cut connections and strike out on their own. So it was, for example, that Miograd Niksic, alias Miska, a man actively involved in Bangkok's diamond and heroin business was killed in Belgrade, as was Dragan Serbes. Goran Vukovic was assassinated in Germany by Ljubo Zemunac, a well-known mafia boss.

Montenegro also has its underworld figures working out of the capital Podgorica, Niksic, and the military port of Kotor. These people and others often appear periodically in newspaper articles reporting on "local crime." As targets of rival gangs, they, as well as their victims, are part of the "collateral damage" of the war, having tampered in dangerous aspects of the informal economy, financed private armies with drug money, or been bold enough to enlarge their market outreach.

In Albania, all aspects of the informal economy have traditionally been in the hands of extended family clans or *fares*. While underworld families made up of ethnic Albanian Montenegrins and Kosovars are involved in drugs and arms trafficking on a north-south axis and eastward toward Turkey, it is the Italian Mafiosi, in association with people of their own choosing who are the main purveyors of drugs in the Adriatic. With heavy investments in coastal real-estate and tourism, the Sacra Corona Unita, the Neapolitan Commorra, and the Calabrian 'Ndranghetta have infiltrated Turkey's southern Balkan route, while arms, cocaine, and amphetamines are also smuggled into Albania Montenegro from Italian coastal ports. The illegal confection of Bulgarian contraband cigarettes is also enmeshed in the drug business.

Although Serbia is still excluded from receiving needed IMF and World Bank credits despite the Dayton accords, the end of UN sanctions and the opening up of the Belgrade-Zagreb Highway in 1995 jump-started a younger generation of drug traffickers into action. These hardened veterans of the war are often protected by political strongmen attached to commercial organizations bearing the stamp of legitimacy. After all, the "black economy," made up of a wide variety of illegally manufactured and traded goods, took five years to build and is said to make up as much as one-third of Serbia's GDP.

The war in former Yugoslavia has encouraged the spread of "Kiosk Capitalism." Hundreds of cafés and small shops supplying multiple needs have appeared in capital cities, seaside resorts, and rural villages in all of the former republics. Suppliers, who have taken over the itinerant business of the caravansaries of old, offer cheap clothing and shoes from Romania and Turkey, or liquor and cigarettes from Bulgaria—bargains to financially strapped citizens. But frequently entrepreneurs investing in these small business ventures are subject to the coercive tactics of the local mafias that stock them and to whom they must pay protection money and a percentage of their profits.

Along with the new routes utilized by narco-traffickers, the classical Istanbul-Sofia-Belgrade axis, long controlled by Turkish *babas (*godfathers*)*, has once again become operational. But this older route competes heavily with one linking Bulgaria via Macedonia, Serbia/northern Albania (across Lake Shkoder by boat), to Montenegro. Essential foodstuffs, gasoline, and other fuel as well as drugs traveled long this line during the war.

However, the final destination of all Balkan routes is Slovenia. Reputed to have one of the most lax drug enforcement capacities in Europe, Slovenia has become the country of predilection for the transportation of banned narcotics and metaamphetimines, as the pipeline can easily funnel them south into Italy and north into Austria. In 1996, at the Yugoslav-Bulgaria-Gradina checkpoint, numerous long-distance freight trucks cleared for Slovenia were found to be carrying hundreds of kilos of heroin. Gradina's 1996 seizure total of 700 kilograms confirmed that Slovenia has surfaced as a prime transshipment depot served by an assortment of vehicles. At this south Central European juncture point for freight cargo and scores of traveling individuals, small-size packages of heroin are not difficult to dissimulate. Whether heroin is concealed in containers labeled raw cotton, handed over to paid couriers to be taped to the torso, or swallowed (body packed) in condoms, or hidden in the false bottoms of pieces of luggage, some of it will be overlooked by the overburdened border inspectors.

ALBANIAN MISERY

Various smuggling strategies, all of which were geared to transgress the UN sanctions imposed on Serbia and Greece's February 1994 economic embargo of Macedonia, have bolstered Kosovar and Albanian *fares* activity, including drug trafficking. Both groups, however, depend on very different pipeline connections.

Marxist-Leninist Albanian Party of Labor (PLA) leader Enver Hoxa (1921–1985), imposed draconian isolation on Albania, banning foreign travel, religious activity, private ownership of cars,[9] and any independent practice of law, while the government's infamous National Information Service (NIS) *Sigurimi* kept secret files on most Albanian citizens. Threat of imprisonment or internal exile successfully eliminated all forms of political dissent. His appointed successor, Ramiz Alia, was slow in enacting political reforms and his widespread unpopularity lost him the 1992 elections. Until recently Albania's political climate has left heroin trafficking the exclusive reserve of the Kosovar Albanians. Granted autonomous status in Yugoslavia's 1974 constitution, these ethnic Albanians were able to work and study outside Yugoslavia with relative ease until 1989, giving them access to drugs from Turkish sources in Istanbul, or in Aegean coastal ports. From southeastern Europe drugs were carried to Schengen member countries and sold at $12,000 to $15,000 a kilo, prices that undercut all competition.

The string of successive upheavals, beginning with the political unrest prompting the mass exodus of 1991–1992, have boosted Albania's market share in Europe's drug business. The 1997 collapse of the country's

"Pyramid" Mafia-directed financial conglomerates in which 80% of the population had invested money hoping for a 35%–100% return, further exacerbated the political climate. This financial meltdown, leading to the spring insurrection with its now only too familiar images of military arsenal looting and balaclava-clad, trigger-happy militiamen firing Kalashnikovs into the sky, speak for the country's recent lapses into anarchy. In addition, Albania suffers from destabilizing factional alliances pitting innovators against old PLA communists, a refurbished intelligence service (SHIK) that acts very much like the one it replaced, and a widening divide between the "nouveau riche" and an impoverished peasantry.

The country's other peculiarity is the *fares* (clan) north-south divide roughly delimited by the Shkumbini River, which cuts the country in half. While the Ghegs are denizens of the north, their Tosk rivals inhabit the south. Ancestral enmity with its oath (*besa*) to honor retributive justice in blood revenge (*gjakmarrje*) has spilled over, seriously affecting political life. This is mainly because the bureaucratic and intelligence elite, formed under communism, came originally from the Albanian capital Tirana and the Tosk south, where the communist-led Partisan movement had been strongest. By contrast, the new leaders, including former president Sali Berisha, ousted in 1997, are almost all northern Ghegs.

Thus, Ghegs and Tosks, both of which had specialized in different black market items during the Bosnian conflict, have become vengeful rivals. However, while the northern Ghegs are more apt to do business with Turkish and Macedonian gangs, the Tosks have teamed up with the Italians. Traffickers shuttle back and forth across the Adriatic from Vlora, Albania's largest port, in high-powered speed boats (*scafi*) transporting a mixed cargo of heroin and "livestock" (illegal immigrants). Dealing primarily with the Italian Sacra Corona Unita, they may collect $100,000 round-trip, while the salary of local customs officials is an irregularly paid $100 a month. Furthermore, these illegal immigrants (Pakistanis, Sri Lankans, Kurds, etc.), who have been forced to pay an exorbitant transportation fee, are often held in bondage and rented out as sweatshop laborers or drug couriers until their debt is repaid.

The fact that former president Sali Berisha, elected in April 1992, was a northerner from Tropja has only intensified Gheg-Tosk rivalry. He purged the state apparatus of hostile Tosks, replacing them with partisan northerners, and disbanded the *Sigurimi*, only to create and fill SHIK with his own Democratic party (DP) members. In addition, during his failed summer 1997 reelection bid, he pledged financial reimbursement to cement the loyalty of his northern supporters, while southern insurgents were derided for their connections with the Italian Mafia and promised nothing.

The Ghegs involved in drug trafficking have several advantages over the southern Tosks, due to their northern location. The recent boom in the Caucasus output of morphine base refined *in situ* by Georgian and Armenian syndicates, and transported westward through Bulgaria and Macedonia, competes directly with the drug-related activities of the Turkish *maffyas*.

Stimulated by the high returns of the Balkan drug trade during the war when the Greek embargo pushed the unemployment figures to 23%, Macedonian traffickers have started plantations of cannabis and poppies in the Varda valley, although on a limited basis. Finally, as a result of the 1997 munitions looting, the abundance of small arms and automatic weapons that ended up in *fares* hands, makes arms-for-drugs exchanges possible and especially interesting to Kosovar guerrillas due to Serb and ethnic Albanian clashes in Kosovo.

Beginning with Serbian leader Slobodan Milosevic's vehement demonstration for a "Greater Serbia," staged in 1989, and the subsequent retraction of autonomy from the province, repression of its ethnic Albanian population (90%) has been constant and brutal. Schools and universities were closed and virulent discrimination drove ethnic Albanians from every kind of work. Exile was one answer to this kind of repression, and passive resistance at home another. For those who remained behind, remittances and donations sent by the Albanian *diaspora* (large *Gastarbeiter* Albanian communities exist in Switzerland and Germany) were vital. As one Kosovar university professor barred from teaching confided, not a single family in Pristina could survive without "Swiss" funding, a euphemism describing foreign contributions. Both Kosovars in exile and Albanians sympathetic to their cause have had to rely on investment schemes with high rates of return and clandestine methods of transferring liquid assets back to Kosovo. Along with generous legal donations, heroin pipelines and money-laundering pursuits have provided an important cash flow. Over the past decade, Macedonian and Kosovar Albanians have become well entrenched in the drug underworld in Austria, Germany, Hungary, the Czech Republic, Poland, and Belgium. In 1996, they were believed to control the quasi-totality of the Swiss drug market, and, as in Germany, make up a growing percentage of incarcerated drug offenders.

It is astounding that southeastern European drug trafficking does not make boldface headlines in the international press more often. Silence may well be on account of the growing focus on the future status of Kosovo now that its frustrated bid for independence has given birth to the Kosovo Liberation Army (KLA). The avoidance of more bloodshed (would have rested)[10] on some kind of agreement involving Kosovo's KLA insurgents, President Milosevic, the Serbian people, and the Kosovo Albanians. In the meantime, as long as there are corrupt and unstable governments, billeted troops, guerrilla insurgents, potential consumers, and economic shortages in the region, drug trafficking will increase exponentially.

THE GLOBALIZATION OF THE DRUG WAR

Ever since prehistoric times, mind-altering or psychotropic substances have been ingested, not as food, but specifically to stimulate dreams, relax or energize the body, escape from the cares of daily life, or find the courage to face them. Along with the awe and fascination that states of altered consciousness have inspired, drugs have also been the object of secret commercial alliances, monopolies, and prohibitions. Many different viewpoints concerning their use including the scientific or the arcane, religious or secular, legal or unlawful, have influenced their production and distribution by monopolistic retainers subscribing to one view or another. It follows that narcotic substances have been employed as a diplomatic tool and a *casus belli* by politicized groups, national movements, and imperial interests.[11] Increasingly, populations the world over are subject to the outcry that the incessant flow of drugs and the parallel economy that it creates has become "the scourge of humanity." Consequently the ongoing drug war, if incapable of total drug-crop eradication, must aim at controlling cultivation at the site of production and limiting incoming shipments and distribution inside national borders, or so goes the litany pronounced by determined and sometimes hypocritical political crusaders. In view of creating a semblance of order, both truant drug traffickers and corrupt governments are singled out and accused of being the source of, or providing the wherewithal for, drug proliferation. But across the former Soviet Union and inside developing countries, huge profits are used as seed money, and immediately invested in murky privatization deals and often legitimate front companies acting as money-laundering devices. Capitalistic business ventures often stand upon politico-military foundations propped up by powerful mafia ties in otherwise fragile democracies, and whole sectors of the legitimate economy and millions of jobs depend on the continuation of illicit dealings, including the most lucrative of all, drug trafficking. Thus both legal and illegal realms are seamlessly stitched together, demonstrating the complexity of the drug problem.

The constant imaging of narcotics as a poisonous foreign invasion spread by immoral outside "others" has been a consistent factor accompanying drug-related power struggles. Propaganda wielded deliberately for this purpose by the ignorant and the powerful has usually succeeded in demonizing the targeted group. For example, the Chinese railroad crews in America's Northwestern states were cursed as "yellow dope fiends," and the Chinese Exclusion Act of 1887 was voted by the Congress into law in order to protect the nation against the influx of coolie labor and the Harrison Narcotic Act of 1914 to outlaw their "pernicious" habit. Likewise the Marjuana Tax Act of 1937 was aimed at discouraging the use of cannabis by incoming Mexican farm workers seen as a job threat during the Depression and quickly adopted by Southern Congressional delegates to cover "crazed Negro dope fiends." In reality, the laws were promoted by industrial interests to cover opium's importation, pharmaceutical preparation and sale; and marijuana's domestic cultivation, experimental use, and commercialization. It is not unrealistic to predict that the same rhetoric will be used with growing frequency to legitimize harsher immigration policies as well as to justify interference in the internal affairs of other nations. Already xenophobic tendencies are growing in Western Europe, and American administrations since the 1980s have mandated the drug policies of its southern neighbors.

Only rarely have political powers openly identified popular drug consumption with the societal and economic malaise linked to the pressures of everyday life since the advent of mass industrialization and the postmodern stresses stemming from a rapidly changing technological environment. But in stigmatizing various current upheavals as a drug problem, the West is able to conveniently reactivate effective control mechanisms of the recent past: economic sanctions, armed intervention, and the imposition of a rigid economic model. Thus the drug issue successfully fills the vacuum left by military alliances and diplomatic accords that have lost their urgency with the end of the cold war, and provides the West with a virtual enemy with infinite guises.

NOTES

1. Ephedrine is a natural component of the plant *Ephidra vulgaris*, which grows wild in parts of Russia and China. From it comes amphetamine sulfate and the more powerful detroamphetamine sulfate. Both substances act upon the central nervous system. The amines are a group of organic compounds of nitrogen that may be considered ammonia derivatives. The illegal fabrication of amphetamines in the 1960s gave them the name "bathroom" or "kitchen" speed. Their misuse causes arrhythmia, hypertension, circulatory-collapse convulsions, coma, and death.

2. Conflicts in these regions include Ossetia, Adjaria, Tchetchia, Balkaria, Azerbaijan, Armenia, etc., in the Caucasus; Kyrgyzstan, Kazakhstan, Bashkortostan, Tartarstan, Uzbekistan, Tajikistan, Kurdistan, Afghanistan, etc. in Central Asia.

3. Chemical precursors consist of a variety of chemical products used to break down the nitrogen-containing alkaloids in both raw opium and crude cocaine: acetic anhydride (opium); sulfuric acid, potassium permanganate, ammonia hydroxide (cocaine).

4. Heroin process: After the poppy flower's petals fall off, the seed capsule swells. Incisions are made with a sharp tool and a milky alkaloid-rich sap seeps from the minuscule tubes in the capsule wall. It dries, darkens and turns to the gummy substance of raw opium that is scraped off before heat makes it adhere too tightly. Raw opium, which can be saved and stored for years without losing any of its potency, is mixed with a precipitating agent and pressed to produce crude morphine or morphine base. The morphine base is then treated with acetic anhydride to produce heroin. It takes approximately 3,000 poppies to produce 1.6 kgs (3.5 lbs) of raw opium. Poppy Straw: When the poppy capsules ripen without incisions being made, the morphine stays in the capsule walls. It can only be extracted in a well-equipped factory. Poppy straw is crushed and dissolved in steel vats. The resulting dark liquid is treated with acids and the exuded crystals are first dried in a centrifuge and then in special ovens to yield a powdery substance. This powder is further treated to produce poppy straw concentrate (PSC) a form of crude morphine.

5. It cost Ankara approximately $12.5 billion in 1994.

6. The Former Yugoslavian Republic of Montenegro formally adhered to rump Yugoslavia after a popular referendum in March 1992.

7. Scott Sullivan, "Drugs in Europe: America's scourge crosses the Atlantic," *Newsweek*, 4 July 1994, pp. 6–12.

8. Until the early stages of the war, Serbian secret intelligence was in the hands of three state organizations: the Information and Documentation Service of the Foreign Ministry (DIS); the Secret Police of the Ministry of Information (SDB), and the Military Counter-Espionage Service of the Ministry of Defense (KOS).

9. Since 1992, Tirana has been flooded with thousands of diesel-spewing

Mercedes cars. They have become a ubiquitous status symbol in a country that prohibited private cars until 1991. Albania is also the end of the line for secondhand taxis coming from all over Europe, and the destination of large numbers of stolen vehicles.

10. Editor's note: Article was completed before the war over Kosovo in 1999.

11. The 1840–42 Opium Wars and the Boxer Rebellion are two cases in point.

Chapter 9

Environmental Security and Civil Society
Oleg Kobtzeff

On 4 April 1986, in the Soviet Socialist Republic of Ukraine, no more than fifty miles north of Kiev, reactor Number Four of a large nuclear plant exploded in the vicinity of Chernobyl. Its radioactive waste was detected in parts of Europe as remote as France, or Lapland, where entire populations of reindeer feeding on contaminated tundra had to be destroyed. Hundreds of deaths and thousands of cases of fallout-related disease struck the Ukrainian, Bielorussian, and Slovak populations. For the first time in recorded history, an exodus of nearly a quarter of a million "environmental refugees" proved that environmental politics could no longer be considered a marginal geopolitical issue.

The progressive flow of uncensored data (eased by glasnost) revealed that Chernobyl was only the tip of the iceberg. For decision-makers, in the Soviet bloc or in the West, even those least concerned by ecology, the risks of geographic, economic, and political instability became too obvious to ignore as it coincided with the collapse of the Soviet bloc. Another revelation was that an environmentalist opposition existed behind the iron curtain. Could it have played a role in destabilizing the regimes?

But Central and Eastern European ecology also became a fad. Sensationalism, then overexposure, then daily routine, devaluated the issue. Whatever was left of our vigilance in the early 1990s was further blunted by the illusion that reforms, democratization, foreign aid, and a free market were to solve all problems. Today, the Central and Eastern Europeans themselves seem to have lost any interest in environmental politics.

Yet, a small but influential chorus of Western analysts is determined to make an issue out of the environmental problems of the "Other Europe." Their main concern is legitimate: how could one expect five decades of catastrophic mistakes in environmental management to have been corrected in less than ten years without any adverse effects on the geography of the region and neighboring countries? The geopolitical consequences alone could be frightening.

ASSESSING THE DAMAGE

For most of the communist period, the state of the natural environment was virtually absent from publications on Central and Eastern Europe: until the 1960s, ecology was rarely acknowledged as a relevant political issue, anywhere. When environmentalism became more fashionable, the Western left never questioned the vague declarations of the Soviet blocs, Albania and Yugoslavia on the natural environment as a "heritage of the People". On the right (if there was any concern for the environment at all), Socialist industry was probably viewed as too unproductive to have done any great harm to nature over a long period. Chernobyl proved that something was terribly wrong in these assumptions. Glasnost and the enormity of the damage made it impossible to deny the crisis any further. More revelations were to follow: the drying of the Aral Sea, the death of the forests of Central Europe, the red rivers of toxic waste pouring into the Danube; the monstrous deformities of plants, animals, and humans in heavily polluted areas; or the frightening statistics on cancer rates, respiratory and skin diseases, and so forth. But what permitted such a monstrosity to ever exist? "Why did a system that made a cult of rationality turn its back on environmental planning?" asks historian Douglas R. Weiner.[1]

The Ideological Factor

Indeed, the destruction of nature perpetrated under all Marxist-Leninist regimes was absurd, according to Marxist philosophy and to the standards set by Lenin's own pioneering environmental policies. So "how could a society that prided itself on its scientific underpinnings, have enshrined Trofim Denisovich Lysenko as a virtual czar in the biological sciences?"[2] How could "scientific" materialism endorse unholy experiments reminiscent of Nazi science (eugenics, bizarre hybridization of animals, Romanian geriatric clinics, hormonal metamorphosis of East German female athletes) or the useless annihilation of entire ecosystems?

The urgency of industrialization in the 1930s to 1950s, combined with totalitarian practices could explain part of the harm inflicted upon nature and the violent repression against environmentalists in those years. It does not explain the unnecessary damage purposefully inflicted against wildlife, nor its scope, nor the mythology of a "New Man" rewriting the laws of nature.

Stalinist demagogy and an extremely vulgar interpretation of the Marxist philosophy of nature are certainly to blame for that. The myth of a new nature appealed to politicians with a very shallow scientific education. Celebrated in song, painting, and sculpture throughout classrooms, museums or concert halls of every nation under Marxist-Leninist rule, the "New Man" and the creation of a new environment for the planet was an immediate crowd-pleaser.[3] Once utopian dreams became the norm, it was easier for charlatans such as Dr. Lysenko or Mrs. Ceausescu to exploit the situation. Did Marxism lack the safeguards that could have protected the environment against such extravaganza?

Forged in a struggle against the predominance of geographic determinism, Marxism reaffirms the power of humankind over nature. At the same time, as abundantly evidenced by Reiner Grundmann, "the concept of domination [over nature] makes sense for Marx only with respect to interests and needs"; it is capitalist production, through its predatory use of resources, which causes ecological damage.[4] However, when in 1917 one of the most typical revolutionary acts was to cut down entire forests protected for centuries by the land-owning aristocracy, prudence and patience was untimely and even suspicious to the enthusiastic lumberjacks. Anti-humanist tendencies in early environmentalism made it even harder for Marxists to notice the nuances in Marx's views of ecology. The nationalist bias found in the romantic movement's fascination with landscapes was already enough to irritate the average Marxist militant in the nineteenth century.[5] Finally, it must be remembered how Leninism opposed peasant culture to urban proletarian culture. Promoting the city proletariat to the status of avant-garde of the revolution, Leninism unavoidably demeaned rural values such as religion, folklore, the traditional family structure, village life, and, also, the feeling of awe and respect for the natural environment that was still strong in many traditional communities.

These dilemmas could explain the extremely ambiguous attitudes of Marxist regimes toward the environment. At times—under Lenin's rule or in the years of communist takeover in Central Europe—environmentalist policies were implemented on a large scale.[6] At least verbally, the governments almost consistently expressed a commitment towards environmental protection; the impressive national parks network demonstrates more than lip service. During other periods, environmentalists were violently repressed and environmental disasters were tolerated. However, there is no trace of *anti*-environmentalist measures comparable, for example, to the anti-religious campaigns. What seems to have prevailed were societal norms demeaning "unrealistic" and "romantic" nature-lovers. But in absence of any democratic institutions, that was enough to inhibit any legal, institutional, or theoretical defense mechanism that could have saved nature from the blind depredations of heavy industry and, as in any other activity, the incompetence of the bureaucrats in charge of land management.

Slowly, but with frightening momentum, pollution and the depletion of natural resources spread like a cancer. In 1957, the Kychym nuclear accident in the Urals already announced Chernobyl. Highly classified until almost the fall of the Soviet regime, the situation was nevertheless sufficiently catastrophic to have spread rumors in the West in the 1960s. As the socialist societies entered the 1970s, then the 1980s, the size of the material damage caused by environmental mismanagement could no longer be hidden.

Toward the Ecological Crisis

Several important changes on the global scene were reshaping the geopolitical position of the Soviet Union and its allies by the mid-1980s, on the eve of the Chernobyl disaster. The true effect of these changes on the power structure of the Soviet bloc and other East European countries is not fully known. But Marxist-Leninist regimes could not have remained unaffected. Were conflicts over the environment an effect, or one of the causes, of these changes? In either case, they were a symptom of a major crisis.

In the 1980s, awareness of the catastrophic results of ecological mismanagement began growing out of the limited circles of environmental scientists, outdoors writers, or tourists. Indeed, the effects of pollution on the geography of every nation in Central and Eastern Europe had become so intense and extensive that even the most stubborn bureaucrats in the regional or national structures of party and government could no longer ignore certain dangers.

One such danger was that a ruined environment spelled declining productivity. This decline did not only concern agriculture or industries relying on natural resources. Emissions of toxic waste had reached such levels that not only flora and fauna were in jeopardy: pollution was beginning to threaten the economic backbone of socialist planned economies by eroding industrial infrastructures. Anyone traveling along the Danube in the mid-1980s could see with the naked eye how the industry of Danubian countries was devouring its own entrails like a diseased stomach digesting its own tissues. In Romania, toxic waste escaping from chemical plants damaged chimneys or sewage pipes, creating zones of deposit in the river, over factory buildings, and all around. The deposit corrugated every architectural structure, and every piece of equipment, choking any mechanical device in the vicinity. In Poland, 65% of the rivers became so polluted that factories began avoiding the use of their water for industrial purposes; the risk of damaging pipes was too high.[7] Glasnost (or the fall of the communist regimes) was to reveal that such situations were typical of many industrial areas (Nowa Huta, or the outskirts of Leipzig, to mention only two examples). It is easy to imagine how such toxic pollution could affect other economic activities, particularly agriculture and its fragile natural resources. At the end of the 1980s, as much as 80% of agricultural land in Bulgaria, 54% in Czechoslovakia, and 30% in Hungary and Romania were considered endangered.[8] In Poland, after acknowledging that 11% of the national territory had become unhealthy, the government had no other choice than to impose, as a short-term priority, the elimination of food production in the most highly degraded regions.[9] By the mid-1980s in Bulgaria, in the Danube plain which makes up 60% of arable land, erosion was washing away 9 million tons of topsoil (9 tons per acre) every year.[10] In countries traditionally relying on timber-based activities, the portion of forests damaged by various forms of pollution was reaching catastrophic levels: 36% in Hungary, 73% in Czechoslovakia, and 82% in Poland.[11] A dramatic decline in catches was a fact already well known to fishermen in Baltic or Black Sea ports, and along lake shores and rivers. In the Danube, from Austria to the Black Sea, commercial species, including the highly profitable caviar-producing sturgeon, had simply become endangered. Worse, fish disappeared entirely from some regions, spelling the end of activities that depended upon fresh water resources; the case of Lake Ladoga is a graphic example.[12] It was frighteningly apparent that Rachel Carson's *Silent Spring* had literally turned into reality. By the early 1980s, this was clear not only to all Soviet or Central and Eastern European hikers, tourists, and villagers in all rural areas, but also to all inhabitants of Finnish, West German, Austrian, Greek, and Turkish regions bordering socialist countries. The reason for numerous unexplained epidemics could no longer be hidden: in Czechoslovakia a housewife explained one day to a reporter that "you cannot hang your clothes outside. If you do, they will be filthy before they are dry."[13] Pollution reaching such a degree was bound to create trouble with local populations or, maybe worse, with neighboring countries.

The obvious "ecological death" of Central and Eastern Europe and the Soviet Union was very untimely. In the Soviet Union as in several other countries, the government was still struggling to reform an inefficient agricultural production. In the USSR, diminishing soil fertility had been identified as the "decisive factor" in the low return on investment in agriculture.

Economic decline alone could have meant social unrest and political instability. The effects of environmental hazard on the health of the populations made the already dramatic situation even worse. Today, the toll taken on humans by the degradation of the natural environment in Central and Eastern Europe is well known: an increase in the statistics in respiratory diseases, circulatory pathologies, and cancer. Mortality rates, especially among newborn babies and active males skyrocketed in the 1980s. In Bulgaria, the environmentalist organization Ecoglasnost revealed, during its famous 1987–1988 exhibit on ecology, that the lung disease rate had leapt from 969 cases out of 100,000 inhabitants in 1975 to 17,386 cases for the same 100,000 inhabitants in 1985.[14] By the mid to late 1980s, one-third of the population of Poland was living in the 11% of the nation's territory that was considered to be unhealthy.[15] In Czechoslovakia in 1991, 57% of the population was living in a highly degraded environment that included 7% of the national territory, while 80% of the territory was endangered by rapidly increasing environmental degradation.[16] In Bratislava alone, from 1981 to 1985, deaths by vascular disease progressed by 42%, and lung disease multiplied at least by three; since 1960, infant mortality rose by 65.2% and, since 1970, miscarriages have increased by 50%.[17] By 1990, the population of highly polluted Nowa Huta (Poland) suffered from twice as many cases of heart failure (due to lack of oxygen) than elsewhere in the country, while in zones generally exposed to air pollution by lead, zinc, and cadmium, the rate of infant mortality rose to 4.4%.[18] In Upper Silesia, local residents have been suffering from 155% higher rates of circulatory diseases, 30% more cancers, and 47% more respiratory illnesses than the national average.[19] Such statistics could no longer be concealed from the public. Signs of an unhealthy environment and decling public health were now in plain view of the population. In the Bulgarian battery factory in Pazardjik (which exported 80% of its production), environmental conditions were so dangerous that employees refused to continue showing up for work and had to be replaced with convicts.[20]

False rumors started spreading, with consequences more dangerous than the mere disclosure of the truth. One of the clearest indications about the geopolitical risks involved was an Organization for Economic Cooperation and Development (OECD) study listing environmental problems as one of the five main causes of massive migration within the countries of Central and Eastern Europe or towards OECD countries.[21] The very legitimacy of the socialist state, the warrant of people's security, was now in danger. The timing was very inconvenient: Polish authorities and the entire Soviet bloc were then coping with Solidarity.

The former president of the Czechoslovak Academy of Sciences Commission for the Environment and councilor for the Ministry of the Environment in 1991, Jaroslav Stoklasa, believed that, in the most affected areas, environmental degradation was disrupting the social tissue and was related to the rise of delinquency and vandalism and a general feeling of disenchantment and loss of self-respect.[22] Dr. Stoklasa's perception of the problem, whether accurate or not, illustrates the sort of pressure that local and national Central and Eastern European officials must have experienced in the second half of the 1980s. Even the most prosaic *nomenklatura* bosses could feel the imminent crisis: the social costs of a spoiled environment would place an unprecedented burden upon the budgets of national and regional administrations.

Other economic implications of environmental degradation were most probably taken into account. In the 1980s, it was clear for every economic analyst and geographer that, for most countries in the world, even the poorest nations, tourism had become a major industry, if not *the* major industry. Yugoslavia, Romania, and Bulgaria, with their Adriatic or Black Sea resorts, Hungary with Lake Balaton, and the Soviet Union and its newly restored monuments and Olympic games, had demonstrated since the 1960s a strong appetite for the revenues in hard currency generated by a regular flow of tourists. Except in Yugoslavia (where travel was almost unrestricted for Westerners) only a modest fraction of the tourist potential of socialist countries had been developed by the mid-1980s. The millions of Western visitors who had already enjoyed the services of the official tour operators and resort facilities proved that the human rights record of Central and Eastern Europe was not necessarily an obstacle for tourist development. But rumors about health hazards due to excessive pollution could certainly dissuade millions more from visiting.

In the meantime, the cost-effectiveness of the heavy industry that was destroying natural sites—now a potential commodity—was showing signs of

Environmental Security and Civil Society

rapid decline, and not only in planned economies but in the West also. Could the choice between a profitable natural environment and inefficient industries have had something to do with the growing competition within the *nomenklatura* between the old guard "dinosaurs" and the "young wolves"?

The degradation of the environment could not last: decisions had to be made by party leaders before the situation would get completely out of control. Any party leader, in any country of Central and Eastern Europe had to be as addicted to wishful-thinking as Ceausescu or Enver Hoxha, not to understand that a crisis was preparing. In addition to economic and social difficulties, an ecological disaster—worse than the Kansas dust bowl that accompanied the Great Depression—was about to threaten the foundations of all socialist systems.

ECOLOGICAL IMBALANCE AND POLITICAL INSTABILITY: THE YEARS OF CHERNOBYL AND VELVET REVOLUTIONS

Could environmental degradation undermine domestic and international stability? How many government officials actually began asking themselves that question? Was the risk of popular anger over the environment great enough to force Marxist-Leninist power structures to reevaluate the foundations of the regimes? Secrecy and *post-factum* testimonies by former party officials (often claiming to have always been reformists at heart) make it very difficult to investigate such a recent past. It will take years before we find out exactly what went on behind the closed doors of party cabinet meetings. Nevertheless, there is one certainty about the content of future history books about the 1980s and not only in Central and Eastern Europe: it was one of the factors of a growing awareness of ecology as a major geopolitical issue.

Pressure from Without: The Crisis of the Environment as an International Affair

The international political consequences of pollution in Central and Eastern Europe developed a long time ago. As early as 1972, very soon after the first UN environmental conference in Stockholm, several Scandinavian states were able to put enough pressure on other European states to obtain the OECD's agreement on monitoring transboundary air pollution in Europe.

The OECD monitoring program from 1972 to 1977 was an international fact-finding program that established that pollution was being exported across boundaries and that the problem required international cooperation. In 1977, these monitoring programs unified under a program sponsored by the Economic Commission for Europe.[23]

Even if they could not admit their responsibilities in transboundary air pollution, Communist countries were now forced to observe the effects of their environmental policies on the geography of other countries and on the international diplomatic scene. For the Communist countries now risked being scrutinized by the Economic Commission for Europe. Strong opposition against any binding regulations on sulfur dioxide and nitrogen oxide emissions first arose in the West, from heavy polluters. These were mainly the United Kingdom and the Federal Republic of Germany, and also the United States, Belgium and Denmark.[24] They created a major diversion and bought the USSR and its allies some time. But pressure was increasing: environmental politics were definitely leaving the ghetto of "alternative groups", communes and other marginal movements of the late '60s. Between 1974 and 1990, the international diplomatic agenda slowly included ecology among questions almost as important as defense. This is when the terms "environmental security" began to appear and when the United Nations qualified the environment and other issues as "nonmilitary aspects of security". In June 1974, scientists shocked public opinion by proposing the hypothesis about chlorofluorocarbons (CFCs) destroying the ozone layer. This was a real menace with a powerful impact upon imaginations. In March 1977, the United Nations program for the environment created a strategy for global environmental security and a coordination committee to monitor the evolution of the ozone layer. This was followed by intense diplomatic activity resulting in numerous multilateral agreements not only on CFCs, but other pollutants as well. After the 1987 conference of Montreal, twenty-four countries signed the protocol banning substances harmful to the ozone layer.

Meanwhile, in Europe, the Soviet bloc was entangled in a web of international environmental government action through its European diplomacy. General Secretary Brezhnev himself (probably for the sake of Soviet image) had asked for provisions on environmental protection in the final act of the Helsinki agreements.[25] In 1979, under the pressure of the Conference on Cooperation and Security in Europe, the UN Economic Commission for Europe organized the Geneva conference of 13–15 November, which adopted a convention on *long distance transfrontier* atmospheric pollution; it came into force on 16 March 1983 and was later completed by the 1985 Helsinki protocol on the reduction, by at least 30%, of sulfur emissions or their transfrontier influx.[26] After Chernobyl, "transfrontier" was obviously only a euphemism for "pollution originating from the Soviet bloc." These issues were particularly sensitive in Scandinavian countries since they were on the front line of transfrontier pollution. Just one example clearly illustrates the problem: until recently Leningrad/St. Petersburg alone was responsible for 90% of all copper and chromium discharge into the Gulf of Finland.[27] Then, after the April 1986 nuclear catastrophe, matters got even worse for the Scandinavians, as shown in the case of contaminated tundra in Lapland. So the next conferences moved eastward: Sofia in 1988, Vienna in 1989, and back to Sofia, in the fall of the same year. That last conference held in Bulgaria from 16 October to 3 November, was to be fatal to the Zhivkov regime.

Pressure from Within: the Environmental Crisis and Domestic Instability

If the Communist leadership did not act rapidly to improve the situation of the environment, could the social and political situation deteriorate? The

Environmental Security and Civil Society 121

risk was real. The victories of Solidarity in the summer of 1980 proved that a Marxist government was no longer guaranteed absolute power over a passive population. The political risks tied to an unhealthy environment became obvious to government and party officials with the emergence of a new form of opposition throughout the Marxist countries and in other socialist countries. Could government circles have become aware of the ecological emergency and become preoccupied with the same concerns as the ecologists?

Barbara Jancar-Webster, Professor at the State University of New York, spent years in the field conducting research on environmental politics in the Soviet bloc; her expertise qualified her as a witness during a U.S. Congress hearing on environmental dangers. She believes that the growing environmental and alternative movements in the West, especially in West Germany, served as a role model. Their influence over Yugoslavs, particularly Slovenes, was manifest. Millions of viewers and listeners enjoyed hundreds of hours of alternative information available through foreign broadcasts that included coverage on environmental affairs.[28]

Information on the state of the natural environment could also have leaked through international contacts. For example, thousands of Socialist-country citizens were allowed to visit Yugoslavia and millions were given visas to Hungary. Hungary, by the late 1970s and early 1980s, was experiencing a comparatively relaxed political atmosphere, as a result of Moscow's extremely prudent handling of Hungarian affairs following 1956.[29] Yugoslavia's regime was even more liberal, with few subjects being taboo in private discussions, especially over environmental issues. Moreover, in the 1980s, "brother socialist countries" were beginning to criticize one another for transfrontier pollution and other environmental problems. This exposure to alternative "official versions" drove wedges into the walls of totalitarian news coverage.

The first traces of environmentalist political activism can probably be found in Slovakia in the late 1960s. Outside Bulgaria, Slovak environmentalism was to be one of the most powerful political forces influencing the changes of 1989 and 1990 in Central and Eastern Europe. The slow evolution of the Slovak environmentalists reveals many interesting characteristics of social and political life in the Soviet bloc. Juraj Mesik, one of the leading figures of the Slovak Union of the Defenders of Nature and Landscape (SZOPK), tells the story.[30] The SZOPK was founded in 1969 as an association officially approved by the government. At first, this was a group enlisting "classic" defenders of nature, that is volunteers mainly interested in defending national parks or threatened species, and educating youths on these issues. As the natural environment deteriorated, the activities of the SZOPK, especially in Bratislava, became more critical, approaching the limits of the regime's tolerance. Nevertheless, the ecologists remained extremely cautious, never provoking the authorities and avoiding extreme actions (i.e., releasing information to the Western media). They were patient enough to ignore any of the government's attacks—harsh criticism in the press and even police harassment. Some environmentalist groups were even dissolved, but the government was also cautious not to transform nonpolitical critics into dissidents or martyrs who could be noticed by Western public opinion.

In the beginning of the 1980s, the Slovak ecologists were ready to climb a new step by establishing contacts with Dutch, Austrian, and other European ecologists. Then, they participated in the creation of a new Central and Eastern European environmentalist network called Greenway. Again, caution was the rule in the activities of this rising movement: the ecologists criticized specific aspects of industrial and environmental management without ever attacking the regime itself. The strategy paid off and the SZOPK, which had grown in popularity, was allowed to continue to exist in its original form, as a semi official organization with Communists participating in its administration. The SZOPK even obtained access to means of communication with the right to publish a periodical, *Ohranca Prirody*. A counterpart now existed in the Czech regions: the Czech Union of the Defenders of Nature, who also enjoyed the right to publish a periodical, *Nika*. Meanwhile, other groups had been struggling for a cleaner environment.

As early as 1980, the association of Czechoslovak fishermen (170,000 members) revealed numerous cases of pollution and its economic cost; it continued spreading such information on a regular basis, and then, from 1988 onward, official scientific publications, such as *Bratislava Nahlas* and *Stav a vyvoj zivotniho prostredi v Czehosloveznsku*, also relayed essential information by publishing objective and nonpartisan reports on the ecological situation of the country.[31] Thus, on the eve of the great political upheavals, a genuine public opinion had been able to develop thanks to this crucial circulation of news.

Let us pause for a moment of reflection. It is true that Husak's government was often repressive: many private lives of ecologists were shattered by persecution. However, it is nothing comparable to the kind of witch-hunt that existed in the Soviet Union in the late 1920s and 1930s. The rise of Czechoslovak environmentalism appears much more as a slow *evolution* rather than a revolutionary movement. In fact, Juraj Mesik's testimony provides no element describing Czechoslovak society divided between environmentalist anti-Communists and anti-ecologist Communists. The divisions seem to be much blurrier. Could we dare suggest that the concern for nature was shared by many social categories with a wide variety of political agendas? Could those categories have included members of the *nomenklatura*? This leads to the next question: were local and national government officials unanimous on the issue of the environment? Were they all hostile to the "defenders of nature"? These questions cannot yet be answered, but they deserve further investigation.

Another country where political environmentalism appeared very early is the German Democratic Republic. There, in the 1960s *Gesellschaft für Natur und Umwelt* (Society for Nature and Environment) was allowed to exist as a forum for public debate on issues concerning ecology. In his detailed article, written before anyone in the West knew about the subject, Hubertus Knabe

Environmental Security and Civil Society

provided some very precious glimpses on the history of the East German ecological movements.[32]

In January 1978, groups of Christian ecologists gathered in Buckow to exchange ideas. From Knabe's account it appears that serious political ecological debates found a haven in East German Protestant churches. If everything is true in the story, it is interesting to note that the themes explored by Protestant intellectuals such as Dr. Heino Falcke or the youths who initiated the first antinuclear groups, were very similar in theme and language to the "Greens" of West Germany. The East German ecologists were proposing a critique of unlimited industrial production using Marxist analysis. In fact it appears that East German antinuclear activism began as a local pacifist movement. To which extent was this pacifism part of the innumerable Soviet-controlled peace movements, and to which extent did Honecker's government try to appear "hip" by encouraging youths to imitate Western anti-war demonstrators? To which extent was the party aware of the risks that this could turn into a critique of its own policies?[33] None of the answers are yet known. In any case, the emulation between West German and East German antinuclear groups tends to confirm Barbara Jancar-Webster's suspicion that West German models had a strong influence upon the ecological movements in the "People's Democracies."

Professor Jancar-Webster believes that the first genuinely independent environmentalist *opposition* was Slovenian. She dates it back to the early 1980s.[34] Compared to the Soviet bloc, the Yugoslav regime was relatively soft on dissidents. Therefore, when the students decided to become politically active in defense of the natural environment, they expected only harassment, not expulsion from their schools. A movement grew in the following manner. Twelve young people founded the original group, and then each one of them contacted a small circle of friends recruiting new members. Then, these new members each approached a small group of trusted friends, asking those to do the same, and so forth, until a larger political movement slowly spread. The government was surprised by such a phenomenon and while officials argued about a strategy to adopt, the movement gained momentum. Then, in the mid-1980s, the environmentalists were encouraged to join the official communist youth movement. They decided to accept.

Again, we find evidence of governments preferring to *channel* the energies of ecologists rather than repress them.

The next country to experience the rise of an environmentalist opposition movement was Poland.[35] The Solidarity union was no stranger to ecological concerns. Proposals for the environment had been included in Solidarity's demands (for example thesis 16 of the program adopted at the September 1981 Gdansk conference).[36] In the months that followed the Gdansk agreements, scientists and intellectuals formed their own environmentalist group, the Polish Ecology Club, in Crakow and a "Green Movement" was started in Warsaw; membership rose quickly and other groups were formed in other towns, throughout the country.[37] There existed a variety of political approaches in those dramatic years: No. 176 of the famous newspaper *Tygodnik Mazowsze* featured a letter advocating the necessity of a "social ecological self-defense movement" independent from any partisan agenda. The particularity of the environmentalist movement in Poland is that it profited from a short but crucial moment when censorship was lifted in the months after the Gdansk agreements and before martial law. Thus, between 1980 and 1981, scores of data on the condition of the natural environment were published and the Polish people received the shock that others experienced only years later, after Chernobyl. One of the most celebrated results of the Polish form of resistance was the closing of the Skawina Aluminum Works outside Kraków.[38] Again, as noticed at the time by "Green Cross" activist Zbigniew Wierzbicki, the line dividing environmental activism from government circles was not always clear-cut. In the Skawina affair, just as in Kielce, or in Walbrzych, opposition to major industrial projects harmful to the environment rose from local protest (including Solidarity members in Skawina) *supported by local administrations.* These local institutions were beginning to "resist more and more frequently the Central power, creating a common front with local communities for the defense of a 'healthy environment.'"[39]

It is now widely recognized by all specialists that one major crisis contributed not only to the birth of environmentalism but to the entire transition in the Soviet Union. It was the nationwide protest against rerouting the rivers of the Russian Great North toward arid lands in Central Asia. The projects that were about to begin by the early or mid-1980s were shocking not only for those who had an ecological conscience, but for mainstream citizens as well, and even hard-boiled Communists with a strong feeling for the landscape. Particularly influential in the opposition to those titanic hydraulic projects, the "ruralist" writers were tolerated by the government for the sake of maintaining official "Soviet patriotism." In Czechoslovakia, an environmentalist opposition began almost in the same way, mainly as a protest movement against the infamous hydroelectric project of Gabcikovo-Nagymaros on the Danube. A comparable situation developed on the other side of the Danube, against the same construction project. There, in Hungary, as noted in the review of French intellectuals and exiled dissidents *Alternatives,*

The birth of an ecologist movement as the one provoked by the dam construction project on the Danube cannot be simply identified as an opposition movement. To reroute the Danube towards Czechoslovakia, irreversibly wrecking havoc upon the ecosystem of the entire region represents, for a great part of the Hungarian population, a national tragedy. Also, the initiatives organized by the "Danube Circle" found a large echo as demonstrated by the massive numbers of signatures on petitions, and the hostile statements made against the project in all intellectual circles.[40]

As in the USSR, opposition to the dam did not mean anti-communism: many *official institutions* joined the protest, despite the bureaucratic obstacles

Environmental Security and Civil Society 125

opposed by the central power.[41]

Events accelerated after Chernobyl. The disastrous condition of the natural environment could no longer be denied or minimized (as it still was in Romania and Albania). Although the catastrophe happened in the Ukraine, millions of citizens outside the USSR began to question the environmental record of their governments. The legitimacy of the regimes was now in danger. Similar accidents could now occur anywhere under socialist rule. Worse, the alliance of the Central and Eastern European countries with the Soviet Union appeared as suicidal. Instead of protecting its allies from a nuclear holocaust, the "big brother" had produced its own nuclear disaster, through a simple blunder, typical of the chronic managerial inefficiency in the Soviet bloc.[42]

In the late 1980s, in most "people's democracies," demands for a safer environment were becoming more and more pressing. Underground publications, political groups small and large, and petitions were becoming an important feature of daily life, while governments tried to stay in control of the situation by multiplying security measures reassurances and declarations on commitment to a cleaner nature.[43]

In the Soviet Union, in response to public opinion, major legislation was passed (the January 1988 decree on "the radical restructuring of nature protection" and the December 1989 "urgent measures for the improvement of the ecology of the country"). With greater political freedom, environmentalist political groups proliferated. In Leningrad alone, more than 300 organizations united in order to present candidates for the 1989 regional elections.[44] But wasn't every measure conceded to popular demand an admittance of the reality of the ecological disaster? This was one of the main risks of glasnost in all its aspects. But it is also important to remember that explaining Chernobyl to the public (after much resistance and weeks of secrecy) was the first manifestation of that very glasnost. It is also important to remember that the January 1988 and December 1989 measures were accompanied by an energetic shakeup in urban administrations. Was Chernobyl the catalyst or the pretext for glasnost and perestroika?

In 1987, the famous Peace and Freedom movement showed that Polish environmentalism was still strong despite the oppression of Jaruzelski's rule. In Estonia, Georgia, and Armenia and particularly in Slovakia and in Bulgaria, environmentalism became the catalyst for the opposition.[45] In Bulgaria it became rapidly clear for observers that the ecologists federated by Ecoglasnost were among the two or three predominant forces on the political scene.[46]

In Bratislava, the SZOPK finally crossed the Rubicon: after developing actions in favor of national monuments, it removed the Communists from its administration.[47] It was now a militant group fighting the government. With the Czech Civic Forum, the Slovak Public Against Violence was one of the two major political groups that lead the Velvet Revolution until the fall of the old regime. One of the main inspirations of Public Against Violence had been ecology; in its first stages, more than half of its management was composed of SZOPK members, and its first headquarters were located in the offices of the SZOPK's municipal secretariat in Bratislava.[48]

And the governments began to yield to the pressure. Only Ceausescu and the Albanian Communist party seemed to be completely oblivious to any ecological concern.

One of the largest and historically significant environmentalist demonstrations under a socialist regime was held in Ljubljana, on the first anniversary of Chernobyl, in 1987.[49] The next great demonstration for the environment gathered 40,000 Hungarians in October 1988. The crowd demonstrated in front of the parliament against the hated Gabcikovo-Nagymaros hydraulic project. This was the first massive popular assembly of the sort since the terrible events of 1956. Some observers believe that the leadership was so impressed by the size of the gathering, that the party, shaken to its foundations, initiated its self-imposed reforms.[50] Construction of the dam was abandoned in May 1989, "democratic centralism" and "dictatorship of the proletariat" five months later.

In Poland, the roundtable talks between the government and the opposition in early 1989 "were unmistakable proof of the influence of the Polish environmental movement on the democratic transition."[51] Representatives of the environmental movement were included in the talks, and the government adopted the totality of the opposition's environmental demands.

In Czechoslovakia, significant environmentalist demonstrations (11 and 12 November 1989 in the coal-mining community of Teplice, or the "Group of Czech Mothers" actions in Prague throughout the fall) marked the protest movements leading to the dramatic conclusion of the Velvet Revolution on 17 November.[52]

The series of mass demonstrations of 1989 and 1990 organized mainly by Ecoglasnost imposed reforms and free elections in Bulgaria. Ecoglasnost and ecology were not the main factors in the destabilization of the Zhivkov regime. However, they served as wedges hammered into the structure of party and government. In the fall of 1989, the Bulgarian Communist power found itself trapped in a situation where it had to manage a double political crisis—the question of Turk minorities, plus rising opposition—and host at the same time an international conference on transfrontier pollution. The Sofia ecological conference of 16 October to 3 November became the arena of all the political tensions in Bulgaria.[53] First of all, the Turkish delegation that reluctantly came to Sofia upon the insistence of its Western allies inaugurated the conference by attacking the host country for its persecution of the Turk minority. Then, because NGOs were expected to contribute their input to the conference (as stipulated by the previous conference in Vienna), it became simply impossible to repress demonstrations organized by Ecoglasnost in the streets of Sofia during the debates. Repression was the government's first reaction, but the conference issued an official condemnation. With the Turkish incident barely out of the way, Bulgaria could not afford multiple diplomatic incidents on another front. Under the pressure of many participants, there was no other choice than to allow Ecoglasnost to recruit new members, collect signatures for petitions, hold a meeting in a facility provided by the government, and organize more demonstrations including a peace march toward the National Assembly. Anton Zapryanov, a famous dissident, was even invited to the public sessions of the conference. Of course, numerous other factors played a role—such as Gorbachev's own interventions—in turning the page of totalitarian rule in Bulgaria. Yet, foreign professionals, such as Geneva's Institut des Hautes Etudes Internationales professor Victor-Yves Ghebali who participated in the international negotiations on the environment, believe that Zhivkov's power structure received a fatal blow during those significant days. A week after the conference, on 10 November, Todor Zhivkov was forced to resign.

We must never forget that the struggle for a clean environment had often left a trail of tears. In a variety of countries, environmental activists had been able to test the limits of the regimes' tolerance, but discovering the boundaries had a price. After martial law was imposed in Poland, Solidarity union activists went underground and ecologists had to do the same.[54] Until the fall of the old regimes, environmental activists could still be fired from their jobs, harassed or persecuted in Hungary, or punished with stiff jail sentences in the Soviet Union, Poland, Czechoslovakia, Bulgaria and Romania.[55] Repression against Romanian environmentalists was so brutal, that their existence became known only after the fall of Ceausescu; only then were they allowed to become actors on the political scene (nine seats in the parliament in 1990). In Chernobyl itself, extreme tensions developed among enlisted men (mostly Balts) and reserve military outfits sent to the Ukraine for the cleanup: protests turned into mutinies and at least twelve executions took place.[56]

Nevertheless, as noted for several countries, and since the earliest stages of communism, the government never seemed to give up on its attempt to channel environmentalism. Also, it was not uncommon for party and state officials to try to control the situation by staying ahead of the activists, by taking the initiative of political action in favor of the environment. In 1986, in the darkest period of the Jaruzelski years, the Polish "green" activist and sociologist Zbigniew Wierzbicki believed that there existed a very wide range of contradictory interests within the party and the administration: channels for a dialog between environmentalists and officials still seemed open.[57] Interviewed almost immediately after the Chernobyl accident, Dr. Nikolai Popov, one of Bulgaria's most famous dissidents, provided a colorful portrayal of the *nomenklatura's* ambivalent attitude:

For several years, committees, centers, commissions, associations—all meant to protect the environment—have proliferated. This proves that the regime has indeed perceived the danger of possible spontaneous popular reactions to pollution. It is probable that since 1983, the attitude of the population towards the problems surrounding the environment has evolved, since its echoes are reaching me as far as my place of exile. This manner of reducing problems by creating *ad hoc* commissions, is the power structure's standard response to the emerging risk of a civil society organizing around any theme whatsoever. When that theme exercises so much pressure that mere repression is no longer sufficient, [that theme] is watered down by a multitude of organisms destined to express the preoccupation of official institutions and make the private initiatives they haven't themselves initiated, seem redundant and insincere. This is what happened during destalinization. A few victims of the trials, such as Tchayko Kostov, were rehabilitated with great ceremonial, their names have been given to streets and two factories, and that settled the problem. After that, it was easy to call anyone who would dare bring up that problem again a malignant provocateur.[58]

But in this process of channeling and subverting a potential political movement, could mainstream communists have been "contaminated"? Could government officials have shared some of the concerns of ecologists? Or could various tendencies have divided the *nomenklatura* into different camps? Were all these dilemmas an occasion for the so-called "young wolves" to put pressure on their elders ("the dinosaurs")?

In any case, the rapid degradation of the natural environment of the socialist countries had become a factor of evolution in Central and Eastern European domestic politics. By 1992, democracy (at least nominal) was the rule in all countries of the Soviet bloc, in Yugoslavia, and in Albania. Central and Eastern Europeans were at least free to debate publicly, publish, and organize political platforms on almost all issues concerning the environment. Foreign powers were now deeply involved in Central and Eastern European environmental affairs.

THE ENVIRONMENT IN THE POST-COMMUNIST PERIOD

The most impressive efforts for the restoration of the natural environment were carried out in reunified Germany. Former East Germany has benefited from the long experience of *Umweltpolitik* that had been a priority in the Federal Republic of Germany for a quarter of a century: the Willy Brandt years had witnessed the recognition and implementation of *Umweltschutz* (Environmental Defense). Then, probably to make a concession to the antinuclear protesters, it became a priority of the Kohl administration under the leadership Klaus Töpfer whose impressive record won him the post of Executive Director of the United Nations Program for the Environment (in 1998). A superficial glance at the daily newspapers or many local TV channels can yield scores of information on the large-scale dimensions of the ongoing cleanup. There was little choice left for the newly unified federation and local governments: some of the measures (i.e., cleaning rivers, and closing unsafe nuclear plants, uranium mines near the Czech border, or cellulose factories on the Elbe) were necessary for the mere survival of the inhabitants. Other measures, such as abandoning brown coal as a source of energy or discontinuing old heavily polluting automobile models, were not only necessary for a safer environment: these symbols of East German heavy industry were economically unviable.

German voters are far from being unanimous over the new environmental challenges and especially over the financial and fiscal implications of *Ökosteuer*. The German Greens became part of the 1999 government coalition and are supported in the European Parliament by a transnational alliance with the French Greens who recently gained great electoral victories. In such a political context, the radical cleanup will probably intensify. This is to be commended, no matter what can be thought of the controversial style or ideology of Green politicians. It would be unfair to forget the numerous federal or local NGOs, nonpartisan groups, associations and clubs only some of which are federated in the Deutscher Naturschutzring (DNR—more than 2.5 million members). The environmentalist lobby BUND, the association NABU, and Greenpeace Deutschland (700,000 donators counted by fundraisers) represent some of the most powerful pressure groups in contemporary Germany. They have been active in West German politics or on specific projects in the field, since the 1970s and are at work today in the new *Länder*. The German initiatives (from the right or the left) for a safe environment can be compared to a war effort and should serve as a model. Although acid rain, automobile pollution, and volatile industrial and domestic substances continue to present a considerable threat, the war to save the environment is forcing "ecological death" to retreat on several fronts: automobile motors (although dangerous by their increasing numbers) are much "cleaner", water quality has improved dramatically and use of energy has decreased by 17% between 1990 and 1995.[59]

Germany is only the best example of serious efforts toward the improvement of the natural environment because of the pressure of the Greens and the financial resources that it can invest. Elsewhere in Central Europe governments are also at work. Having assessed the past damage and the present threats, they are creating new government institutions, helping private initiatives and implementing strategies for the protection of nature and sustainable development.[60]

Based on such information, it is tempting to believe that the end of a certain form of communist rule calls for an "all clear" on the front of the environment. Does this mean that environmental issues will become less important in Central and Eastern European domestic and international politics? The latter could explain why today, Central and Eastern European "green" movements seem less influential than in 1980s. It is as if life goes on, and more "serious" issues than the environment should mobilize the energies of Central and Eastern Europeans and their foreign partners, now that communism and its inept land and resource management is a part of history.

But the seriousness of the damage sustained under the old regimes should forbid us from closing the chapter on environmental security in Central and Eastern Europe too quickly. The issue is more relevant than ever to global geopolitics.

International Cooperation

That is the message apparently sent out by developed nations and their international institutions in their ongoing effort to define and implement environmental policies in Central and Eastern Europe. But how many of these efforts are efficient, how many are purely cosmetic?

The international organizations, as we have seen particularly well in the Bulgarian case, were already deeply involved with Central and Eastern European states in ecological affairs. It was only natural that diplomatic activity would continue in that area, and would intensify after the removal of old regime ideological and infrastructural barriers. Therefore, international conferences (sponsored by the UN, European, or other institutions) were held almost every year until now, while other important activities were taking shape. Here are only a few examples.

The OECD, the European Council, and the European Bank for Reconstruction and Development have been particularly active in Central and Eastern Europe, already on the eve of the transition to market economies.

A good example of the West's concern for the environment in the Central and Eastern Europe is the funding of the numerous activities of the OECD. The Paris-based international institution's first mission in this field is to collect, centralize, process, and analyze a voluminous bulk of scientific and socioeconomic data on all aspects of the human impact on the natural environment of Central and Eastern Europe. The other mission is to assess the damage and investigate the consequences on local economies and societies and their international impact. Then, the OECD becomes involved in policy-making.[61]

One of the purely financial aspects of OECD action has been to support the so-called environmental funds—an important source of finance for environmental expenditures in transition economies. These institutions provide resources for environmental projects and investments at a time when enterprises and government programs face severe financial constraints. The New Independent States' Environmental Funds Network (under the auspices of the Environmental Action Program Task Force) is one of these institutions. Its first meeting was held in Almaty on 27–28 November 1997 with more than 50 participants from environmental funds, government ministries, and international organizations.[62]

But a significant project to restore a healthy environment in half of a continent without private efforts would be unrealistic. To finish the job and guarantee sustainable development, only one incentive can, in the long term, mobilize the private forces and money needed for such a gigantic project: profit. As we will see in the last paragraphs of this chapter, "ecobusiness" could play a crucial role in the future, not only in the management of Central and Eastern Europe's natural environment. Ecobusiness could not only benefit the economy of the countries (as in Kenya, Costa Rica or parts of the North American Pacific coast), but also, it could help restore a sense of civil society. That is why on 25–26 November, 1996, an OECD/CCET workshop organized with the Regional Environmental Center in Szentendre, Hungary, brought

Environmental Security and Civil Society

together thirty-three environmental entrepreneurs, representatives of business associations, the European Bank for Reconstruction and Development (EBRD), EC/PHARE, and "green equity funds" to precisely discuss such matters as local environmental businesses, the services they provide in waste and-water treatment systems or soil and water remediation, and the important role "that they will play" (or *could* play?) "in correcting past damage and promoting sustainable development."[63] The workshop's list of suggestions for entrepreneurs, Central and Eastern European business associations, financial institutions and government organizations highlighted the need for:

— greater awareness and use of environment-specific credit lines;
— provision of seed capital for enterprises;
— better advertised funds and resources for equity investments among enterprises;
— continuous management training and expanded business association activities; and
— information exchanges, particularly covering management and environment market issues.[64]

As noted by the workshop organizer Graham Vickery, "transition economies are still addressing the policy, legislative and institutional issues which drive environmental investment and create the demand for environmental goods and services."[65] The 1998 Ministerial Conference, "Environment for Europe," assisted with the implementation of the above-mentioned recommendations, in coordination with PHARE, the EBRD and the multilateral Regional Environmental Center.[66]

Such debates allow for some optimism since they at least demonstrate that important practical questions have not met with complete indifference by Central and Eastern European governments, important international institutions, or large business corporations. As noted further at the Szentendre workshop, of the countries surveyed, "Poland and the Czech Republic have the most mature environmental business sectors, followed by Hungary and the Slovak Republic."[67]

The importance of Central and Eastern European affairs is also recognized in comparable activities undertaken to a greater or lesser degree by other government institutions, such as the United Nations Conference on Environment and Development, UNESCO, the European Union, the EBRD, semi governmental organizations (like the French Defense Ministry-backed Cousteau Society project for the Danube, funded by the European Bank for Reconstruction and Development or EBRD), or powerful NGOs connected with governmental circles, such as the International Union for the Conservation of Nature.

The EBRD is probably best known by the public at large for its involvement in Captain Cousteau's research along the Danube at the helm of the *Calypso*. Other than those expeditions, the EBRD, created essentially to develop market economy and democratic regimes in Central and Eastern

Europe, has manifested a strong commitment to environmental issues by incorporating ecological criteria in all its investment and technical aid projects.[68]

In its earliest stages, the EU's Technical Assistance for the Commonwealth of Independent States (or TACIS) only referred to environmental issues without expressing clear commitments about ecology; but already by 1993, 20% of the regional activities of TACIS were focused on the environment.[69] The Black Sea became an area of particular efforts for TACIS, where it helped to establish "the political, legal, institutional, technical and financial measures necessary to act as a framework for the safeguard of the environment and sustainable use of the local natural resources. In the long run it is hoped that economic growth and investment in the tourism and fishing industry of the region will increase."[70] The PHARE program, created in 1990 to contribute to the democratization process and encourage investments and transfers of knowledge, also became involved in nuclear security and environmental affairs. Pollution control, teledetection, treatment of sewage waste, nature conservation and education, plus financial aid awareness campaigns are among the various accomplishments of PHARE.[71]

A significant example of the new ecological dimension of present "East-West" international cooperation is the signature in December 1991 by Poland and the European Community of a "European agreement to associate the European Communities and its member states with Poland" which requires, in its Article 71, that "environmental considerations are fully incorporated into [other] policies from the outset."[72] The legal and political implications are important: the agreement forced Polish law to be modified to conform to "the spirit and details of EC directives."[73] The European Commission helped the Polish government adapt its structures and integrate EC environmental law through the PHARE program, and it provided considerable financial support.

In 1995, the Association Agreement with the European Union entered in force after ratification by Bulgaria and the fifteen EU member states.[74] As with Poland and the former EC, the agreement calls for "harmonization of laws . . . regulations, standards, norms, and methodologies," which entails substantial legislative action and financial responsibilities. The political significance of these environmental provisions of important East-West agreements is worth noting: the West considers environmental safety in Central and Eastern Europe sufficiently important to make it *a condition of Europe's enlargement.*

Individual nations have also demonstrated a strong commitment to a safer environment in Central and Eastern Europe. For example, hundreds of smaller documents on more precise and immediate issues (water pollution, sulfur dioxide emissions, wildlife management, etc.) have been already signed or are being negotiated on a *bilateral* level, between countries of Central and Eastern Europe and Western European states. This confirms once again that at least some political leaders in the West have recognized the importance of ecological matters in the former Soviet bloc, former Yugoslavia, and Albania.

Environmental Security and Civil Society 133

The U.S. Environmental Protection Agency has been very active in Central and Eastern Europe, establishing such programs as funding for the regional environmental center for Central and Eastern Europe in Budapest, institution building, and intense training projects (with a particular concern for the technological aspects of environmental management).[75]

Such examples can be multiplied. The results of this international attention to the environmental question in Central and Eastern Europe are still modest but, nevertheless, encouraging.

The outlook on the domestic front is also rather good. It is safe to announce that in the 1990s, most national governments in the region have at least recognized the emergency. Environmental agencies or ministries have been created and there exists some political will to solve the problems left behind by the Marxist-Leninist regimes, or to avoid repeating their most serious mistakes. Although some "taboos" continue to limit the action of environmentalists, the freedom they enjoy is incomparably greater than before 1989 and environmentalist parties are represented in the Parliaments. Local and international NGOs and environmental publications have sprouted throughout Central end Eastern Europe. All over the former Soviet bloc, Yugoslavia and even Albania, an abundance of NGOs, local or "imported," proliferated after 1989-1990. The West German Greens stormed the East German political arena immediately after the Wall fell; their presence and influence became so important that many found it overwhelming, literally crushing whatever local environmentalism there had existed before. The World Wildlife Fund (WWF), Friends of the Earth, Greenpeace, the Sierra Club, and the Audubon Society also established Central and Eastern European operations very rapidly.[76] The Central East European Environmental Center, which opened in Budapest in 1990 with a $4 million grant from the United States, is only one of the most active agencies promoting NGO development in the field of the environment.[77]

However, numerous problems remain. Unfortunately, the record of the previously mentioned organizations can be just as discouraging as it is sometimes impressive. The resignation of the EBRD's first president, Jacques Attali, raised some of the first doubts about the reliability of current aid programs in the area of environmental safety and other domains as well. It had been found that half of the EBRD's budget had been spent on decorating its headquarters with extravagant luxuries. How many environmental projects could have been funded with the sums spent on the infamous marble of the EBRD building? Less scandalous but no less disturbing are the limitations shown by the PHARE program. Although in 1989, 25% of its budget was earmarked for environmental projects, by 1994 only 11% of the appropriated sum had been allocated.[78] Among many other anomalies, critics have noted the excessive amounts of money spent on consulting fees and studies rather than on concrete projects.[79]

Critics will inevitably deplore that all these efforts—domestic and international, governmental, and private—are no more than drops in the ocean and it is difficult to find sufficient proof to the contrary. Are there no indications that the condition of the natural environment in Central and Eastern Europe improved in any way?

The OECD's lukewarm analysis of the situation and complete statistics are available in print and on the Internet.[80] They allow evaluating the news from the front. Fortunately, there is room for some optimism: the catastrophic rate of deterioration of the environment, as a whole, has been halted, for the moment. Deterioration continues in some sectors but seems under control, in other words no "point of no return" has yet been reached and most of the damaged ecosystems can still recover (if and when sufficient funds and efforts will be invested). All indicators present a less than spectacular, yet clear decline in pollution, in its various forms. Particular aspects of the aggression against the environment have been discontinued (at least for several consecutive years), such as the use of fertilizers harmful to water supplies and oceans.

One of the major problems in such evaluations is that the decline of pollutants is, to a large extent, due to a decline of productivity. A cancer that ceases to spread is not necessarily a sign of remission: the patient is maybe dead. This metaphor is applicable to many industrial infrastructures and their surrounding landscapes in Central and Eastern Europe. In Russia, for example, the declining curb of toxic air emissions parallels the decline of the GDP. Therefore, it is necessary to search for a so-called "decoupling" in GDP and pollution trend indicators for a real sign of a return to environmental health. The real good news would be a decline in pollution accompanied by a rising GDP. Fortunately, this "decoupling" was observed in 1996 in Hungary and Poland where the GDP has risen while at the same time, sulfur dioxide emissions continued to fall and carbon dioxide emissions appeared to be relatively stationary.

However, in its January 1996 review of the Czech and Slovak republics, Hungary, Poland, Bulgaria and Russia, the OECD candidly deplored the following setbacks: the use of fertilizers is slowly increasing again (except in Russia and Bulgaria). Energy intensities and air pollution levels are still unacceptable, despite the progress observed. The OECD adds that monitoring techniques and data quality cannot indicate clear trends in ambient air and water quality improvement. But in a sense, that is almost a euphemism. In other words, no spectacular improvement has been noticed yet.

More data should become available shortly, but the warning of the 1996 OECD report is still valid: environmental challenges remain significant. A look at the data that is already available, listed above, one is left with the disturbing impression that government documents seem to contain more wish-lists than actual results. This leads to two serious questions. First of all, has the West done enough to help restore a healthy natural environment in the countries in transition? More bluntly: are the efforts no more than the old Communist regimes' cosmetic repairs? The EBRD scandal even brings back memories of Communist *nomenclatura* incompetence and corruption. Does the West have sufficient vision to lead international cooperation toward more

Environmental Security and Civil Society

efficient results? The second question concerns the political will of the people in Central and Eastern Europe. Do *they* have any vision? The answer to that might be the worse news, yet.

The Decline of Political Mobilization for the Environment in Central and Eastern Europe

Recent trends in domestic politics in the former Soviet bloc, former Yugoslavia and Albania leave no doubt. The environment has become less than a secondary concern for Central and Eastern European voters. In Hungary, in the mid-1990s, there was even talk of eliminating the Environmental Ministry.[81]

As mentioned earlier, demands for a cleaner environment and the "Chernobyl effect" gave a strong environmentalist dimension to the opposition in the late 1980s. But what could have been expected did not happen: no powerful "green" movement ever rose to the summits of political life in the 1990s nor even gained any noticeable influence. The Central and Eastern European ecological activists even appear to have lost in a few months whatever authority they enjoyed before 1989. The first semi-free elections in Poland (after the "Round Table" agreements) are significant. As many as 35% of the seats in the Sejm and all seats in the newly created Senate were to be filled with any candidate elected by the voters; Solidarity won all seats available in the Sejm and 99% of those in the Senate. Only four prominent environmentalists obtained seats in the Sejm and only after being endorsed by Solidarity, after a long electoral campaign.[82] The first (and last) East German free legislative elections of 18 March 1990 yielded no more than 1.96% of the vote for the Greens (in coalition with Women's Union), who won only eight parliamentary seats. Between 1990 and 1992 free elections were also held in Romania, Hungary, Poland, Bulgaria, Czechoslovakia, and Albania; environmentalists won seats in only two of these countries: in Romania (nine out of 387 seats) and in Bulgaria. Bulgarian environmentalists ran as candidates for the Union of Democratic Forces, the coalition, which obtained 34,36% of the vote of October 13, 1991. Filip Dimitrov, founder of the Green party (born from the divisions inside Ecoglasnost) was the president of that coalition and would eventually become Prime Minister on 8 November and again on 20 May of the following year. Valentin Vasilev, minister of the environment was the only member of Ecoglasnost in those two cabinets and was replaced by former communist Valentin Bosevski in the Berov cabinets. This modest Bulgarian example is the highest level of partisan influence gained by "green" activism in the post-communist period. Indeed, in Bulgaria, the opposition rose in great part from the environmentalist movement. But that is precisely why the destiny of Bulgarian environmental politics after 1990, appears as an anticlimax: their place in Bulgarian politics could barely even compare to the status of Greens in Germany.

Is this to say that the environmental movement was only incidental in the history of communism in Central and Eastern Europe? Did the articles printed in the publications exaggerate the "green" aspirations of Central and Eastern

Europeans? After all, has the December 1986 issue of *Alternatives* on the environment, not been honest about warning Western public opinion against wishful thinking if they viewed Central and Eastern European environmentalists as a mass phenomenon?

It is tempting to notice this apparent decline of ecology in the light of an earlier discussion: if the environmental movement had such shallow roots, could it have been only a decoy to lure popular energies and discontent into reformism, or technical and practical battles—e.g., the defense of nature— while the real struggles for power took place within the *nomenklatura*?

There are several prosaic explanations for the public's relative disaffection toward environmental politics. First of all, post-communist reconstruction and the social problems caused by the abrupt transition to market economies create numerous distractions. Government priorities have shifted to problems like falling production and rising unemployment, while for millions of citizens, solving the planet's problems could seem less urgent than solving daily personal problems of survival such as food, clothing, health and employment. Barbara Jancar-Webster presents the same issue from the following point of view:

> Once the scientists took up their new positions (i.e. in environmental ministries), they had little time for the movements. Since movement membership was informal and tended to rise and fall with the political saliency of issues, members simply drifted away. Pre-transition environmental education had not been in progress long enough to produce a mass public awareness of the severity of environmental problems. As a result, the public had an extremely high expectation of what the new government could do, and no idea of what actions were required of them to ensure government responsibility.[83]

Czech officials personally explained to Barbara Jancar-Webster that they were expected to solve all problems immediately, and "while people demanded instantaneous results" with no idea of the legislative implications and their timetables "they themselves abandoned their activism to turn to more immediate concerns": job security and inflation.[84] To this we could add criminality and housing problems; these are less threatening than a potential nuclear accident but they are more immediately perceptible.

Most characteristic is the case of Slovakia, where environmentalism had apparently played a central role in the transition. Today, the influence of ecology is almost a marginal issue. Juraj Mesik's explanation is very honest and lucid:

> As soon as it was proven that the Communists were not to intervene with armed forces against the [Velvet] revolution, and that it had a real chance to win, new persons appeared at the head of VPN [Public Against Violence] and the ecologist spirit was more and more pushed aside by economic pragmatism. By accepting its role as the driving force of the Democratic Revolution, the ecologist movement in Bratislava, as in all of Slovakia, lost many leaders. It appears that a part of the activists of the ecological movement are not real ecologists, but sympathizers seeking in their wake a

social and political battle. A portion of the members of the VPN's direction swapped their social function as creators and controllers of sustainable development for the role of free market promoters.[85]

Was all this noise about the great environmental issues in Central and Eastern Europe only a fad? Could it have been the last incarnation of the "red scare" and of the atomic menace? Or a subtle environmentalist addition to the pop-culture of backyard fallout shelters and schoolchildren drilling for nuclear attacks in the American suburbia of the 1950's and 60's?

The New Ideological and Geopolitical Temptations

The environment in Central and Eastern Europe is becoming a lesser priority on some agendas, but not all agendas. Still unnoticed by a large public, a notion of "environmental security" is gaining influence since it was first introduced at the UN's General Assembly in 1987.[86] Is there a risk that, some day, the fear of Central and Eastern European environmental *insecurity* may affect the judgment of Western leaders and fuel new East-West confrontations?

In the early 1990s, terms like "lebanization," "africanization," or "balkanization" were frequently used by the press in its attempts to find pseudo-academic labels to describe political instability in the post-Cold War "chaos." Later, it almost seems as if this chaos gained in stature, becoming a fully accomplished character on the stage—an *autonomous* political force. The vocabulary found in certain titles is quite evocative: "The Geopolitics of Chaos," the "Anarchy *Problèmatique*," "Rogue States," "The New World: From the Order of Yalta to the Disorder of Nations," and so on.[87] Robert Kaplan, in his "Coming Anarchy," explores the ecological dimension of the alleged chaos.[88] Kaplan's article is only the best-known example of a rich series of reflections in the early 1990s upon the environmental causes of geopolitical instability. The White House itself acknowledges that these reflections had a direct influence over the Clinton administration's integration of "environmental security" into its national security policy.[89] Reputed author of *Balkan Ghosts. A Journey Through History* (New York 1994), Robert Kaplan, receives support from the U.S. Institute of Peace and Foreign Policy Research Institute. His theory of anarchy can be summarized in his own formula: "environmental scarcity, cultural and racial clash, geographic destiny and the transformation of war."

There is a strange analogy between the various chaos theories—especially those concerned with environmental security—and Samuel Huntington's theory about the "clash of civilizations" in their compulsion to divide the globe into clear-cut "impenetrable" borderlines (Kaplan often repeats the expression).

After frequent exposure to chaos theory or to Huntington, it is almost inevitable to look at the world and draw a line, between "them" and "us," between "chaos" and "order," between "democracy" and "violence," between countries with a tradition of the Enlightenment and countries without that tradition. To those fatal differences, Kaplan and a few others would add, safe, pure environment vs. unsafe, impure environment.

Are we witnessing the emergence of a new geopolitical doctrine justifying the struggle for an environmentally clean *Lebensraum*? The perspectives are frightening as we notice how far European thinkers have already gone in that direction.

France is the birthplace of the "duty to interfere" theory, that is the right to intervene in a foreign territory when basic human rights are being violated, even against the will of the sovereign state. "*Droit d'ingérance*" was made famous by former NGO founder and member of several socialist cabinets Bernard Kouchner, and lawyer Mario Bettati, dean of Paris-Sud University. Their revolutionary concept can be summed in one of their expressions: "humanitarian aid may be a continuation of politics by other means."[90] The United Nations introduced this essentially French principle in Resolutions No. 43/131 of 8 December 1988 and No. 43/131 of 5 April 1991, demanding free or "immediate access" to victims of natural catastrophes or political oppression in the case of the Iraqi Kurds. Many governments and private individuals fear that this might be used as the legal instrument to legitimize hegemony "with a human face" or to make warfare "politically correct."

Critics even include conservatives who see this as the most dangerous departure from *Realpolitik* to date, and as a serious threat to global political equilibrium. During their 1996 conference, the theorists of the "right to intervene" acknowledged all the risks of humanitarian operations being used as beachheads for military invasions.[91] However, these critiques were immediately dismissed on the assumption that only humanitarians (such as the "French doctors" and NGO field operators) have the experience required for successful humanitarian interventions, their democratic values being the safeguards against militaristic exploitation.[92] The irony is that such reassurances originate from former May 1968 radical militants whose articles appear, side by side, in the proceedings of the conference, with no less than three papers on military tactical support signed by General Morillon, veteran of Bosnia and an ardent Catholic with contacts in the *Opus Dei*. The UN resolutions mention "natural catastrophes" as sufficient causes for overruling the principle of sovereignty. Environmental disasters could easily fall under this category.

Former UN civil servant Michel Bachelet defends an environmentalist version of the "duty to interfere" in his *L'ingérence écologique* (*Ecological Interference*) published in Paris in 1995. Many constructive legal and practical solutions to international environmental threats make it a valuable monograph. However, it is revealing to look at the foreword signed by renowned *Nouvelle vague* cinematographer Claude Chabrol. It could be quite typical of the voters' perception of these issues. After listing some of the innumerable disasters found in Bachelet's book, Chabrol agrees with the author, that the size of environmental threats is "proportionate to the irresponsibility of many governments and nation-states" and concludes: "that is when the sovereignty of states appeared to me as essentially debatable."[93] This echoes Bernard

Environmental Security and Civil Society 139

Kouchner and Mario Bettati when they "lay claim to the right of humanitarian intervention against a *wrong interpretation of the sovereignty of nations.*"[94] The temptation to militarize the entire issue is all too clear in the expression "environmental security," which borrows from defense and military vocabulary.

If the situation of Central and Eastern Europe's natural environment does not improve faster, international conflicts could indeed erupt as a direct consequence of rarified natural resources (as in the Middle East of Africa) or be used as a pretext for geopolitical struggles between the great powers. However, in the light of recent events, the shape of future ecological conflicts might resemble the blunder in Somalia rather than any great victory for American or French geopolitical interests and a clean environment. Marie-Christine Delpal, Bernard Hours, and other critics of the "right to interfere" (such as Régis Debray) stress that the new concept is not part of any rational vision of global order but that it is "a convenient substitute for a deficient policy."[95] It is only a side effect of feeble foreign policies. New idealistic doctrines (we should say attitudes) only fill the gap left by the absence of any consensus over which foreign policy to pursue. Part of it can be explained after *Realpolitik* had been demonized (following Vietnam), after the collapse of the Marxist world-vision, or after the weakening of France's or Europe's position. There is an implicit fear in Delpal and Hours, that weakening the state by shattering the notion of sovereignty can only make matters worse. A good illustration is the situation in which peace-keeping forces find themselves in Bosnia and Kosovo. After the American hesitations—between isolationism and military intervention—or Europe's inconsistencies and its inability to prevent the conflict, troops from a variety of Western powers are facing the challenges of the terrain without a clear policy (we are told that to find a political solution in Kosovo could take fifty years).

Therefore, when governments will be faced with the unavoidable problems of "environmental security" in the future, it would seem reasonable to explore the virtues of classical approaches, particularly through state-to-state diplomacy which preserves the authority of sovereign states while seeking *political* solutions.

Restoring the Environment, Restoring a Civil Society

Tackling the structural problems of Central and Eastern European societies causing both ecological damage and political instability is the only reasonable defense against environmental insecurity. It excludes both charity (or financing corrupted administrations), and military adventures. Reestablishing state structures necessarily implies heavy expenses for law enforcement, science, education, cultural policies, and a rational tax system to finance it all. Unfortunately, strengthening state structures is not very popular in this age of triumphant neo-liberalism, when reestablishing a free market seems to be the only relevant issue. Yet, just as there can be no genuine free market without an effective state to guarantee safety, freedom and opportunities for all potential entrepreneurs, without solid state structures there can be no environmental security.

The choice is difficult: reconstructing the state and a civil society is extremely complicated. But it would be less realistic to implement policy aimed at protecting the West from new Chernobyl scenarios without reinforcing the state and society in transition countries. Also, it is sometimes the extreme challenges that eventually bring the greatest rewards and even profit, in the long term.

As mentioned earlier, Robert Kaplan's merit was to awaken the West's vigilance in matters of environmental security. Huntington deserves credit as well, for underlining an important factor in modern conflicts: culture and identity. There could exist a close link between identity crises and environmental security. But why should environment and national identity only be discussed in terms of violence, intolerance, and conflict?

Throughout Central and Eastern Europe small groups of volunteers are adding small dots of color on the gray map of post-communism. In Slovenia, natural park rangers devote their last energies to the preservation of wild bears and other mammals. Along the Danube, teachers take their schoolchildren to clean up soiled banks of the river. On the coast of Dalmatia, skin divers spend long hours removing tons of garbage from the bottom of the sea, while youth groups struggle to find boats and fuel to observe Marine mammals, all in the midst of wars following Yugoslavia's breakup. In Hungary, the NGO *Ormánság Alapítvany* rallies people with very diverse ethnic backgrounds to build organic farms and a new village lifestyle with environmentally friendly manufacturing activities and ecological educational facilities.[96] As far as Siberia, young men and women struggle with poverty and risk their lives against poachers, to save the last tigers of northern Asia. These efforts are very modest. But for those who know Central and Eastern Europeans well, they are far more typical than the excesses of Kaplan's "skinhead Cossacks" and they deserve the attention of Western policy-makers.

Will the opportunities be recognized? Grassroots projects favorable to sustainable development or "ecobusiness" could not only heal nature but also help rebuild a civil society; ecobusiness has already started in Central and Eastern Europe.[97] But why do we hear so little about it? Is it because ecobusiness is unrealistic that it exists on such a modest level? The problems that are preventing their development are once again linked to the lack of solid state structures. Today, in some areas, it is literally impossible for an individual (a foreigner or a local) to create such simple and inexpensive businesses as an organic vegetable cannery, a recycled paper factory, or a photo-safari outfitting operation. Before any equipment is even bought, an outrageous amount of money will be spent on taxes, on bribes to bypass overwhelming bureaucratic obstacles and on "protection" money to a wide variety of parasites. Any economic initiative is blocked by opposition in all forms (legal or illegal) from any established company perceiving the small businessman/businesswoman as a real or imagined competitor or a client to be squeezed out of his/her capital in a hit-and-run operation as fast and as ruthlessly as possible without the slightest concern for any future business opportunities.[98] The problem here is neither economic, nor logistical. It is essentially political: the state's presence is overwhelming when it comes to taxes, land ownership, and small business regulations; on the contrary, it is hopelessly wanting when it comes to protect small business from unfair competition, monopolies and racketeers. But consolidating state structures is irrelevant for the gurus of the free market who are less concerned with freedom of enterprise for small businesses than multinational corporations, not. Yet, it is small business only that is one of the most realistic solution to exploit the full potential of eco-business in Central and Eastern Europe.

The identity crises in Central and Eastern Europe are a symptom of poverty, social injustice, conflicting standards of social behavior, weak legal institutions, and the disintegration of all social bonds in rural communities, urban quarters, and in the family unit itself. The result is social isolation and anomie. In a time of historic turmoil and uncertainty, standing in a crowd that shares the same fears and shouts the same slogans, creates a momentary feeling of community and an impression that one can control the forces of history and one's own destiny after all. The great causes that can rally Central and Eastern Europeans can be aggressive, intolerant or violent. Or not: restoring the natural environment and creating the infrastructures for wildlife management and sustainable development, outdoor public recreation and international tourism could serve as an outlet. Moreover it could provide an existential purpose for those who have a dire need to find a place in their society—whether as employees, small businessmen/businesswomen, or volunteers.[99] The protection of nature is indeed, to a certain extent a neoromantic Western fad. But it is also a creative and non-violent cause addressing genuine dangers of global proportions. As such, it can transcend national barriers, and, properly channeled, it could possibly become a substitute for the cultural marks destroyed in the process described by Antonin Liehm in chapter 4 of this volume.

Creating the structures and the educational programs that could bring Central and Eastern Europe's agriculture, national parks, fish and game, freshwater and forest resources management to the level of those in the United States, Canada, or at least Kenya, would require gigantic efforts. But if Central and Eastern Europeans could achieve feats such as Nowa Huta under communist industrialization, the environmental cleanup, under a less dictatorial regime, is yet feasible. The size of the challenge could provide the grandeur that is lacking so much in the present "transition." Native and visitor alike will find this grandeur in the natural heritage. There, intense physical and aesthetic sensations, provide an immediate gratification that can be shared by all.

If this can be turned to the economic benefit of the local inhabitants and restore some of their national pride and civil society along the way, a new environmental *Ostpolitik* through peaceful cooperation deserves all the support it can get.

NOTES

1. Douglas R. Weiner, *Models of Nature. Ecology, Conservation, and Cultural Revolution in Soviet Russia* (Bloomington: Indiana University Press, 1988), p. 1.
2. Ibid.
3. The forms of expression were extremely diverse. Utopian visions of a remodeled nature appear in the early to mid-1800s, in Vladimir Odoevskiiy's "Year 4338" and Chernychevskiiy's hymn to skyscrapers in one of Lenin's favorites: *Chto Delat'? (What Is To Be Done?)*. In the era of Stakhanovism, muscles of blond proletarian superheroes were filmed and sculpted by the communist competitors of Leni Riefenstahl and Arno Brecker (Andrzej Wajda's caricature of the movie director in *Man of Marble* was a self-portrait). Promethean aesthetics ranged from the highly sophisticated avant-garde (Andrej Mikhalkov-Konchalovskiy's ambivalent *Sibiriada*, expresses both nostalgia for the unspoiled wilderness, and the necessity of its anihilation to make way for dams, electricity and other necessities of socialist happiness) to the trashy (science-fiction novels beginning with the sentence "when communism finally triumphed throughout the planet, the world government turned to the stars"—spoonfed by Mikhail Bulgakov in his censored play *Blazhenstvo*).
4. Reiner Grundmann, *Marxism and Ecology* (Oxford: Clarendon Press, 1991), p. 92. I have borrowed the term "predatory" from the vocabulary of Communist geographic literature.
5. These esthetics were pushed to the extreme by Nazi ideology, and even to this day by other extreme-rightist thinkers, who equate the "purity" of nature with the purity of race. See Luc Ferry, *Le nouvel ordre écologique: l'arbre l'animal et l'homme* (Paris: Bernard Grasset, 1992); in addition, see Douglas R. Weiner, "Demythologizing Environmentalism," *Journal of the History of Biology*, 25, no. 3, Fall, 1992, pp. 385–411. Gordon Marsh, "The Goths in New England; a Discourse Delivered at the Anniversary of the Philomathesian Society of Middlebury College," August 15, 1843, Middlebury, 1843, p. 18, shows how easily the great figures of environmentalism could be inclined to racist historiosophy through the ideal of "purity" (fortunately absent from his classic *Man and Nature*—see David Lowenthal, "Introduction" in *Man and Nature* [Cambridge: Harvard University Press], 1965, p. xv).
6. In the 1940s, even under Stalin, Central European conservationists did not risk, as in the USSR, to be prosecuted as criminals. On the contrary, not only were conservation movements tolerated, but the new Communist governments even found it necessary to express conservationist views to gain supporters. See Zbigniew T. Wierzbicki, "Entre le socialisme réel d'hier et le néo-capitalisme de demain," in Krystyna Vinaver, (ed.), *La crise de l'environment `a L'Est* (Paris: l'Harmattan, 1993), p. 34. Lenin's very moderate policies for nature conservation are analyzed in Weiner's *Models of Nature*.
7. Larry Tye, "Pollution a Nightmare Behind the Iron Curtain," *Arizona Republic*, February 25, 1990, p. C. 1; quoted in Zachary A. Smith, *The Environmental Policy Paradox* (Englewood Cliffs, NJ: Prentice-Hall, 1995), p. 231.
8. OECD, *Reforming the Economies of Central and Eastern Europe* (Paris: OECD, 1992), p. 98, and Krystyna Vinaver, "Le désastre est-européen," *L'etat de l'environnement dans le monde* (Paris: La Découverte, 1993), p. 198.
9. OECD, *Reforming the Economies*, p. 98.
10. Nikolaï Popov, interviewed by Freddy Foscolo, "Pollution de l'esprit et de la nature," *Alternatives*, no. 4, December 1986, p. 34.
11. OECD, *Reforming the Economies*, p. 98.
12. See the documents and interviews in G.A. Goryshina, *Ladoga* (Moscow: Planeta, 1989). In 1992 and 1993, I was among the first Westerners to penetrate the

area—one of the most remote and supposedly pristine forests of Europe. There, I traveled by rowboat along the Finish border and hiked near the Eastern shore of the lake. Many other grim discoveries only confirmed Goryshina's documents: vandalism caused by unregulated camping, deforestation, topsoil erosion, entire herds of cows suffering from leukemia, etc. But more frightening was my progressive awareness that all animal life was missing from the forest scenery. An experienced observer of wildlife, I spotted no animals, except frogs, toads, eight ducks, and one woodpecker and heard no nocturnal animal activity after twenty nights sleeping outdoors.

13. Mark M. Nelson, "As Shroud of Secrecy Lifts in Eastern Europe, Smog Shroud Emerges," *Wall Street Journal,* 122, no. 42, March 1, 1990, p. A1; quoted in Smith, *The Environmental Policy Paradox*, p. 231.

14. Richard Crampton, "The Intelligentsia, the Ecology and the Opposition in Bulgaria," *The World Today,* 46, no. 2, February 1990, p. 23.

15. Wierzbicki, "Entre le socialisme réel d'hier," p. 34.

16. Jaroslav Stoklasa, "L'état de l'environnement, la réforme économique et la coopération internationale," in Vinaver, *La crise de l'environment*, p. 69.

17. Ibid.

18. Roger Cans and Daniel Schneidermann: "Europe de l'est: la nature en ruines," *Le Monde*, March 14, 1990.

19. Ferenc Juhasz and Aldea Ragno, "The Environment in Eastern Europe: From Red to Green?" *The OECD Observer*, 181, April/May 1993, p. 34.

20. Nikolaï Popov, interviewed by Freddy Foscolo, "Pollution de l'esprit et de la nature," *Alternatives*, no. 4, December 1986, p. 34.

21. OECD, *Reforming the Economies*, pp. 109–114.

22. Stoklasa, "L'état de l'environnement," p. 71. Central and Eastern European observers are not always aware of similar social disturbances in the West, occurring in large industrial zones struck by recession and poor suburbs in the richest capitalist societies. There, "dehumanized" housing, unemployment and the marginalization of large immigrant populations are the obvious causes of all social problems. The same problems occur on Indian reservations in North America, in some of the world's most beautiful and protected natural environments. The distinguished Hungarian sociologist Elemer Hankiss presents very rich examples of the same phenomena in Central Europe, and shows how the communist regime worsened the situation by complicating social relations. This should not mean that the environmental dimension of the social problem in Central and Eastern Europe is negligible. Apparently the common denominator among all of these ghettos, suburbs, or industrial zones, worldwide, is a loss of social identity after an abrupt acculturation to a modern industrial society. This society can no longer provide enough means for subsistence and social advance. And no solace is to be found in cultural activities since the dominating culture—be it WASP, French bourgeois, or official Soviet culture—has put to shame all earlier reference. References to rural cultures and nature were often denied by the Marxist-Leninist tendency to put forward the proletarian, therefore urban, culture.

23. Gareth Porter and Janet Welsh Brown, *Global Environmental Politics* (Boulder, CO: Westview Press, 1996), p. 69.

24. Ibid.; Lars Bjorkbom, "Resolution of Environmental Problems: The Use of Diplomacy," in John E. Carroll, (ed.), *International Environmental Diplomacy: the Management and Resolution of Transfrontier Environmental Problems* (Cambridge: Cambridge University Press, 1988), p. 128; Harold Dovland, "Monitoring European Transboundary Air Pollution," *Environment*, 29, December 1987, p. 12.

25. Victor-Yves Ghebali, *La diplomatie de la détente: la CSCE, d'Helsinki à Vienne (1973–1989)* (Bruxelles: Bruylant, 1989), pp. 244–245 and V.-Y. Ghebali, "Les

trois dimensions de la coopération ecologique Est-Ouest," *Le Trimestre du Monde* (Paris: Observatoire des relations internationales, 3rd quarter, 1990), p. 61.

26. Ghebali, "Les trois dimensions de la coopération ecologique," p. 61.

27. Janusz Kindler, and Stephen F. Lintner, "An action plan to clean up the Baltic," *Environment*, 35, no. 8, 1993, p. 9, quoted by Gabrielle Rhebinder, "The European Union and the Environment in East and Central Europe," unpublished manuscript, p. 7. As far away as Alaska, the press warned that pollution from Soviet rivers was one of the causes of a decline in marine animal populations in the Arctic and northern seas. Misguided accusations of over-hunting fur-seals provoked tragic conflicts between uninformed environmentalists and aboriginal hunters who were forced to abandon century-old hunting traditions that provided annual incomes for entire villages. See my editorials and articles on the Pribylov islands in *The Kodiak Fisherman*, vol. 1, no. 2, 1987 and W.E. Butler, "Pollution Control in the Soviet Arctic," *International and Comparative Law Quarterly*, 21 (1989).

28. See Marcin Frybes' article (note 2) in this volume. Gorbachev himself, immediately upon his release from detention in August 1991, admitted that Western propaganda stations were indispensable during a political crisis. Therefore, efforts to scramble the signals were very inconsistent since Communist leaders themselves needed uncensored news for information concealed by rivals or their own inefficient subordinates. Western broadcasts penetrating through thousands of miles of borders fashioned the opinions of whoever understood German (in western Bohemia, in southwestern Slovakia near Bratislava, in western Hungary and in almost all of Slovenia), Italian (in Slovenia and across the Adriatic in Albania), Finish, Greek, or any other foreign language. in Carelia, Estonia, Albania, or Macedonia and Bulgaria, TV programs in English, French or German could penetrate from Finland or Greece subtitled rather than dubbed.

29. Timothy Garton Ash, "The Hungarian Lesson," *The New York Review of Books*, 32, no. 19, December 5, 1985, pp. 5–9, shows nevertheless that the "freedom of tone" and lax censorship coexisted with more insidious and effective forms of self-censorship and peer pressure within the intelligentsia.

30. The rest of this paragraph is based on Juraj Mesik, "Les organizations non-gouvernementales, hier, aujourd'hui et demain," in Vinaver, *La crise de l'environnement*, pp. 87–95.

31. J.-P. A. (initials), "La nature menacée, une nouvelle marge de contestation?" *Alternatives*, no. 4, December 1986, p. 33.

32. These paragraphs on the German Democratic Republic are based on the article by Hubertus Knabe, "Débats écologistes au sein des Eglises de R.D.A," *Alternatives*, no. 4, December 1986, p. 38.

33. It must not be forgotten how organized religion was always supervised—if not infiltrated—by the government "organs" throughout Warsaw Pact countries. As a tribute paid to the government for an extremely limited and fragile religious freedom, the antinuclear protest almost immediately became an essential feature of authorized religious activity under communism. Official declarations against NATO's nuclear arsenal, and workshops "for peace" were ritual in great religious events, not only inside the Soviet bloc but in any international conference with Central and Eastern European participants. This is how East German Protestant groups first became involved in antinuclear debates and were noticed on the international arena. Their new ecological activism could only make them more appealing to Western public opinion.

34. Barbara Jancar-Webster, "Eastern Europe and the Former Soviet Union," in Sheldon Kamieniecki, (ed.), *Environmental Politics in the International Arena. Movements*,

Parties, Organizations, and Policy (New York: State University of New York Press, 1993), p. 209.

35. Ibid.

36. Z.T. Wierzbicki, "Entre la crise et la catastrophe écologique," *Alternatives*, no. 4, December 1986, p. 41.

37. Ibid. and Jancar-Webster, "Eastern Europe and the Former Soviet Union," p. 209.

38. Ibid.

39. Wierzbicki, "Entre la crise," p. 41.

40. J.-P. A., "La nature menacée," p. 33.

41. Ibid. G. Dénes, one of the founders of the Danube Circle, provides an excellent history of Hungarian environmentalism in "Petite histoire des bleus," *Nouvelles Alternatives*, March 1987, no. 5, pp. 29–30.

42. Such were the arguments (to mention one example) of the underground Hungarian review *Hirmondo*, in 1986 (one of its significant articles, signed Szilard Remenyi, was published in French in the March 1987 issue of *Nouvelles Alternatives*, no. 5, pp. 39–40).

43. See for instance Jaroslav Blaha, "Un désastre écologique provisoire," *Nouvelles Alternatives*, March 1987, no. 5, pp. 33–35.

44. Barbara Jancar-Webster, "The Environment Attractor in the Former USSR: Ecology and Regional Change," in Ronnie D. Lipschutz, and Ken Conca, (eds.), *The State and Social Power in Global Environmental Politics* (New York: Columbia University Press, 1993), p. 175.

45. Jancar-Webster, "Eastern Europe and the Former Soviet Union," p. 209; and Campbell, Petra, "Ecoglasnost," unpublished manuscript.

46. St. Kervandzhiyev, "Du chlore sur le Danube," *Nouvelles Alternatives*, no. 10, June 1988, pp. 46–47.

47. Mesik, "Les organizations non-gouvernementales," p. 90.

48. Ibid. and Orbis Press Agency, Prague, press release no. 387/VI.

49. *Utne Reader*, no. 31, January/February 1989, p. 87 and Jancar-Webster, "Eastern Europe and the Former Soviet Union," p. 212.

50. Jancar-Webster, "Eastern Europe and the Former Soviet Union," p. 212.

51. Ibid., p. 213.

52. Ibid., and Mesik, "Les organizations non-gouvernementales," p. 91.

53. This entire paragraph is based on the analysis and personal recollections of Victor-Yves Ghebali, "Les trois dimensions de la coopération ecologique Est-Ouest," pp. 62–65.

54. Jancar-Webster, "Eastern Europe and the Former Soviet Union," p. 209.

55. "Les gens ne savent rien du nucléaire," *Alternatives*, no. 4, December 1986, p. 45; Jan Krivan, "Ecology as Deviance: the Case of Pavel Krivan," *Across Frontiers*, 2, nos. 3 and 4, pp. 15–18; Jancar-Webster, "Eastern Europe and the Former Soviet Union," p. 209.

56. Agnès Dorka, "Des Estoniens à Tchornobyl," *Nouvelles Alternatives*, March 1987, no. 5, p. 37.

57. Wierzbicki, "Entre la crise," pp. 44–45.

58. Nikolaï Popov interviewed by Freddy Foscolo, "Pollution de l'esprit et de la nature," *Alternatives*, no. 4, December 1986, p. 35. My translation from French.

59. Most of my data on Germany is drawn from the German local and national daily news media and especially Gilles Leroux, "Ecologisme et politique écologique en Allemagne," *Allemagne d'Aujourd'hui*, no. 145, Juillet–Septembre 1998, pp. 28–47.

60. See for example the documents provided by the Government of Macedonia (Skopje: 1996); also Center for Co-operation with the Economies in Transition, *Environmental Performance Reviews: Poland* (Paris: OECD, 1995), and Center for Co-operation with the Economies in Transition, *Environmental Performance Reviews: Bulgaria* (Paris: OECD, 1995), and the OECD web site for other countries.

61. http://www.oecd.org/sge/ccet/. Policy-making includes defining objectives, considering options and studying the financial implications and funding usually leading to legislative and fiscal action (such as the famous polluters-payers practice) and important law-enforcement strategies. During the entire process, OECD experts, civil servants, or representatives of the government of member nations (including all the ministers of the environment) participate in diplomatic meetings and international negotiations to define the objectives of all these concerted efforts, and to solve the inevitable legal and political problems resulting from this new form of East-West cooperation. The OECD homepage on the Internet will provide sufficient guidance on the organization's activities for the environment, and in other domains. The impressive amount of data and references includes online publications and a catalog of OECD publications. The latest news on the environmental front is usually reported in the online and printed periodical *Transition in Brief* (click on "newsletters") and through E-mail (for more information, contact Olga Savran, Environment Directorate, olga.savran@oecd.org).

62. "Environmental funds network," *Transition in Brief*, no. 6, winter 1997, p. 5. The Network's objectives are described in the following manner:

support the development of funds as environmental policy and financing mechanisms in transition economies; maximize the effectiveness and efficiency of the funds in financing environmental protection activities; strengthen the management and other human resource capacities of the funds; and facilitate dialogue and cooperation between the funds and with donors and international financial institutions.

63. "Providing environmental Goods and Services," *Transition in Brief*, no. 6, winter 1997, p. 4.

64. Ibid.

65. Ibid.

66. Ibid., see the article by Fianna Jesover, "OECD at the Aarhus Environment Ministerial[Conference]," http://www.oecd.org//sge/ccnm/news/outreach2/aarhus.htm

67. "Providing environmental Goods and Services," p. 4. On the other hand, we are warned that the environmental business sectors "in Bulgaria, Romania and the Russian Federation are somewhat less developed than in the Visegrad countries, while in the other New Independent States they remain in the embryonic stages."

68. Rhebinder, "The European Union," p. 9.

69. Ibid. p. 4; Parlement Européen, *Rapport sur l'état de l'environnement dans la communauté des Etats Indépendants, les états baltes et la Géorgie* (Paris: Sources d'Europe, 1994), p. 5.

70. Europe Information Service, *L'Europe de l'Est et l'environnement* (Bruxelles. Eis, 1994), p. 32, quoted in Rhebinder, "The European Union," pp. 4–5.

71. Europe Information Service, *L'Europe de l'Est*, p. 8; Europe Information Service, *Rapport sur les aspects environementaux du programme PHARE*, (Bruxelles: Eis, 1994); Rhebinder, "The European Union", p. 6.

72. See Center for Co-operation with the Economies in Transition, *Environmental Performance Reviews: Poland* (Paris: OECD, 1995), pp. 136–137.

73. Ibid., p. 136.

Environmental Security and Civil Society

74. Center for Co-operation with the Economies in Transition, *Environmental Performance Reviews: Poland* (Paris: OECD, 1995), Center for Co-operation with the Economies in Transition, *Environmental Performance Reviews: Bulgaria* (Paris: OECD, 1995), p. 128.

75. Ronnie Lipschutz, *Global Civil Society and Global Environmental Governance: The Politics of Nature from Place to Planet*, (New York: State University of New York Press, 1996), pp. 154–155. The Peace Corps has also invested many efforts for environmental education in the region.

76. Jancar-Webster, "Eastern Europe and the Former Soviet Union," p. 203 and Lipschutz, *Global Civil Society*, pp. 151–168. Gilles Leroux, "Ecologisme," pp. 28–47, presents a clear and concise anatomy of West German political groups and volunteer associations in the historic context of the past twenty years.

77. Ibid. The examples are simply too numerous to list here. One chapter on Hungary by Ronnie Lipschutz in his *Global Civil Society*, lists dozens of large foreign and local NGOs with international backing, for more than seventeen pages. Jokingly titled "Environmentalism in One Country," that lively and inspiring (although never idealistic) chapter is also one of the best descriptions of the many small but motivated and efficient grassroots organizations. In the present atmosphere of post-communist pessimism and cynicism, Ronnie Lipschutz presents an army of forgotten restorers of something that might resemble a civil society.

78. Europe Information Service, *l'Europe de l'Est*, p. 27; Europe Information Service, *Rapport sur les aspects environementaux*, art. 2, § 4; Rhebinder, "The European Union", pp. 6–7.

79. Europe Information Service, *Rapport sur les aspects environementaux*, p. 24; Rhebinder, "The European Union," 7.

80. Center for Co-operation with Economies in Transition, *Environmental Indicators: A Review of Selected Central and Eastern European Countries* (Paris: OECD, 1996). The OECD's figures and interpretations will be compared to those published in William F Martin, Ryukishi Imai, and Helga Steeg, *Energiesicherheit im globalen Kontext. Ein Bericht an die Trilaterale Kommission*, Arbeitspapiere zur Internationalen Politik, no. 97 (Bonn: Forschungsinstitut der Deutschen Gesellschaft für Auswärtige Politik e. V, Februar 1997).

81. Lipschutz, *Global Civil Society*, p. 130.

82. All election results in this paragraph are based on the wide variety of sources collected in Edith Lhomel and Thomas Schreiber, (eds.), *L'Europe Centrale et Orientale* (Yearbook of the CEDUCEE), (Paris: La Documentation Française, 1992); and Georges Mink, *Europe de l'Est, la transition* (no. 636 of *Problèmes politiques et sociaux, dossiers d'actualité mondiale*), (Paris: La Documentation Française, July 6 1990), pp. 31–33.

83. Jancar-Webster, "Eastern Europe and the Former Soviet Union," p. 215.

84. Ibid.

85. Mesik, "Les organizations non-gouvernementales," pp. 90–91.

86. See J. Kakonen, "The Concept of Security: From Limited to Comprehensive," paper presented at the 25th Annual International Peace Research Conference, Groningen 3–7 July 1990 and Matthias Finger, "The Military, Nation, State and Environment," *The Ecologist*, 21, no. 5, September/October 1991. Gareth Porter, "Environmental Security as a National Security Issue," *Current History*, 94, no. 592, May 1995, presents the debate in the context of U.S. foreign policy-making and, contrary to Finger, defends the timeliness of a defense and foreign policy based on the concept of environmental security. The seriousness and extent of this debate in North American academic and political circles is reflected in Alexander Carius and Andreas

Kraemer, "Complexificação of Environmental Security," in William Burros, (ed.), *Global Security Beyond 2000: Global Population Growth, Migration, and Transnational Organized Crime*, Nov 2–3, 1995, Pittsburgh, PA, USA, conference report, (Pittsburgh: Center for West European Studies, University of Pittsburgh, 1996), and in Simon Dalby, "Security, Modernity, Ecology: The Dilemmas of Post-Cold War Security Discourse," *Alternatives: Social Transformation and Humane Governance*, 17, no. 1, 1992; Norman Myers, *Ultimate Security: The Environmental Basis of Political Stability*. New York: Norton, 1993; G. Pris, (ed.), *Threats without Enemies: Facing Environmental Insecurity* (London: Earthscan, 1993). Extensive bibliographic materials will be found in all those titles. Last but not least, two of the most influential pioneers of the notion of environmental security, with sometimes conflicting interpretations, the visionary Thomas F. Homer-Dixon and the more self-critical Daniel Deudney, must be recognized for their regular and abundant contributions to a variety of publications.

87. Ignacio Ramonet, *Géopolitique du chaos*, (Paris: Galilee, 1997); Richard K. Ashley, "Untying the Sovereign State: A Double Reading of the Anarchy Problématique," *Millennium: Journal of International Studies*, no. 17, 1988, pp. 227–262; Michael T. Klare, "The New 'Rogue State' Doctrine," *The Nation* (May 8 1995); Pierre Lellouche, *Le nouveau monde. De l'ordre de Yalta au désordre des nations* (Paris: Grasset, 1992).

88. Robert Kaplan, "The Coming Anarchy," *Atlantic Monthly*, 273, no. 2, February 1994, pp. 44–76.

89. The emergence of the concept of environmental security, its relevance, and its influence today is the subject of Gareth Porter's "Environmental Security as a National Security Issue," *Current History*, 94, no. 592, May 1995.

90. Marie-José Domestici-Med (ed.), *Aide humanitaire internationale: un consensus conflictuel* (Paris: Economica, 1996), p. 343. This title includes the proceedings of one of the conferences that helped advance the right to intervene. Better known to academic, legal and political circles was the conference organized by Bernard Kouchner and Mario Bettati in 1987 "Droit et morale humanitaire." (See Bernard Kouchner and Mario Bettati (eds.), *Le devoir d'ingérance* (Paris: Denoël, 1987); and Bernard Kouchner, *Le devoir d'ingérance: mutation de l'ordre international* (Paris: Odile Jacob, 1996).

91. Domestici-Med, *Aide humanitaire internationale*, p. 343.

92. Ibid.

93. Claude Chabrol, "Préface" in Bachelet, *L'ingérence écologique* (Paris: Editions Frison-Roche, 1995), pp. 11–12 (my translation).

94. Kouchner and Bettati, *Le devoir d'ingérance*, p. 22, quoted in Hours, Bernard, *L'idéologie humanitaire ou le spectacle de l'altérité perdue* (Paris: L'Harmattan, 1997), p. 148.

95. Marie-Christine Delpal, *Politique extérieure et diplomatie morale: le droit d'ingérance en question* (Paris: Fondation pour les études de défense nationale, 1993), p. 114; see Bernard Hours, *L'idéologie humanitaire* and Domestici-Med, *Aide humanitaire internationale*, p. 343 and the paper by Régis Debray included in the same volume.

96. Lipschutz, *Global Civil Society*, pp. 163–164.

97. See OECD, *The Environment Industry and Markets in Selected Central and Eastern European Countries* (Paris: OECD, 1995); and The Ecologists' Movement of Macedonia–DEM, *Towards Sustainable Agriculture in the Republic of Macedonia* (Skopje: DEM, 1998).

98. OECD analysts discuss only a few examples of the amazing bureaucratic and financial obstacles to small businesses at http://www.oecd.org/sge/ccnm/

news/trans8/russia/fosterin.htm. With the exception of the former East German *Länder* such occurrences are unfortunately widespread in transition economies.

99. The possibilities of using environmental action as an outlet is discussed at length in Daniel Deudney, "Global Environmental Rescue and the Emergence of World Domestic Politics," in Lipschutz and Conca, *The State and Social Power*, pp. 280–305 (see "Green Culture as Earth Nationalism," pp. 293–301). Deudney being one of the pioneers of environmental security, this offers great hope about a possible evolution of this theory toward less conflictual representations.

Chapter 10

The Genesis of NATO Enlargement and of War "over" Kosovo
Hall Gardner

INTRODUCTION
The decision to enlarge the North Atlantic Treaty Organization came about as a result of the geostrategic interplay between a newly unified Germany, the former Soviet Union/Russia near disaggregation, a resurgent United States, and the newly liberated states of eastern Europe. This geostrategic interplay consisted of:

1. The effort of the United States to sustain NATO credibility, if not its very legitimacy, in the face of the collapse of the Warsaw Pact. Ostensibly, NATO not only had to enlarge its membership, it also had to go "out of area or out of business" if it was to justify its very existence.

2. Essentially German interests in forming a secure buffer from the potential for "instability" expected to emanate from the "east" in the aftermath of Yugoslav and then Soviet collapse.

3. Interrelated American interests in "double containing" the potential political-military capabilities of the newly unified Germany and to forestall Bonn/Berlin from pursuing the "re-nationalization" of German defenses.

4. The fact that many eastern European states hoped to draw the United States and NATO into protecting their newly achieved political and economic independence against the feared possibility of a *revanchist* Russia, if not the largely unspoken fear of a revisionist Germany.

The debate as to whether NATO should enlarge into east-central Europe arose in early 1990 in the midst of discussions over German unification. The latter step had raised the crucial question as to the appropriate relationship between the newly unified Germany and NATO. Political pressure to enlarge the alliance was then given an extra push following the October 1991 *Krakow Declaration* by Poland, Czechoslovakia, and Hungary.

By mid-1993, German elites began to urge NATO to enlarge its membership into Central Europe. As the war in Bosnia heated up, President Clinton announced in January 1994 that enlargement was no longer a question of "if," but "how" and "when." Concurrently, "out of area" actions taken by NATO during the war in Bosnia in the former Yugoslavia—coupled with perceived weaknesses of the UN as a security organization—then accelerated demands for enlargement. By March 1999, Poland, the Czech Republic, and Hungary entered NATO as "full" members. Not entirely haphazardly that same month, NATO engaged in an "out of area" and "humanitarian" intervention against Serbia in response to the latter's campaign of "ethnic cleansing" in Kosovo-Metohia (the official Serbian name for the province)—following U.S.-NATO threats to Serbia since December 1992.

GERMAN UNIFICATION OR CONFEDERATION?

Throughout the Cold War, the United States and the Soviet Union competed for the political, economic, and military allegiance of both West and East Germany. Each side claimed it would support a unified Germany, but on its respective terms. In general, Moscow's propaganda sought a unified, but "neutral" Germany; American propaganda sought a unified Germany, but one that would remain in NATO. As the Cold War dragged on, and as the two sides could not reach a possible compromise involving the formation of a new Germanic confederation, it ironically appeared that Washington and Moscow had forged a tacit agreement: A unified Germany was not really in the interest of either "superpower." At the same time, however, neither side could ultimately stop the process driven by Bonn—and *indirectly* backed by NATO.

In just two years after German unification in 1989, Moscow's worst fears had come true. The collapse of Soviet controls over East Germany, the keystone for Soviet domination over the entire region, not only resulted in the collapse of the Warsaw Pact as had generally been expected, but also, by late 1991, the collapse of Soviet controls over European Russia and central Asia. Soviet disaggregation thus resulted in the independence of the Baltic states, Belarus, and Ukraine, as well as former Soviet republics in central Asia. Moreover, the Russian Federation found itself confronted with a significant number of potential secessionist movements, most notably, that in Chechnya.

From the American perspective, it was feared that a united Germany would shift the geopolitical and economic equilibrium in Europe. As a potential political and economic rival to the United States, a unified Germany could increasingly assert its hegemony over much of eastern Europe. While the loss of Soviet controls over eastern Europe appeared, for the most part, to represent a positive gain for the United States, the EU, and Germany itself, German unification could also mean that Germany might act upon threats to leave NATO altogether. Accordingly, a united Germany might seek out a *Sondersweg* or its own "special way," and engage in actions that were possibly contrary to the interests of the United States and the European Union.

It was feared (correctly or incorrectly) that Bonn/Berlin could possibly renounce its membership in NATO and forge a separate pact with Moscow over the heads of the eastern European states in between. Whatever the case, Germany's future allegiance appeared uncertain.

As negotiations over German unification intensified in the period 1989–1990, Washington argued vehemently that a "neutral" Germany outside of NATO might not necessarily be a pacific Germany. The fact that Bonn had yet to sign a formal peace treaty with its neighbors, and that it continued to claim its 1937 borders, raised fears that it could use political and economic pressure to regain lost territories in Poland and in Czechoslovakia. (Never publicly stated, Germany could also pressure to obtain Russian Kaliningrad, formerly German Königsberg.) Washington thus argued that a united Germany-in-NATO would prevent Bonn from becoming a potential threat to its neighbors. As the possibility of a renewed German "threat" against the Soviet Union/Russia appeared greater than the possibility of German-Soviet/Russian alliance, Gorbachev began to accede to American demands to keep a unified Germany within NATO. The Soviet leadership, however, demanded in return that specific limitations be placed upon both NATO and German military capabilities.

German unification under a federal West German model was not, however, the only option. A feasible alternative (which would have had to resist the political pressures of pan-Germanism by means of effective leadership) would have been to unify Germany upon a confederal basis.[1] Prior to the rule of Chancellor Otto von Bismarck, Germany had, in fact, been a *loose* confederation; it need not automatically be presumed that a *tighter* confederal model would necessarily break down into intra-German conflict in post-1945 circumstances. Moreover, such a confederation between West Germany and East Germany *in the process of democratization* may have better served the long-term interests of the United States and the Soviet Union/Russia, if not that of the Germans themselves. The option of a confederal Germany had been briefly considered by the German Länder themselves in the aftermath of World War II, but abandoned as the Cold War heated up by 1947.[2] Soviet premier Nikita Khrushchev then supported the concept of the two Germanys plus the "free" city of West Berlin in the late 1950s and early 1960s, but the proposal was not given serious consideration (even as an initial bargaining position) by either the American or West German leaderships. The proposal was only vaguely supported by French leader Charles de Gaulle.

The concept of unifying Germany on a confederal basis was then resurrected in the 1970s when the two Germanys began to reach out for a *modus vivendi*. It was raised again in 1989–1990 but fell upon deaf ears. A leading proponent of German confederalism, novelist and Nobel Prize winner Günter Grass argued in 1990, "A confederation of two German states dovetails better with the current process of European integration than does a single powerful state, since an integrated Europe will itself be confederate in structure and must therefore transcend the traditional divisions into nations." Grass added that a German confederation could become a model to emulate "wherever one political entity has aggressively established borders or seeks to extend them at the expense of another."[3] He then mentioned Korea, Ireland, Cyprus, and the Middle East, as examples.

A German confederation could have also served as a model for Mikhail Gorbachev's New Union Treaty and efforts to formulate a new relationship between Moscow as the center of a "New Union" and each of the former Soviet republics. A confederal Germany could also have shown the way toward new arrangements for Czechoslovakia, prior to the peaceful breakup of the latter in 1993—if not for the former Yugoslavia which did not break-up peacefully. Perhaps a German confederation could even have served as a model for a possible confederation between China and Taiwan. In regard to NATO-Soviet relations, a confederal Germany could possibly have permitted NATO and the Soviet Union/Russia to forge overlapping or conjoint security guarantees for the entire eastern European region.[4]

In regard to overall European security, the formation of a confederal Germany could have helped lend greater consideration to a number of divergent proposals that were made in the period 1989–1991. Vaclav Havel— at least initially—argued that a reassociated Germany tied temporarily to NATO, and then ultimately tied to an all-European system of security, would have been in the enlightened self-interest of the United States and the Soviet Union; Havel called for a Europe "capable of defending itself" that would not need the protection of the two "superpowers." Zbigniew Brzezinski proposed membership of Germany in both NATO and the Warsaw Pact. Membership of Germany in NATO with "associate" status for East Germany in the Warsaw Pact was another possibility.[5] Membership of the Soviet Union in NATO was likewise proposed.[6]

An additional option could have been considered, at least when Mikhail Gorbachev was still in power: UN blue helmets could have been deployed in eastern Germany and then into the other states of eastern Europe at the same moment that Soviet forces pulled out. This would have provided reassurance to the Soviet Union that neither Germany nor NATO would remilitarize its newly unified eastern Länder by means of a "forward deployment." At the same time, the deployment of UN blue helmets would have helped to secure these countries in their transition to democracy, while West Germany remained "double contained" in NATO.

The fact that the German leadership opted for unification under a West German federal model, however, resulted in an entirely different regional and global geostrategic calculus—and a radical reconsideration of American and NATO strategy in regard to Europe as a whole. Here, the Bush Administration and the Kohl government feared that a confederal approach to the German question would open a destabilizing constitutional debate that could possibly, although not necessarily, lead to a "neutral" Germany. The Basic Law provided Germany with two alternative paths to unification. The first option under Article 146 envisioned all-German elections which could then create an

The Genesis of NATO Enlargement and of War "over" Kosovo 155

entirely new form of government with a new constitution. The second option under Article 23 would urge East Germany to dissolve into its former Länder which in turn would be brought directly into the Federal Government without a significant change in the system of West German governance. The Bush administration supported the less risky path. As Brent Scowcroft put it: "Kohl (and we) strongly preferred Article 23, which avoided the possibility of changes to the West German system, especially if the SPD, east and west, won control of the constitutional assembly and sent the new Germany down a neutral (and possibly more socialist) path. This was a real danger."[7]

At the same time, the Kohl government worked out a compromise with its critics. In the effort to forge solidarity in the coalition over Article 23, Kohl overrode the advice of his Defense Minister Gerhard Stoltenberg who had pressed for full German membership in NATO. In a joint statement, West German Chancellor Helmut Kohl and Foreign Minister Hans Dietrich Genscher proposed the demilitarization of East Germany. Washington, however, refused the latter option and continued to insist, with the support of Kohl, that NATO "jurisdiction" (in the words of U.S. Secretary of State James Baker) reach into the eastern region of Germany, despite Soviet objections.

German "success" in achieving unification consequently lent support to general demands for "national independence" throughout the world—as opposed to more compromising positions for "confederation." German unification, for example, helped reinspire Japanese aspirations to regain the Kurile Islands.[8] Although Germany cannot be blamed for the outbreak of the hostilities, it was Bonn that initially—contrary to the policies of the EU, UN, and the United States who then changed their policy in response—gave diplomatic support to Slovenian and Croatian demands for independence. Germany overtly supported demands for Ukrainian and Kazakh independence, in addition to that of the Baltic states—after the ratification of the March 1991 "two plus four treaty." Soviet leader Mikhail Gorbachev considered German steps in late 1991 toward recognizing the former Soviet republics negligent in that the latter had yet to clearly demarcate their borders prior to independence, thus risking prospects of conflict in the not-so-long term.

Soviet Collapse and NATO Enlargement

Faced with the NATO's military, political-economic, as well as ideological, superiority, Mikhail Gorbachev could only cut his losses by means of a traditional Russian retrenchment. (Soviet tank defenses of eastern Europe, for example, had become obsolete in the face of NATO and American military-technological innovation.) Gorbachev's 7 December 1988 UN speech promised significant unilateral weapons cuts and troop withdrawals. Moreover, East Germany was largely bankrupt; Moscow could no longer sudsidize the country.

Ironically, however, Gorbachev's strategy of retrenchment became increasingly regarded by the Bush administration as "threatening" the NATO alliance. While the Soviet "threat" had to a large extent served throughout the

Cold War to sustain alliance cohesion against both *external* and *internal* Communist challenges to NATO members, the sudden reversal of Soviet policy upset U.S. policy-makers. By significantly reducing troops and forces throughout eastern Europe, Gorbachev seemed to be beckoning West Germany to seek out unification on Soviet terms, that is, as a neutral state outside NATO. Gorbachev's geostrategic gambit seemed to be aimed at splitting the alliance, taking advantage of Washington's ostensible weaknesses and inter-allied differences.

The latter pessimistic scenario depended, however, upon the assumption that Washington could not ultimately forge an entente with Moscow—if not bring the latter into the alliance itself. Yet rather than reaching out for an entente or alliance with Moscow, the Bush administration elected to counter Gorbachev's diplomatic offensive and to "play offense" by supporting the "liberalization" process in eastern Europe. As former President George Bush put it: "We must take the offensive. We cannot just be seen as reacting to yet another Gorbachev move. *We need to do it to keep public opinion behind the Alliance*. Maybe eastern Europe is it—get in there in his end zone. Not to stir up revolution, but we're right on human rights, democracy, and freedom."[9] (Emphasis mine.) The United States thus continued its efforts to "get" into the Soviet "end zone" as a means to "keep public opinion behind the Alliance" at the same time that Germany continued to press for unification. As time proceeded, the option of enlarging NATO jurisdiction beyond Germany itself became the preferred option—despite Washington's initial denials to the contrary.

It was in March 1989 that Gorbachev renounced the Brezhnev doctrine, and promised that Moscow would not intervene in Hungarian affairs. Yet, the decision to renounce the Brezhnev doctrine did not immediately result in the collapse of the Warsaw Pact. As Gorbachev proceeded with Soviet reforms, eastern European states continued their efforts to take advantage of glasnost and perestroika. Between August and September 1989, Polish Premier Tadeusz Mazowiecki vowed to keep Poland in the Warsaw Pact, but urged the Soviet Union to respect its internal political and economic order. Hungary then declared itself a free nation on 23 October of that year. While the Hungarian Democratic Forum argued for a gradual shift toward neutrality, it was stated that Hungary would remain in the Warsaw Pact's political structures but withdraw from its military structure.

Significantly, the step-by-step removal of Soviet troops from Hungary would ultimately open the door to conflict in the former Yugoslavia (and open the supply of arms to Croatia). As Serbia and Croatia would no longer feel the threat of possible Soviet intervention—a contingency feared ever since Marshall Tito split with Stalin and broke out of the Soviet orbit—the two could more "safely" go to war without the apparent threat of outside intervention. Once the war in Bosnia erupted, however, the Soviet military presence on Hungarian bases would be not-so-gradually replaced by a NATO presence—prior to any formal offer of "full" Hungarian membership in

NATO. (By 1992, NATO would also forge close ties with Turkey's ally, Albania, which had not been a member of the Warsaw Pact.) While a Soviet interventionism had been feared throughout the Cold War, few in the former Yugoslavia expected NATO to intervene in the post-Cold War period.

Concurrently, the "velvet revolutions" in east-central Europe took place as West Germany debated the appropriate process and format of unification. Despite its 1970 nonaggression treaty with Poland, and agreements with Czechoslovakia, debate revolved around the fact that Bonn had not signed formal peace treaties and continued to sustain its claims to its 1937 borders. Tensions between the Social Democrats and Chancellor Kohl's Center Right coalition soon emerged over the question of the German populations living in Danzig/Gdansk as well as in Stettin/Szczecin, in addition to questions related to pre-1948 German property rights in Poland and Czechoslovakia.

THE RAZING OF THE BERLIN WALL

The Berlin Wall was razed in November 1989. Chancellor Kohl seized the moment to reunify Germany as a federal state—despite his previous support for confederation, or West-East "reassociation." Neither Washington nor Moscow (nor NATO allies, England and France) could stop West Germany as it took steps to unify the country. (In December 1989, François Mitterrand had visited East German leader Eric Honnecker, angering Bonn; Margaret Thatcher admitted that her steps to slow down or halt German steps toward unification had failed miserably.)

Chancellor Kohl's 28 November 1989 "Ten Point Program for Overcoming the Division of Germany and Europe," which originally envisioned the establishment of confederative structures, suddenly transformed into a plan for outright annexation (the latter plan not shared with the allies). Steps toward unification were based upon the West German federal model—in what U.S. Secretary of State James Baker called "the largest leveraged buy-out in history."[10] Point five of Chancellor Kohl's plan had envisioned the development of "confederative structures between the two states in Germany with a view to creating a federation. But this presupposes the election of a democratic government in the GDR." Here, Bonn was certain that democratic elections would overthrow the East German Communist party (SED)—opening the door to absorption by West Germany.

Point ten then stated: "Reunification—that is regaining national unity—remains the political goal of the Federal Government. We are grateful that once again we have received support in this matter from our allies in the declaration after the NATO summit meeting in Brussels in May." The May 1989 Brussels summit had stated that "(t)he Wall dividing Berlin is an unacceptable symbol of the division of Europe. We seek a state of peace in Europe in which the German people regain its unity through self-determination." In effect, in addition to helping to transform Soviet policy, NATO's May 1989 Brussels Summit provided the aegis for unification under a federal West German model. The May 1989 Brussels Declaration had likewise permitted Moscow to save face by promising to strengthen the Conference on Security and Cooperation in Europe (CSCE) and in return for accepting German membership in NATO.[11] Consequently, one of the major factors resulting in the Soviet decision to fold up the Warsaw Pact was based, at least in part, from the significant change in NATO's strategic concept—despite fears generated by German unification.

The possibility of a confederal model (that may not necessarily have led to a "special way" between capitalism and communism, as proposed by the then East German Communist party [SED], as well as by some intellectuals of the East German New Forum) was thus toyed with, but ultimately ruled out by Chancellor Kohl. On 1 February 1990, East German Premier Hans Modrow called for a new German "confederation" and neutrality. West German Foreign Minister Hans Dietrich Genscher responded that West Germany would remain in NATO, but that East Germany should become a demilitarized zone in order to protect the security interests of the USSR. Washington, however, opposed a totally demilitarized eastern Germany and worked diligently to forge an agreement with Moscow that would provide NATO "jurisdiction" (in James Baker's terms) over all of Germany. The Baker plan and the "two plus four" agreement promised not to deploy "foreign forces" at least initially, in the eastern region of the new Germany

Although Washington had yet to finalize its plans for NATO's enlargement into east-central Europe, that option was already in the air. Russian sources argue persuasively that key Western leaders gave verbal promises not to enlarge NATO beyond the eastern Länder of Germany. On 2–3 February 1990, both German Foreign Minister Hans Dietrich Genscher and Secretary of State James Baker stated their agreement that the United States had no interest in extending NATO's area of defense and security eastward. On 9 February 1990, James Baker is reported as telling Gorbachev that the consultations and discussions in regard to the "two plus four" mechanism should guarantee that the reunification of Germany would not lead to an eastern extension of NATO's military organization. English Prime Minister John Major is reported as telling Marshal Iazov that he did not envision the possibility that eastern European countries would belong to NATO. German Chancellor Helmut Kohl is quoted as telling Mikhail Gorbachev on 10 February 1990 that he did not expect NATO to enlarge its field of action.[12]

The 11–13 February Ottawa Agreements on German unification set troop levels; between 18 and 24 February, both Poland and Hungary backed the Genscher plan. Likewise in February 1990, Foreign Minister Gyula Horn suggested that Hungary play a nonmilitary role in NATO, at roughly the same time that talks on a complete Soviet withdrawal from Hungary began to break down. Foreign Minister Horn did not endorse withdrawal from the Warsaw Pact, but proposed that the two defense organizations could eventually merge—a proposal rejected by then NATO Secretary-General Manfred Wörner. As Europe could eventually move to a new system of collective security, "it therefore could not be excluded that Hungary could become a member of NATO's political wings." Assistant Secretary of State Lawrence Eagleburger jumped on the idea of a Hungarian role in NATO as "revolutionary . . . the world is changing. NATO will have to change with it."

On 12 June 1990, Gorbachev asked East Germany to maintain associate membership in the Warsaw Pact—a proposal rejected by West Germany. In July 1990, at its London Declaration, NATO invited Mikhail Gorbachev and Warsaw Pact leaders to address the North Atlantic Council and to establish relations with NATO. The latter likewise began to emphasize the political importance of the CSCE—a policy strongly supported by German Foreign Minister Hans Dietrich Genscher and Czechoslovak President Vaclav Havel. NATO's London Declaration also announced a dramatic change in strategy, moving away from a "forward defense" and, *where appropriate*, "towards a reduced forward presence." In addition, NATO sought to modify its "flexible response" doctrine to reflect a reduced reliance on nuclear weapons. The change in NATO strategy helped to grant Gorbachev more flexibility in dealing with Warsaw Pact states, and led Gorbachev to accept all of Germany in NATO. NATO's new strategy, at least as it appeared at the time, helped to strengthen Gorbachev's hand against Soviet hardliners, that is, before the alleged "coup attempt" in August 1991 would force him from power.[13]

The German Unity treaty was signed on 31 August 1990; it promised that Germany would not sustain any territorial claims to territories belonging to Poland or to the USSR, but claims to property rights were largely left unresolved; by September 1990, East Germany formally left the Warsaw Pact. On the 12 September, the Treaty on the Final Settlement on Germany was signed (the "two plus four" treaty) which confirmed the final nature of the frontiers and terminated four power rights and responsibilities in Berlin and Germany as whole, and asserted that Germany possessed no "territorial claims" whatsoever against other states. (The "two plus four" accord was jokingly referred to as the "one and one half" or "one and one-third" agreement in that an indebted East Germany could hardly be considered a fully sovereign state and due to the fact that the four powers, the United States, the United Kingdom, France, and the USSR, had relatively little say in the agreement. In addition, in an effort to influence the question of German borders [in regard to the Oder-Neisse line], for example, Poland unsuccessfully petitioned to be permitted to participate in unification discussions.)

On the 13 September, the German and Soviet Treaty on Good Neighborliness, Partnership and Cooperation was signed. The latter raised fears of a separate German-Soviet deal at the expense of the eastern European states in-between, despite the promises of the "two plus four" agreement to confirm existing borders. Not-entirely-exaggerated fears of Soviet-German complicity at the expense of eastern Europe—and of the European Union—may have provided an additional impetus to enlarge NATO beyond the borders of eastern Germany alone into east-central Europe, working to rule out viable alternatives.[14]

The 14 November 1990 Polish-German treaty guaranteed the sanctity of the Polish-German border, as did the "two plus four" treaty. The fact that the Polish-German treaty was, however, protested by a group claiming to represent Silesian Germans appeared to indicate that the question was not entirely resolved, at least in regard to property claims. (The 1992 and 1997 German-Czech treaties would likewise be protested by groups representing Sudeten Germans.)

On 21 November 1990, in Paris, a joint declaration of twenty-two NATO and Warsaw Pact countries declared that each country was free to become a member of the alliance of its choice. Then, in the midst of rumors of a coup d'état, Soviet Black Berets moved into Vilnius to prevent Lithuanian secession in December 1990—raising fears of the newly liberated eastern European states. On 31 January 1991, the Hungarian Parliament voted to join the North Atlantic Council as an "associate" nonvoting member. The resolution, however, stated that Hungary was neutral and that it had no interest in joining NATO's military structure. The Czechoslovak Premier Marian Calfa likewise stated that Prague would seek "some form of cooperation with NATO."

On 11 February 1991, Gorbachev notified heads of state that the Warsaw Pact would disband by 1 April and tried to keep the pact alive as a potential political format, yet failed. Poland and the Czech Republic signed a military accord after disbanding. In spirit with the Warsaw Pact treaty, former members called for a transition to all-European structures of defense under the control of the CSCE. Since 1954, the Soviet Union had called for a General European Treaty of Collective Security Organization in Europe, which would supplant both NATO and the Warsaw Pact. The latter option, generally regarded by the West as a ploy to undermine NATO, had been written into the 1955 Warsaw Pact. The Warsaw treaty had provided for its own dissolution, but only once an inclusive system of security was implemented for all of Europe.

On 21 March, Vaclav Havel, who had strongly supported an all-European security framework and the dissolution of both blocs, not-so-ironically became the very first head of a Warsaw Pact country to visit NATO headquarters in response to the July 1990 open invitation. Havel did state that Czechoslovakia might someday enter NATO, but that the time was not yet quite right for such a move. On 31 March 1991, Tass warned former Warsaw Pact states that they would jeopardize Soviet security interests if they joined NATO. In addition to opposing the modernization of NATO short-range nuclear weapons, a policy dubbed "Genscherism" (and resented by the White House), Genscher also stated that it would be unwise for eastern European states to try to become part of NATO.[15]

On 3 October, in part as a response to the attempted coup against Mikhail Gorbachev in August, a joint German-American declaration announced the formation of the North Atlantic Cooperation Council (NACC). Urged primarily by Germany as a means to reassure Moscow, the latter represented a new forum for NATO and former Soviet bloc states, including Russia, to discuss security issues. (At that time, France opposed NACC, as Paris wanted to strengthen security dialogue within the CSCE where the United States was not predominant.) By 5–6 October 1991, however, citing the dangers caused by the breakup of Yugoslavia, and continuing political-economic instability in the Soviet Union, Poland, Czechoslovakia, and Hungary stated their intent, in the *Kracow Declaration*, to act in union for a united Europe, and asserted that their security would be best served by integration with NATO.

The Rome 1991 Summit of 7–9 November declassified NATO's new summitry, and then formally introduced the NACC. In that same month, President George Bush ruled out NATO intervention in the former Yugoslavia—in the false expectation that the EU could handle the crisis diplomatically. A crisis arose as Germany broke ranks with EU and UN policy by formally recognizing the independence of Slovenia and Croatia in December 1991—without establishing a means to guarantee the rights of Serb and Muslim minorities in Croatia. The latter fact consequently worked to internationalize the civil war in the former Yugoslavia, and worked to widen the war between Serbia and Croatia into Bosnia. Both the EU and the United States initially refused to recognize the break-away republics for fear the war would spread to Bosnia, Kosovo, and Macedonia. (The United States waited to extend formal recognition to the republics until UN peacekeepers arrived in February 1992.)

In December 1991, Boris Yeltsin sent a letter to NATO declaring Russian interest in joining the Atlantic Alliance, although no formal application was filed. Concern, however, was raised that once new members entered, NATO consensus would collapse. The issue of how to sustain NATO consensus-building if new members, and Russia in particular, entered, tended to stall the enlargement process altogether, at least until mid-1994. Concurrently, despite Russian interest in joining, it appeared that NATO, if it were to enlarge, possessed a definite preference for the membership of states in east-central Europe.[16]

By February 1992, Pentagon Defense Planning Guidance (DPG) documents were leaked to the *New York Times*. These documents warned of a possible Resurgent Emergent Global Threat (REGT) should a *revanchist* Russia (perhaps linked to a resurgent China) arise from the ashes of Soviet collapse. To counter such a threat, the documents then advocated "extend(ing) to east and central European nations security commitments similar to those extended to Saudi Arabia, Kuwait, and other Gulf states."[17] Ironically enough, this hard-line policy statement stopped short of advocating the far more intensive policy of NATO enlargement.

Then in May 1992, a subsequent "politically correct" version of the Pentagon's DPG was published. This latter draft toned down the language of the February draft: Germany, Japan, and India were no longer deemed potential military threats as stated in the February 1992 DPG draft! Instead of warning of REGT, the May draft called for a "democratic partnership" with the new Russia. The latter document would represent a foretaste of the Partnership for Peace (originally called Partnership for Peacekeeping), said to be developed in SHAPE headquarters in March–April 1993.

Its importance perhaps overlooked at the time, Albania was the first former Communist country to ask for NATO membership. In a visit to NATO headquarters on 16 December 1992, Albanian President Sali Berisha demanded a peacekeeping force in Kosovo. NATO defense ministers declared their intention to step up NATO's contribution to peacekeeping forces in Bosnia-Herzegovina. NATO backed a UN decision to send peacekeepers to the Former Yugoslav Republic of Macedonia (FYROM); it also favored a UN presence in Kosovo and called for further preventive measures by the UN or CSCE. NACC members were ready to consider peacekeeping on a case-by-case basis under UN or CSCE auspices.[18] The deployment of UN war-preventive forces in Kosovo, however, would have required that Kosovo return to its pre-1989 status as an autonomous region—a status illegally taken away by Slobodan Milosevic in 1989 upon his rise to power.[19] Serbia, backed by Russia, refused to place Kosovo under a UN protectorate, as demanded by moderate Kosovar leader, Ibrahim Rugova; at the same time, the United States did not resolutely sustain diplomatic pressure over time on this issue. Nor did Washington work closely with Moscow on this issue—a crisis soon recognized to be a greater potential threat to the collective interests of NATO than Bosnia itself.

While Washington took a backseat behind the EU and UN in regard to the ongoing war in Bosnia, Acting Secretary of State Lawrence Eagleburger warned Serbian leader Milosevic in a private letter in late December 1992, that "in the event of conflict in Kosovo caused by Serbian action, the United States will be prepared to employ military force against the Serbs in Kosovo and in Serbia proper."[20] Secretary of State Warren Christopher and President Clinton publicly repeated this overly general warning in February 1993 and December 1994, as pressure built for greater U.S. and NATO involvement in Bosnia. By June 1993 the United States committed troops to the first UN war preventive force, UN Preventive Deployment (UNPREDEP) in FYROM. UNPREDEP was consequently deployed before any significant conflict broke out in an effort to contain Serbia and to prevent the war from spreading to this former Yugoslav republic—if not to preclude Moscow from unilaterally deploying its forces in FYROM, which had asked for Russian supports.

In March 1993 Volker Rühe, the German defense minister stated, at an Alistair Buchau lecture, that NATO must not be a "closed shop." Then, on 21 May 1993, in a speech at the North Atlantic Assembly in Berlin, he stated that "the accession of new partners is not so much a question of 'if' as one of 'how' and 'when'"—almost the same words President Clinton would use in January 1994.[21] Yet while Rühe pushed for the membership of east-central European states (that surrounded the newly unified Germany) in NATO, German Foreign Minister Klaus Kinkel advocated a "go slow" approach, much like his American counterpart, Secretary of State Warren Christopher.

German Chancellor Helmut Kohl feared Russia's reaction and the possible effect NATO enlargement might have on German-Russian relations as well as on his personal relationship with Boris Yeltsin.

Needless to say, Poland, the Czech Republic, Hungary, and Slovakia were first proposed for "full" NATO membership by Germany in 1993, at roughly the same time that the Partnership for Peace was being formulated by the Pentagon. A newly unified Germany, whose sovereignty was to a large extent "double contained" by its Basic Law, was consequently able to draw NATO into support as an ultimate guarantee of its security from feared "instability from the east." Bonn was then in a position of strategic leverage to argue that NATO would also be needed to guarantee the security of an enlarged European Union.

On 22 April 1993, President Clinton met privately (without his political advisors) with Lech Walesca and Vaclav Havel at the opening of the Holocaust Museum in Washington. The Polish and Czech leaders are said to have impressed upon the president the importance of an enlarged NATO for their respective countries. The meeting at the Holocaust Museum also coincided with fierce fighting between Bosnian Croats and Bosniak Muslims; a renewed Serbian siege against Srebenica took place in which the UN was regarded as "appeasing" Bosnian Serb expansion. Human rights activist Elie Wiesel pleaded, in reference to Bosnia, "Mr. President, this bloodshed must be stopped. It will not stop unless we stop it." The next day, 23 April, President Clinton stated that he would give serious consideration to limited airstrikes against Bosnian Serb positions. Yet despite these strong political-ethical pressures, airstrikes were not immediately forthcoming; nor did NATO opt immediately for enlargement. In June 1993, Secretary of State Warren Christopher told NAC foreign ministers in Athens that NATO enlargement was "not on the agenda."

In a diplomatic offensive intended to press for the concept of overlapping NATO-Russian security guarantees, Boris Yeltsin appeared to accept the possibility of NATO membership for Warsaw on 25 August 1993 and for Prague on 26 August.[22] Here, in a strongly worded statement in support of Poland, Russia appeared to be signaling that it would support NATO enlargement—but only as long as it was also part of the process. Later that month, Boris Yeltsin suggested that Russia should be on the fast track like other states in eastern Europe—if NATO was to expand. (Hungary, Poland, the Czech Republic, and Bulgaria, all declared their desire for membership.) On 30 September, however, Yeltsin appeared to reverse himself—in the midst of his crackdown on the Russian Parliament.

At this point, the U.S. State Department was hesitant to support enlargement into east-central Europe for fear of pushing Russia over the edge. Secretary of State Christopher, under the influence of Ambassador at Large for the Newly Independent States (NIS), Strobe Talbott, opposed the NATO "fast track" approach, but was still open to a gradual expansion. Secretary of Defense Les Aspin and the Pentagon were strongly opposed to NATO enlargement, largely in the fear that expansion could dilute NATO defense capabilities.[23] Whereas the Pentagon generally favored strengthening the Partnership for Peace initiative, National Security Council Advisor Anthony Lake continued to push for enlargement.

On 21 September 1993, in his first major policy address, "From Containment to Enlargement," National Security Advisor Lake argued that "the successor to a doctrine of containment must be a strategy of enlargement—enlargement of the world's free community of market economies." He added that the NATO summit in January 1994 would "seek to update NATO—so that there continues, behind the enlargement of market democracies, an essential collective security." Lake also reflected that conflict in Bosnia represented a vast humanitarian tragedy that "can all too easily explode into a wider Balkan conflict." [24]

On 30 September, Yeltsin and his "pro-Western" foreign minister Andrei Kosyrev warned NATO against expansion. In the midst of his crackdown on the Russian Parliament, Yeltsin ostensibly flip-flopped upon his joint declaration in Warsaw in August 1993 and argued that NATO enlargement would not be in conformity with the 1990 Russo-German Treaty of Good Neighborliness, Partnership, and Cooperation dealing with German unification. Yeltsin also stated that NATO should consult Moscow first before drawing in new states into security arrangements. Yeltsin's late September 1993 protest appeared to cause the Germans and the Americans to backtrack on NATO enlargement; yet the Pentagon had already been concerned that enlargement could water down NATO collective defense capabilities and political consensus.

The Partnership for Peace (PfP) was launched at the 20–21 October 1993 NATO Defense Minister meeting at Travemuende. Yet as eastern European states were upset that NATO had yet to offer them full membership, Les Aspin replied in response that membership would happen sooner rather than later. Manfred Wörner stated "we have reached consensus to fundamentally open the gates of NATO." Radically shifting away from his position in support of an all-European system of security of 1990, on 21 October 1993, Vaclav Havel stated in Poland, "Any dialogue on associate or observer status [in NATO] is welcome but cannot exclude our eventual full membership."

In September–October 1993, the RAND trio of Ronald D. Asmus, Richard L. Kugler, and F. Stephen Larrabee, argued that "if NATO does not address the primary security challenges facing Europe today, it will become increasingly irrelevant. NATO must go out of area or it will go out of business."[25] The last phrase became a political mantra for pro-NATO expansionists such as Senator Richard Lugar. Then Republican presidential candidate, Bob Dole, concomitantly pushed for more forceful NATO action in the former Yugoslavia and for the entrance of as many states as possible into NATO—with the exception of Russia. Calls for NATO to go "out of area or out of business" represented a traditional realist motivation for the expansion of an alliance; this demand contrasted with the more idealist and liberal tone of NSC advisor Anthony Lake, who justified enlargement upon the basis of protecting newly emerging democracies and market economies—even if such enlargement appeared largely selective.

In November 1993, President Bill Clinton publicly announced the PfP initiative, which was formalized in January 1994. PfP, however, was attacked from both sides for either not sufficiently strengthening the NACC or for not pushing for enlargement fast enough, hence representing a "partnership for postponement." The December 1993 victory of Vladimir Zhirinovsky's pan-Russian Liberal Democratic Party in the Russian *Duma* (the lower house) then forewarned of the possible rise of a Russian *revanchist* movement. Secretary of State Warren Christopher responded that "swift expansion of NATO eastward could make a neo-imperialist Russia a self-fulfilling prophecy." But he also warned "if there's a reversal, if they're a *revanchist* country, then. . . NATO would have to consider the erection of a security barrier of the kind we had in the past."[26]

The apparent betrayal of promises to expand NATO membership more rapidly, coupled with the rise of *revanchist* movements in Russia, upset most eastern European elites who desired "full" NATO membership as soon as possible. Accordingly, just before the January 1994 NATO summit, Poland and Lithuania pressed for a more precise timetable for NATO membership; Poland threatened a strategic alliance with a then nuclear Ukraine—if membership in NATO was not soon granted.

In a statement revealing the German "connection" to NATO enlargement, President Clinton repeated almost the exact May 1993 words of German Defense Minister Volker Rühe after he announced in January 1994 that NATO enlargement was "no longer whether NATO will take on new members, but when and how." This statement was then interpreted by expansion proponents as the go-ahead to enlarge but it was still unclear whether President Clinton actually made a formal executive decision or whether the policy was pushed by zealous proponents within the National Security Council and the State Department.[27] Later in February 1994, President Clinton restated U.S. interest in "preventing a broader conflict in Europe" and in "showing that NATO, history's greatest military alliance, *remains a credible force for peace in post-Cold War Europe.*" (Emphasis mine.) At the end of June, Senator Richard Lugar then sought a clear timetable for enlargement; PfP was labeled "policy for postponement."

The Pentagon, at least up to September–October 1994, had been strongly supportive of the PfP, and did *not* interpret President Clinton's general support for enlargement in January 1994 as a definitive executive order. Richard Holbrooke, however, asked a reluctant Pentagon in September 1994 for a preliminary study of what it would take to enlarge NATO. (As former U.S. ambassador to Germany brought back to the State Department as assistant secretary of state, Holbrooke was fully informed of German security concerns as argued by German Defense Minister Volker Rühe.[28]) Former Defense Secretary William Perry still refers to Holbrooke as having "presumed" at that point that the president had decided to enlarge NATO, whereas Clinton had yet to make a decision.[29]

It is clear that U.S. policy toward enlargement began to toughen by the November 1994 congressional elections, both in regard toward a more engaged role for NATO in former Yugoslavia as well as in terms of congressional pressure to enlarge NATO. Among other acts proposed by Congress, the July 1994 NATO Participation Act, for example, advocated membership for Poland, the Czech Republic, Hungary, and Slovakia—the same states given support by Germany in 1993. (By 1995–96, however, Slovakia largely dropped from the list following Prime Minister Meciar's rise to power and ostensibly due to Slovakia's lack of respect for basic democratic and free market principles.) Concurrently, the United States and NATO began to engage in a "lift and strike" in regard to Bosnia, dropping support for the UN arms embargo on the former Yugoslavia, and engaging in NATO airstrikes. (Enlargement also obtained support from Madeleine Albright, who became Secretary of State once Warren Christopher stepped down. Albright, much like Czech leader Vaclav Havel, had initially opposed NATO enlargement. Former National Security Advisor Zbigniew Brzezinski likewise exerted considerable influence from outside the Clinton administration.)

Through the NATO-Russian bargaining process, Russia continued its efforts to forge more positive relations with the United States and NATO, but closer to its terms. Moscow accordingly pressed for the possibility of establishing overlapping or conjoint security guarantees for states in eastern Europe, at the same time that it threatened states against joining NATO. In May 1994, General Pavel Grachev, then defense minister, had proposed the creation of a block-free system to be coordinated by the NACC and the CSCE (to be renamed the Organization for Security and Cooperation in Europe [OSCE]), for example. In June 1994, Russia had signed onto the PfP framework agreement, but then stalled on endorsing the NATO-Russian Individual Partnership in the period July–December 1994, particularly once the United States had opted to engage in a NATO enlargement study. By December 1994, Russia protested the apparently sudden push toward NATO enlargement, and, at least initially, refused to agree to an Individual Partnership with the PfP. Moscow was concerned that its membership in the PfP might not stall NATO enlargement after all. At same time, by late 1994, Moscow had intensified preparations for intervention in Chechnya and did not desire possible NATO interference in its internal affairs.[30]

The 10 May 1995 U.S.-Russian summit was unable to resolve the issues dividing the two states. Indicating that no decision had been made (a fact that would appeal to Moscow), President Clinton (perhaps disingenuously) stated "even NATO has not made such a decision . . . who knows, perhaps there are still disagreements within NATO itself."[31] By 1 June 1995, Russia finally agreed to an Individual Partnership with NATO, but as Russian influence in this agreement was still limited, Moscow threatened to leave the PfP if NATO did opt to enlarge eastward. Although Moscow had taken positive steps toward the alliance (and in the same month that Senator Sam Nunn had opposed enlargement for fear of antagonizing Russia) in July 1995, Assistant Secretary of State Richard Holbrooke publicly ruled out the possibility of conjoint or overlapping NATO-Russian security guarantees as "historically discredited."[32] Concurrently, in July 1995, NATO removed the "dreadful dual-key" control system (in Richard Holbrooke's words) over military operations in the former Yugoslavia. Then by 30 August, NATO engaged in its first massive airstrikes, at that time the largest military action in its history.

In September 1995, *The Study on NATO Enlargement* was finally published. The document set the ground rules for NATO membership, but gave no clues as to which states might enter NATO, nor did it give a precise estimate of the costs. Likewise in September, Russian President Boris Yeltsin stated that NATO bombings in Bosnia "are only the first sign of what could produce NATO's enlargement . . . [which could] reconstitute the two military blocs." By October, however, by then bringing Russia into the peace process in Bosnia, Holbrooke stated that Russia's role in Bosnia helped the United States to understand how to approach the next strategic goal—the enlargement of NATO.[33] At the same time, Holbrooke failed to strike a deal over Kosovo as Serbian leader Slobodan Milosevic threatened to derail the Dayton peace package—if Kosovo was included in the accords. Washington consequently excluded the Kosovar delegation from participating in the November 1995 Dayton peace talks over Bosnia—in deference to Milosevic.

In December 1995 (and despite promises that it would make a decision by late 1995), NATO decided that no public invitations to prospective members would take place before 1997. Instead, NATO opted to postpone the announcement of new members for a number of reasons: (1) The lack of progress in civil-military relations and problems of irredentist demands among prospective member states; (2) to make certain Moscow would support the Dayton agreement and NATO activities in the former Yugoslavia; and (3) to be certain that the announcement of NATO enlargement would not provoke a backlash in the 1996 Russian presidential elections—a point subsequently reinforced by President Clinton in September 1996 to Boris Yeltsin.

Both domestic and external pressure for NATO enlargement continued to swell, however, in spite of, if not because of, apparent Russian opposition. In October 1996, in a speech in Detroit intended to attract the "swing" votes of some 20 million Americans of eastern European origin located in fourteen key states that represented 194 electoral college votes, President Clinton called for the first "full-fledged" members to join NATO by 1999 (the year of NATO's fiftieth anniversary). The new timetable for expansion raised the question whether the proposed members would actually be able to meet NATO qualifications for entry or whether NATO would simply overlook weaknesses in order to window dress these states for membership. PfP advocates continued to argue that all states, including Russia, needed to be more fully involved in the process of building European security over the long term before taking steps to enlarge NATO's membership.

On 26 June, just prior to the 8 July 1997 decision in Madrid to enlarge

NATO's full membership to include Poland, the Czech Republic and Hungary (dropping Slovakia as a candidate), opponents of NATO enlargement, published the *Open Letter to the Honorable William Jefferson Clinton*, arguing that

The U.S.-led effort to expand NATO . . . is a policy error of historic proportions . . . [that will] decrease allied security and unsettle European stability. NATO enlargement will tend to strengthen the non-democratic opposition in Russia, draw a new line of division between the "ins" and the "outs," overextend NATO's ability to carry out its primary mission, and will involve U.S. security guarantees to countries with serious border and national minority problems, and unevenly developed systems of democratic government. . . . In the United States, NATO expansion will trigger an extended debate over its indeterminate, but certainly high, cost and will call into question the U.S. commitment to the Alliance.[34]

Despite the high status and significant foreign policy experience of many of its signers, the open letter did little to derail the NATO enlargement process once it got rolling. The opposition of George Kennan, among others, and an information campaign on NATO enlargement led by Susan Eisenhower, likewise had little effect on Senate opinion. As one leading senator put it to me, "we don't agree with Ms. Eisenhower." In addition, alternatives such as strengthening the PfP initiative by extending NATO security guarantees, but not its integrated command, to as many states as possible within eastern Europe, so as to form a separate Euro-Atlantic defense and security identity, were given short shrift in the haste to enlarge NATO's "full" membership by 1999.[35] Once the timetable was set, it was said that support for NATO enlargement represented a test of loyalty to President Clinton himself.

Interestingly, in a signal to Moscow, the 27 May 1997 Founding Act between NATO and the Russian Federation, which established the NATO-Russian Permanent Joint Council that was intended to give Russia "a voice but not a veto" in the alliance decision-making process, was signed *prior to* the Madrid summit of 8 July 1997. This fact at least appeared to grant Moscow an ostensible political *primacy* over the newly entered NATO members. Concurrently, however, the Madrid summit raised the expectations of a further enlargement, and to consider Romania and Slovenia, if not one or more of the three Baltic states, on a promised future round. Following U.S. Senate ratification on 30 April 1998, with a resounding 80–19 vote, Poland, the Czech Republic and Hungary formally entered an ostensibly "new" NATO in the midst of rapid transformation on 12 March 1999, as "full" members.

WAR "OVER" KOSOVO

Roughly two weeks after the inclusion of three new states, on 24–25 March 1999, NATO shocked the world (as well as its own membership) once it found itself engaged in the first full-scale war of its fifty year history.

The reluctant decision to engage in high altitude airstrikes "over" the sovereign state of Serbia was taken without a UN Security Council mandate in support of NATO "enforcement" actions—as required by the North Atlantic Treaty itself. NATO did base its actions on UN Resolution 1160 (1998) and UN Resolution 1203 (1998), although neither resolution explicitly mandated the use of force. NATO also acted on the basis of the January 29 meeting of the Contact Group (backed by the UN Security Council) which confirmed the view that the situation "remains a threat to the peace and security in the region, raising the prospect of a humanitarian catastrophe." The North Atlantic Council then stretched the latter Contact Group statements "to take whatever means necessary . . . to avert a humanitarian catastrophe."[36] NATO subsequently rationalized its decision to go to war following Serb failure to agree to conditions set at the hastily-arranged negotiations at the Rambouillet summit in France in February 1999.

NATO had additionally based its actions upon the 3 October 1998 ACTORD in which NATO allies argued that NATO could threaten the use of force without an explicit Security Council mandate to do so—once it became clear that such a step was the only likely solution: "Such a step would constitute an exception from the rule, not an attempt to create a new international law."[37] Yet, as UN Secretary-General Kofi Annan put it when the war broke out: "It is indeed tragic that diplomacy has failed, but there are times when the use of force may be legitimate in the pursuit of peace." But then he added, "The Security Council has primary responsibility for maintaining international peace and security—and this is explicitly acknowledged in the North Atlantic Treaty. Therefore the Council should be involved in any decision to resort to the use of force."[38]

In February 1998, Serbia had engaged in a serious offensive in the Drenica region against Kosovo Liberation Army (KLA) acts of "terrorism" against Serbian police, raising the question as to whether the general threat against Serbia made by the Bush administration in December 1992 remained valid. As the fighting escalated (and despite public recognition in February 1998 by U.S. envoy Richard Gelbard that the KLA represented a "terrorist" organization), Serbia was regarded as mocking NATO credibility. A cynical Serbian joke purportedly ran "a village a day keeps NATO away." Madeleine Albright on 7 March 1998 swore that "We are not going to stand by and watch the Serbian authorities do in Kosovo what they can no longer get away with doing in Bosnia."[39]

That summer, U.S. ambassador to NATO Alexander Vershbow proposed a conjoint U.S.-Russian plan to impose a political settlement by means of deploying 30,000 to 60,000 troops in Kosovo under a general UN mandate. Yet the Clinton administration largely ignored the proposal due to the fact that it was concerned with terrorist attacks on U.S. embassies in Africa, not to overlook the political risks involved in deploying forces in advance of the November 1998 mid-term elections.[40] As time ran short, "Monicagate," coupled with the effort to impeach President Clinton, additionally prevented the administration from focusing more resolutely on resolving these crises through preventive diplomacy. Washington would most likely have needed to provide significant political and economic incentives—including closer Russian ties to NATO, if not ultimately "full" NATO membership—to bring Moscow on board and to induce the latter to engage in a more positive role in the Balkans.

On 13 October 1998, NATO issued its first "activation order" in an effort to get Serbian leader Slobodan Milosevic to accept a ceasefire agreement brokered by U.S. envoy Richard Holbrooke and involving the deployment of some 2,000 ineffective, largely untrained, unarmed OSCE "verifiers" under a Kosovo Verification Mission (KVM). NATO threats did lead Belgrade to accept the withdrawal of 10,000 members of its special forces, although some 20,000 military, paramilitary, and special forces remained. Concurrently, however, the KLA moved into formerly Serbian positions, and attempted to draw the Serbs into committing atrocities so as to obtain Western support (actions openly admitted by KLA militants). By the Fall of 1998, it was reported that some 200,000 to 300,000 Kosovars had fled their homes. What the Serbs called "Operation Horseshoe," conceived by Milosevic and his advisors in October 1998, set in motion a "humanitarian crisis" with profound implications for regional stability.

After a long debate, NATO stated that UN authorization to take military action outside the NATO area was not necessarily mandatory, but only in exceptional cases. As NATO members Greece and Turkey were only *indirectly* threatened by Serbian actions, the North Atlantic Assembly (NAA) essentially based its argument for enforcement upon a vaguely defined self-declared right to a "collective defense of interests" within the Euro-Atlantic area as opposed to the more traditional Cold War notion of a "collective defense of territory" sanctioned by Article 51 of the UN Charter. (The NAA had voted on the issue on 14 November 1998, following the 3 October 1998 ACTAD accord.)[41]

NATO issued a second "activation order" on 30 January (following the "Racak massacre") and set a deadline for the peace talks to reach a decision between 6 and 19 February. As talks stalled, the deadline was postponed. Although NATO representatives had been excluded from the peace talks in deference to French/EU interests (a fact protested by the Kosovar delegation), on 22 February NATO Supreme Commander General Wesley Clark belatedly attempted to persuade the reluctant Albanian delegation to sign the Rambouillet accords—the first *direct* intervention by NATO itself in the talks. (EU allies had wanted to play a larger role in the Kosovo talks, seeing themselves as snubbed by the United States at Dayton in 1995.)

As the Rambouillet accords envisioned the KLA's dissolution, the KLA was opposed—even more so as the Serbs were to maintain some 5,000 police and military forces in the region as part of the agreement. The initial Kosovar reluctance to sign the accord resulted in a significant loss of Western public support for the KLA. At the same time, it is clear that the Rambouillet summit was hastily prepared. On the one hand, U.S. and Contact Group strategy appeared to give the upperhand to KLA hardliners as opposed to the more

The Genesis of NATO Enlargement and of War "over" Kosovo 171

moderate leadership.[42] On the other hand, NATO's proposed role in the post-Kosovo peace settlement represented too great an infringement upon Serbian sovereignty (as defined by Annex B) to be accepted by the Serbian leadership.

Once the KLA belatedly and reluctantly agreed, the failure of the Serbs to sign on then provided the rationale for NATO airstrikes over Kosovo, Montenegro, and Serbia itself beginning 24–25 March. Ostensible U.S.-European efforts to play "honest broker" were put to a sudden end. One unnamed assistant to Madeleine Albright put the issue bluntly: Rambouillet had "only one purpose: to get the war started with the Europeans locked in."[43] In effect, the U.S. and NATO decided to make their threats credible (regardless of EU proposals) in light of Slobodan Milosevic's repeated refusal over seven years to take American and then NATO warnings seriously—as Acting Secretary of State Lawrence Eagleburger had initially stated in his "Christmas warning" to Slobodan Milosevic in December 1992.

The decision to intervene was also taken prior to the arrival of the Russian Prime Minister Yevgeni Primakov in Washington on March 23; the latter then broke off discussions.[44] Russia then dropped out of the NATO-Russian Permanent Joint Council (PJC) established by the May 1997 NATO-Russian Founding Act (but then rejoined the PJC in July once the war was over). NATO accordingly opted to act on its own without a clear mandate from the UN Security Council in a calculated risk that its actions would not alienate non-NATO members of the UN Security Council—Russia and China.

According to President Clinton, NATO action "over" Kosovo was based upon three principles: (1) to demonstrate the seriousness of NATO's opposition to aggression (i.e., NATO credibility); (2) to deter Milosevic "from continuing and escalating his attacks" in Kosovo; and (3) to damage Serbia's capacity to wage war.[45] In addition, a fourth consideration (and perhaps the primary one in terms of NATO interests as a collective defense/security organization) represented the unverifiable fear that the expulsion of Kosovar refugees and destabilizing sociopolitical conflict could *potentially* spread to FYROM and Albania and then to NATO members Greece and Turkey.

After the seventy-eight day NATO bombing campaign (which began with "surgical strikes" against largely symbolic targets), NATO Supreme Commander General Wesley Clark stated that the incremental nature of NATO's air campaign—dubbed "war by committee"—was necessary to keep NATO allies (particularly Germany, Greece, and Italy) on board. NATO officials also stated that they did not anticipate the fact that the bombing campaign would accelerate ethnic cleansing (despite CIA analysis to the contrary). President Clinton and NATO leaders were also surprised that Milosevic did not fold after the first wave of cruise missile attacks in late March, although the decision to triple the number of aircraft in April (when weather conditions generally improved) then helped to secure success.[46]

The war "over" Kosovo represented a kind of litmus test for the loyalty of the new members, particularly if a ground war had proved necessary. A joke circulated throughout NATO that "the Poles are in" (being the most supportive of NATO actions); "the Czechs are out" (being the least supportive); and "the Hungarians are in-between."[47] As a front-line state, Hungary found itself confronted with direct Serbian threats, as well as with indirect threats to ethnic Hungarians within Serbian territory, primarily in Vojvodina province. On one hand, NATO launched aircraft from bases in southern Hungary; on the other, Budapest was impelled to hold up a Russian convoy of "supplies" on its way to Serbia, and prevent Russian planes from flying through Hungarian airspace. Concurrently, Bulgaria and Romania have hoped to be rewarded—by means of increased economic assistance and "full" NATO membership—for the high political and economic costs incurred for their role in helping to isolate Serbia. (Five NATO missiles accidentally struck Bulgarian territory, for example.)

A multiplicity of factors led to the Serbian decision to withdraw from Kosovo: (1) Milosevic failed to break the alliance's will and play upon allied differences; (2) Serb efforts to destabilize the neighboring states of FYROM and Albania by means of the mass expulsion of refugees and border clashes failed, as did efforts to stage a coup in Montenegro; (3) NATO moved in to guarantee the territorial integrity of Albania and Macedonia, and promised assistance, if necessary to Romania and Bulgaria as well; (4) the threat of a ground campaign (as called for by the United Kingdom partly in an effort to assert *primacy* over France and Germany within the Alliance) appeared more serious; (5) NATO devastation of Serbian military and civilian infrastructure; and (6) perhaps most importantly, Milosevic did not expect Russia to abandon the Serb cause by endorsing NATO demands to retreat from Kosovo.

Moreover, behind-the-scenes negotiation took a different direction once Viktor Chernomyrdin became Russia's Balkan envoy and Deputy Secretary of State Strobe Talbott stepped into the limelight and Secretary of State Madeleine Albright withdrew into the State Department. EU special envoy, Finnish president Martii Ahtisaari also played a key role.[48] Negotiations to end the war established a very different set of conditions than did the Rambouillet summit. Contrary to Rambouillet, there was to be no referendum on the political status of Kosovo after three years. NATO's Kosovo Force (KFOR) could only operate within the province of Kosovo; KFOR was to be deployed under a general UN mandate (UN Security Council Resolution 1244)—*providing a post facto legitimacy for NATO actions*.

THE QUESTION OF "HUMANITARIAN INTERVENTIONISM"

NATO justified its use of force as an exceptional "humanitarian intervention" yet for NATO to claim its actions as morally justified largely depends upon the argument that the United States and its European allies had thoroughly attempted all possible diplomatic options prior to opting for the use of force. Intervention upon the basis of "humanitarian" concerns raises questions of double standards and of *triage* in an era of relatively limited resources, i.e., why intervene in this state rather than another which is similarly engaging in significant human rights abuses or crimes against humanity.[49] Waging war on "humanitarian" grounds also risks opening the door to unilateral military intervention by third states on the ostensible basis of defense of persecuted minorities. In effect, NATO argued that it had a "right," if not a "duty," to intervene, at least in exceptional circumstances, regardless of the international legal implications involving questions of state sovereignty.[50]

NATO's actions must also be regarded in light of the way the war was fought. NATO targets included dual-use military/civilian infrastructure (as well as targets of historical, religious, and cultural value); high altitude bombing (intended to reduce the risk to pilots) made targets difficult to distinguish and locate despite the use of "smart" weaponry. The fact that Serb forces accelerated acts of "ethnic cleansing" during the bombing campaign (resulting in the expulsion of an additional 850,000 Kosovars) ironically made NATO's attacks on dual-use infrastructure less ethically messy than would have been the case had NATO actions caused an even greater number of ethnic Serb and Albanian civilian casualties. Likewise, the punishment and "collateral damage" inflicted upon the Serbian civilian population (as targets of "surgical strikes" and as displaced "internal refugees") must not prove to be disproportionate to the injury suffered by the ethnic Albanian population. Most "ethnic cleansing" by Serb forces occurred where the KLA had been most active; Serbian actions tended to be selective as opposed to indiscriminate.[51] It is absolutely certain that heinous crimes against humanity were committed, yet the proof of a planned "genocide" is still lacking.

A related concern is that an effective system of justice and enforcement has yet to be established in Kosovo. Concurrently, NATO has been reluctant to serve as a police force for controlling criminal activities, drug smuggling, and acts of terrorism and revenge—in addition to apprehending individuals indicted by the International War Crimes Tribunal. This has raised questions as to the ultimate purpose of NATO's intervention (in regard to issues of "justice"), its appropriate role as a "police force" in the aftermath of a conflict, as well as the nature of its interaction with governmental and non-governmental organizations (NGOs). Will NATO, the UN, the EU and NGOs be able to establish a modicum of a "just" social and political order?

The roots of the tragedy really stem from the UN's inability to deploy preventive war forces in Kosovo in December 1992—an action that NATO itself had supported at the time. Although Russia continued to back the Serbian position on Kosovo in the UN Security Council, Moscow may have changed its policy if offered greater political and economic incentives. Had Russia been promised a closer relationship with the Alliance at that time, Moscow may have been more willing to work with Washington to pressure Serbia to accept the deployment of UN-NATO war-preventive forces in Kosovo at an earlier date. A closer NATO-Russian-UN-OSCE relationship could have been forged by means of strengthening the Euro-Atlantic Partnership Council and Russia's role in the "new" NATO.

Another possible option was that of "partition." U.S. policy, however, had opposed a "partition" as an act of "appeasement" that would ostensibly vindicate Serbian acts of "ethnic cleansing" and then establish a precedent that would jeopardize the multiethnic peace in Bosnia. Moreover, if Serbia were to obtain the mineral-rich north, partition, it was argued, could also open the door to demands for a greater Albania to protect the southern regions. On the other hand, a "partition" that would divide Kosovo into two "autonomous" regions, and backed by the joint deployment of NATO-Russian forces under a general UN mandate, could have been designed to counterbalance both pan-Serb and greater Albanian claims. Such a "partition" could also have been coupled with negotiations leading toward joint Serb-Albanian stock ownership/control of key industries and sharing of tax revenues. A policy of "appeasement" (defined not as capitulation, but as diplomatic compromise backed by the *threat* to use force from a position of strength) may appear, at first glance, to be ethically repugnant, yet it cannot be overlooked that acts of forceful intervention also carry with them significant ethical ambiguities involving the killing of innocent civilians. Military intervention may, in addition, result in the "appeasement" of "lesser evils" as a by-product—much as the human rights abuses and territorial demands of Croatia (the "lesser evil") in Bosnia were largely "appeased" by NATO in the effort to contain Serbia (the "greater evil").[52]

In essence, a more realistic alternative—one that recognized that the two opposing sides were largely irreconcilable in the near term—may have been possible to implement. Such a policy could have avoided an extremely costly war whose unintended (but largely foreseeable) consequences in the name of "humanitarianism" could potentially destabilize the reform process in countries throughout southeastern Europe—if not ultimately provide cannon fodder for a revanchist backlash in Russia.

PROBLEMATIC CONSEQUENCES OF THE CONFLICT

Key questions surrounding NATO involvement in the Balkans have yet to be answered. The initial American reluctance/refusal to incorporate Russia more thoroughly in diplomacy, or in the decision to engage in enforcement actions, followed by general reluctance to include Russia in the peace settlement, does not augur well for the future development of a Euro-Atlantic system of "collective security" that incorporates both eastern European and Russian security interests.

Without a clear UNSC mandate as stipulated by the North Atlantic Treaty in regard to enforcement, NATO actions lacked a solid international legality and legitimacy. In addition to stretching the terms of the North Atlantic Treaty itself (as previously argued), NATO actions called into question the role of the NATO-Russian Founding Act and the Permanent Joint Council. These actions also questioned NATO's ability to move beyond "collective defense of territory" and toward a system of "collective security" with the Russians on board. Here, NATO has appeared to have redefined "collective security" to mean the "collective defense of interests." The latter remains an ambiguous concept, involving an unclear mix of geostrategic and "humanitarian" concerns, and which may or may not incorporate the interests of non-NATO members such as Russia.

At the end of the conflict, Russia essentially forced its way into the post-Kosovo peace settlement by marching troops officially assigned to SFOR in Bosnia to the Pristina airport in Kosovo ahead of the NATO advance—risking conflict with the latter.[53] Although Russia did agree to rejoin the Permanent Joint Council, suspicions remain. Russia's revised national security concept for the year 2000 argues that the "level and scale of the threat in the military sphere is increasing" and it points (unlike its previous national security doctrines) to the West as a potential threat. NATO's use of force outside alliance borders, without sanction from the UN, and the incorporation of this new policy into alliance strategic doctrine, was viewed as "fraught with the threat of destabilization of the whole strategic situation in the world."[54]

NATO's actions also lacked clear-cut political goals, as well as a clear exit strategy.[55] In the aftermath, it is still not certain how the general map of the Balkan region is to be formed, involving multinational units which link differing communities together, or else more or less ethnically homogeneous enclaves or mini-units? It is not certain that the essentially American multiethnic integration strategy that emphasizes, and largely depends upon, the development of a balanced and prosperous civil society will necessarily succeed in Kosovo (or in Bosnia, for that matter).

Also problematic is NATO's relationship to Serbia and the future political status of Kosovo. The alliance has appeared to waffle between its goal to return Kosovo autonomy within the Serbia, or to support Kosova independence—if not to ultimately eliminate Milosevic. As has been the case for fairly well-substantiated accusations of Bosnian government links to Islamic mujaheddin, accusations that the conflict has already transformed Kosovo-Metohia into Kosova (and therefore into a defacto Albanian state run by the KLA and Albanian mafia with the UN as a fig leaf) have served to discredit the efforts of both NATO and UN. NATO difficulties in protecting Serbian and other minority populations (particularly Romani [gypsies] but also Turks and Muslim Slavs accused of "collaboration") remaining in Kosovo have raised doubts about NATO's ability to play "honest broker" and to sustain an "ethical" balancing act between Serb and Albanian interests and then to implement a "meaningful autonomy."

As has been the case in Bosnia,[56] rival factions in Kosovo have yet to give up their particularistic demands; the KLA and other Albanian parties have been reluctant to dissolve power structures set up to parallel those of NATO and the UN.[57] At the same time, the Serb presence in Pristina and Kosovo has, as a whole, dwindled substantially; Serbian leaders have proved reluctant to participate in the new internationalized structures of government and multiethnic power-sharing arrangements. The extent to which KLA fighters will fully integrate into the Kosovo Protection Force established by the UN remains to be seen. Will a defacto partition of Kosovo be implemented as has appeared to be the case in the city of Mitrovica near the Serbian border (the mineral-rich northern part of the city is 90% Serb)? Or will Kosova ultimately seek "independence" forcing the remaining Serbs out?

Moreover, sustained peacekeeping and international investment cannot be guaranteed. Washington asked the EU to provide the needed assistance to much of southeastern Europe after the war; yet it was not clear how much aid would be forthcoming, what form it would take, and to whom it would go. $2.1 billion was pledged for Kosovo alone in late July 1999 at the Sarajevo summit, which inaugurated the EU Stability Pact for Southeastern Europe. Yet it was not clear if the Europeans will continue to sustain sufficient political, military, and economic supports to maintain stability, and sustain economic growth, for both Bosnia and Kosovo, and to integrate these economies into a larger Balkan/Danube economy—of which Serbia is the heart.[58] Here, disputes between rival Kosovar political factions have worked to hinder the aid process as has the question as to whether Serbia should receive humanitarian assistance, particularly if Milosevic stays in power. Serbia and Montenegro may undergo a period of political-economic instability, adding additional headaches to the region's chance for recovery. In effect, economic sanctions against Serbia indirectly threaten the process of political-economic reforms in Romania, Bulgaria and FYROM. The Balkan region as a whole may need as much as $30 billion over five years to an estimated $100 billion over the next ten years if political stability and the political-economic reform process is to be sustained.[59] Both the EU and United States may need to choke up greater funding and investment.

Having intervened by force rightfully or wrongfully, NATO now needs to carry out its peacekeeping mandate to the end (for a decade if not longer)—in order to sustain a modicum of "order" and "justice" and in cooperation with the UN and other international organizations. Most crucially, the repercussions of this war must not ultimately provoke a new round of hostilities. Perceptions that NATO helped Kosova achieve "independence" may lead to a perpetual Pandora's box of secessionist movements throughout the region possibly beginning in Montenegro and FYROM. Should the UN, EU, and NATO (due to burgeoning costs or other considerations)[60] ultimately opt to leave the region *prior to a full resolution of the outstanding political disputes*, the political-ethical foundations of the whole venture—if not the basis of NATO's legitimacy—could, this time, be fundamentally jeopardized.

GEOHISTORY

In advocating NATO enlargement to cover all of a newly unified Germany, it was not generally recognized that NATO would also be drawn into protecting former Imperial German and Austro-Hungarian spheres of influence and security in the era before World War I. NATO efforts to forge a new system of security in eastern Europe can also be compared and contrasted with French efforts to implement an "eastern Locarno" in the interwar period. Moreover, while never the sole bone of contention, Balkan conflicts were at the center of tensions among the major powers before World War I, World

The Genesis of NATO Enlargement and of War "over" Kosovo 177

War II, and the Cold War. Continuing instability in the region now threatens to thoroughly undermine the post-Cold War U.S.-EU-Russian detente.

From a geohistorical perspective, NATO enlargement into Poland, the Czech Republic, and Hungary has worked to extend NATO protection to states of the former Imperial German and Austro-Hungarian empires, but now including most of Poland (except the significant region granted by Stalin to Belarus) and not including Slovakia. (Prussia, Austria, and Russia had partitioned Poland in the late eighteenth century until the latter gained independence after World War I.) Likewise, German recognition of Slovenia and Croatia as independent states, while not causing the war, indirectly worked to extend NATO's post-Cold War "community of interests" into southeastern Europe at the extreme borders of the former Austro-Hungarian empire, once NATO opted to engage itself in the former Yugoslavia.

U.S. and NATO support for Albania (now as an ally of Turkey) to a certain extent mimics the strategy of the Austrian empire before World War I. As tensions spiraled after the 1875–1876 Serb uprising in Bosnia against Ottoman rule, both pan-Serb and greater Albanian ideologies were given an extra impetus. Through the Mürzteg program of 1903, Austria and Russia obtained significant rights of interference in Bosnia and in Balkan affairs at the expense of Ottoman interests in an effort to contain tensions. (In contemporary circumstances, there is no country equivalent to the Ottoman empire as a "sick man of Europe"; yet Turkey, Iran, Pakistan and Saudi Arabia have all been vying to influence pan-Islamic movements in many of the regions once controlled by the Ottomans, exacerbating regional tensions from Bosnia to central Asia.)

The 1903 Mürzteg program appears to possess some important geohistorical parallels (and differences) with contemporary international peacekeeping in Bosnia (and now Kosovo) in terms of NATO-Russian cooperation; yet in the present situation the United States has thus far been reluctant to grant Russia any significant influence in the region. The collapse of Austro-Russian collaboration over the Balkans after the 1908 Austrian annexation of Bosnia represented one of the major factors that worked to undermine relations between Russia, Austria, and Imperial Germany. Yet the rupture in Austro-Russian relations also resulted in closer Anglo-French-Russian ties after the unexpected formation of the Anglo-Russian entente in 1907.

In the 1912–1913 Balkan conflicts, Serbia, along with Greece and Italy, claimed Albania, once the latter obtained independence. Having annexed Bosnia in 1908, Austria, on the other hand, backed Albania against pan-Serb expansion. Serbian behavior in burning whole villages in the battle to forge a greater Serbia (and preclude the establishment of a greater Albania) appears to parallel contemporary acts of "ethnic cleansing." Serb actions took place at a time when Belgrade was, at least indirectly, backed by Franco-Russian Dual Alliance and when Imperial Germany backed Austria and sought hegemony over the Ottomans. In the present era, however, Russia has thus far turned its back on support for pan-Serb ambitions.

NATO efforts to implement a new system of security in eastern Europe can also be compared and contrasted with those of interwar France. Before World War II, the 1934 assassination of Yugoslav King Alexander and French Foreign Minister Louis Barthou by the Croatian *Ustashe* served to destabilize French efforts to achieve a collective security pact or an "eastern Locarno." The latter (which involved the Little Entente states of Romania, Czechoslovakia, and Yugoslavia as well as the Balkan entente of Greece, Romania, Turkey and Yugoslavia) represented an effort to achieve a regional counterpoise to Nazi German and Soviet pressures.[61] Once World War II erupted, the Nazi-backed *Ustashe* continued its attacks against its Serb and Communist rivals; fascist Italy occupied Tirana and supported the claims of a greater Albania.

Throughout the Cold War (which was, in part, sparked by Yugoslav, Bulgarian, and Albanian support for Communist insurgents in Greek Macedonia), a feared Soviet thrust into Yugoslavia was regarded as a potential flash point for World War III. As Soviet troops had been perceived as massing near the border of Yugoslavia in 1950, it was believed that the Korean War might possibly represent a flanking maneuver to cover a Soviet thrust into Belgrade. (Marshall Tito had prepared for such a contingency by building bomb shelters throughout the country.) It is thus a tragic historical irony that the war over Kosovo began just as NATO announced its fiftieth anniversary and its enlargement into former Soviet/Russian spheres of influence and security. This time, however, it was NATO—and not Moscow—that opted for war in response to Yugoslav actions.

Following the signing of the North Atlantic Treaty in 1949, the Soviet Union and China entered into formal alliance in 1950, much as contemporary Russia and a much stronger China have reached out for a strategic partnership at least in part in response to NATO enlargement and to the war "over" Kosovo. Chinese opposition to NATO actions intensified following NATO's "accidental" bombing of the Chinese embassy. China argued that the embassy bombing was intentional (due to its diplomatic support for Serbia) and not accidental (due to inaccurate maps) as claimed by Washington. Both Moscow and Beijing have consequently strengthened their "strategic partnership" (including Russian sales of advanced arms and dual-use technology to China) in opposition to American "hegemony" and "unilateralism."

The risk is that NATO actions may have opened the door for other states or alliances to engage in unilateral actions based upon "humanitarian concerns." Pointing to NATO intervention, Moscow rationalized its own intervention against the Chechen republic in 1999–2000, for example, as a "civilizing" crusade against Chechen "gangs" and "acts of terrorism." Russia, China, and India had all opposed NATO's "humanitarian intervention" as a fundamental violation of the principle of state sovereignty. The latter countries have feared that NATO actions in support of ethnic Kosovar Albanians could set a precedent that would help to strengthen secessionist movements in Chechnya, Tibet and Taiwan, and Kashmir, among others.

There is, however, no reason for the long history of intra-European or global conflict to repeat itself. It is quite feasible that Russia could, in the not-so-distant future, align itself with NATO, much as tsarist Russia shocked the world by aligning with Great Britain in 1907, but in very different geohistorical circumstances. This latter scenario will largely depend upon whether Washington and Moscow can ultimately find sufficient common interests—and common threats—to cooperate actively in a sustained entente or alliance relationship in regions within and beyond the new Europe.

ENLARGEMENT AND NATO'S NEW MISSION

The enlargement of NATO's "jurisdiction" into eastern Germany provided the essential model upon which Washington would negotiate with Moscow for further NATO enlargement into east-central Europe despite Washington's initial—but informal—promises not to do. German unification not only dragged NATO into a defense of a newly unified Germany's eastern borders, but NATO also found itself drawn into east-central and southeastern Europe in the effort to protect Germany and other NATO members from feared "instability from the east." NATO enlargement was intended to sustain the "double containment" of German power capabilities and additionally forestall the slim, but historically demonstrated, contingency that Germany and Russia might opt for an alliance at the expense of the countries in-between. The enlargement of NATO also served to secure American, German, and EU political-economic interests in the eastern European region. It remains to be seen whether Russia will be able to sustain any significant political-economic or military influence in the area.

The importance of German influence in the NATO enlargement process can be inferred from the following statement by former permanent representative to NATO, Robert E. Hunter, who argued that "(G)eographic location between NATO and Russia in the center of Europe" and "proximity to Germany, with its ambition to surround itself by NATO and the European Union" represented two of the six "standards" to decide which states were to enter NATO. Poland and the Czech Republic were only two countries on a "direct strategic line" between NATO and Russia. (What a "direct strategic line" meant in terms of NATO-Russian relations was not explicitly stated.) Although Hungary entered NATO for other reasons (such as direct support for IFOR and SFOR in Bosnia), "no other future NATO applicant meets the full range of criteria." At the same time, Hunter also forewarned that "the next round of enlargement, if there is to be one, will . . . be hotly contested.[62] In response to the decision, Russia warned that enlargement would result in "new dividing lines."[63]

The key dilemma is that proposals to accept new members into NATO by the year 2002 may well make or break the positive aspects of the new found NATO-Russian relationship depending upon which states enter and under what *qualified* conditions. Having looked beyond eastern Germany to east-central and southeastern Europe, NATO may look for new members in northeastern Europe including the Baltic states, as well as to former neutral states, such as Austria, Sweden, and possibly Finland. At the same time, Bulgaria, Romania, and Slovenia in southeastern Europe all possess great expectations of entering NATO after having loyally provided diplomatic and/or logistical supports for the war "over" Kosovo. This raises the question of NATO's potential overextension and too great a dispersal of resources among its east-central, southeastern and northeastern flanks. NATO may have to undergo more radical reforms in its command structure and its mission if it is to accept even more members.[64]

On the one hand, the more members NATO accepts, the more it risks overextension and a breakdown of its political consensus; on the other hand, the closer NATO approaches Russia, the greater the possibility of a Russian backlash. Moscow has warned that it would consider Baltic state membership in NATO as a casus belli. On the other hand, Russian opposition to NATO membership for Lithuania, for example, might be mitigated if the two sides could find a way to guarantee Russian access to Kaliningrad, among other geoeconomic and geostrategic concerns. NATO would also need to draw Russia closer to the Atlantic Alliance and ultimately into "full" membership.

NATO enlargement into eastern Germany, east-central Europe, as well as NATO intervention in Bosnia and then Kosovo, has, to a large extent, been justified upon the ostensible need "to go out of area or out of business" which is more in line with traditional "realism" than with NATO's new found humanitarian "idealism." As argued, at each step of the NATO enlargement/engagement process, it was claimed that NATO's credibility and legitimacy were at stake. In effect, during the Cold War there had been no effective political pressure for NATO to engage in "out of area" intervention to counter the repressive actions of the Soviet Union (or third states) in countries that indirectly affected NATO's "collective interests." NATO's legitimacy and appropriate role were thus only questioned following the collapse of the Soviet empire and NATO's initial reluctance to engage forces in "out of area" conflict in former Yugoslavia. NATO consequently needed to *construct* a new legitimacy beyond that of traditional "collective defense" in order to justify its very existence by re-defining its mission and adopting a new role.

NATO intervention in Bosnia in close, albeit tense, interaction with the UN at least initially appeared to move NATO closer toward its new ideal of "collective security." Yet NATO intervention in Kosovo without a UN mandate has raised questions as to its ability to move beyond its concepts of a "collective defense" of "territory" or "interests" and toward a new system of "collective security" that will thoroughly incorporate Russia and other non-NATO members in the decision-making process—despite the fact that the deployment of KFOR under a general UN mandate provided a post facto legitimacy for NATO's "humanitarian" intervention.

NATO has undertaken an extremely ambitious task. It seeks to "fully" integrate new members from eastern Europe, at the same time that it implements a new relationship with Russia and Ukraine and permanently defuse the historical Balkan cliché of a "powder keg." Whether NATO can successfully engage in such an ambitious mission without ultimately overextending its resources and undermining its political consensus and legitimacy will largely determine whether the peace of the Euro-Atlantic community can be sustained well into the new millennium.

NOTES

1. See arguments of Jürgen Habermas, *The Past as Future*, translated and edited by Max Penskyi (Lincoln and London: University of Nebraska Press, 1994), 45–54.

2. French proposals were largely killed in 1945 when Moscow proposed that Soviet troops be deployed in each region of a proposed German confederation; George Kennan's post-World War II "Plan A" for German unification never saw the light of day once it was leaked to the press. The 1947 conference of German Länder ended with a walkout of pro-Soviet East German states.

3. Günter Grass, "Short Speech by a Rootless Cosmopolitan," *Two States-One Nation?* (New York: Harcourt Brace, Jovanovich, 1990), 5. See also Günter Grass, "Don't Reunify Germany," *When the Wall Came Down: Reaction to German Unification*, eds. Harold James and Marla Stone (London: Routledge, 1992), 59.

4. See my argument in *Surviving the Millennium: American Global Strategy, the Collapse of the Soviet Empire, and the Question of Peace* (Westport, CT: Praeger, 1994); *Dangerous Crossroads: Europe, Russia, and the Future of NATO* (Westport, CT: Praeger, 1997).

5. Hannes Adomeit, "Gorbachev and German Unification," *Problems of Communism*, 39 (July–August 1990).

6. In 1982, Ronald Reagan is said to have proposed Soviet membership in NATO at a North Atlantic Council meeting, shocking German officials in particular, who wondered if the president was serious. See also Ira Straus, "Russia-in-NATO," Committee on Eastern Europe and Russia in NATO http://www.fas.org/man/nato/ceern/index.html.

7. George Bush and Brent Scowcroft, *A World Transformed* (New York: Random House, 1998), 146.

8. The 3 October 1990 Japan Times drew the lesson: "Observing Germany's trauma has made us determined that the 'northern territories,' which have been under Soviet occupation since 1945, be very soon once again part of the nation." James and Stone, *When the Wall Came Down*, 347.

9. James A. Baker III, *The Politics of Diplomacy* (New York: G.P. Putnam and Sons, 1995), 86.

10. Baker, *The Politics of Diplomacy*, 232.

11. Philip Zelikow and Condoleeza Rice, *Germany United and Europe Transformed* (Cambridge: Harvard University Press, 1995), 344, 473 fn.

12. See Andrei Gratchev, "La Russie à la recherche d'une politique étrangère," *Relations internationales: les Études de la Documentation Française, La Russie 1995–1996*. (Paris: La Documentation Française, *1996*).

13. Amy Knight, *Spies Without Cloaks: The KGB's Successors* (Princeton: Princeton University Press, 1996). Knight has argued that the alleged coup attempt was really botched effort by Gorbachev to prevent the dissolution of the empire by declaring a national emergency. In Knight's account, Gorbachev calls President George Bush to warn him of the coup. Seymour Hersh, however, argues that U.S. intelligence knew of the coup and illegally shared U.S. intelligence intercepts with Yeltsin. President Bush then called Gorbachev to warn him. Yet if U.S. intelligence was as good as Hersh claimed, did Washington know that the coup had really been

staged by Gorbachev himself, as Knight argues, or had Gorbachev simply given the green light to his underlings for some form of radical action? The truth may be in a phone call. See Seymour M. Hersh in "The Wild East," *Atlantic Monthly*, June 1994.

14. NATO enlargement into east-central Europe may, in part, have been intended to forestall a German-Soviet condominium over the region, but it may not necessarily prevent a NATO-Russian partition, that is, unless NATO can bring Moscow into closer participation, if not "full" membership. See my argument in *Dangerous Crossroads*.

15. Quitting his post on April 29, 1992, Genscher was responsible for the early recognition of Croatia. *Facts on File* 1991, 247.

16. See Ira Straus, "Russia-in-NATO." "It is assumed without discussion that Russia-in-NATO would mean a Russian veto power that could destroy NATO."

17. *International Herald Tribune*, 18 February 1992; 12 March 1992; 25 March 1992.

18. *Keesing's* Record of World Events, December 1992, 39250. By March 1999, Albania and FYROM became tacit NATO protectorates.

19. In the process of eliminating Kosovo's autonomous status between 1989 and 1991, Serbia added the region, Metohia to Kosovo province (Kosova in Albanian), in an effort to further downplay the Albanian regional identity and demographic majority, and better assimilate the region.

20. Antony Lewis, "Words and Deeds," *The New York Times* 11 April 1994, cited in Terry Terriff and James F. Keeley, "The United Nations, Conflict Management, and Spheres of Influence," *International Peacekeeping*, 2, No. 4 (Winter 1995), 533, fn. 47. The December 1992 warning served to reduce U.S. diplomatic flexibility as it dealt with the Milosevic regime by putting NATO's credibility on the line.

21. Quoted in Gerald B. Solomon, *The NATO Enlargement Debate, 1990–1997, Blessings of Liberty* (Westport, CT: Praeger, 1998), 30.

22. For discussion, see Gardner, *Dangerous Crossroads*, 19.

23. For more on the inner bureaucratic debate, see James M. Goldgeier, "NATO Expansion: Anatomy of a Decision," *Washington Quarterly*, 21, No. 1 (Winter 1998).

24. U.S. Department of State Dispatch, Bureau of Public Affairs, 4, No. 39 (27 September 1993). http://pdg2.usia.gov/scripts. Lake also argued, "The second imperative for our strategy must be to help democracy and markets expand and survive in other places where we have the strongest security concerns and where we can make the greatest difference. This is not a democratic crusade; it is a pragmatic commitment to see freedom take hold where that will help us most. Thus, we must target our efforts to assist states that affect our strategic interests . . . the most important example is the former Soviet Union. . . . If we can support and help consolidate democratic and market reforms in Russia and the other new independent states, we can help turn a former threat into a region of valued diplomatic and economic partners." But then Lake argues for a third element of strategy of enlargement "to minimize the ability of (backlash) states outside the circle of democracy and markets to threaten it. . . . Our policy toward such states, so long as they act as they do, must seek to isolate them diplomatically, militarily, economically, and technologically." While mentioning Iraq and North Korea, and in arguing that the United states can help to "steer" China down the proper path, Lake did not mention what would happen if Russia, or another significant power, did begin to act as such a "backlash" state.

25. Ronald D. Asmus, Richard L. Kugler, and F. Stephen Larrabee, "Building a New NATO," *Foreign Affairs* (September/October 1993).

26. U.S. ambassador at large, Strobe Talbott convinced Secretary of State Warren Christopher, who initially supported NATO enlargement, to take a "go-slow" approach. *International Herald Tribune*, 3 January 1994.

27. James M. Goldgeier, "NATO Expansion."

In general, Spain, Portugal, and Greece opposed enlargement, for fear of draining away NATO resources allocated to them; Norway, Denmark, Turkey and Germany supported enlargement. Turkey, however, sought a southeastern enlargement that included Bulgaria, Romania, and Albania, but not east-central Europe. France, Italy, and Canada sought to include Romania and Slovenia—in addition to Poland, the Czech Republic, and Hungary.

28. James M. Goldgeier, "Keeping the Door Open" in *NATO at Fifty*, ed. Susan Eisenhower (Washington, DC: Center for Political and Strategic Studies, 1999), 94.

29. James M. Goldgeier, "NATO Expansion."

30. For details, see Gardner, *Dangerous Crossroads*, 18–30.

31. Solomon, *NATO Enlargement*, 80–81.

32. Holbrooke, letter to Richard Davies, 25 July 1995.

33. Holbrooke, *To End a War*, 214.

34. "Open Letter to the President" *Center for Political and Strategic Studies*, 26 June 1999. http://www.cpss.org. Signers of the letter included Sam Nunn, Bill Bradley, Gary Hart, Jack Matlock, Arthur Hartman, Richard T. Davies, Paul H. Nitze, Robert McNamara, Stansfield Turner, and former NATO Assistant General Philip Merril.

35. See Hall Gardner, "Toward a Euro-Atlantic Compromise," *Focus* November 1997 (www.cpss.org/nato/nato.htm).

36. Mark Weller, "The Rambouillet Conference on Kosovo," *International Security*, Vol. 75, No. 2, 1999.

37. Javier Solana, "NATO's Success in Kosovo," *Foreign Affairs*, November/December 1999. NATO expected UNSC members Russia and China to veto intervention, but another option would have been for NATO to obtain a Uniting for Peace resolution from the General Assembly to legitimize its intervention, as Washington did during the Korean war.

38. "Text of Annan's Statement on NATO bombing," Reuters, 24 March 1999.

39. *International Herald Tribune*, 19 April 1999, 2.

40. William D. Hartung, "Costs of NATO Expansion Revisited," *A World Policy Issue Brief*, 21 April 1999. http://www.nyu/globalbeat/nato/Hartung0499.htm. See also, *New York Times*, 18 April 1999.

41. Debate in NATO circles centered on the concept of the "collective defense of interests" which is considered a "non-Article V action." Moreover, NATO is mandated by the U.S. Senate as a "collective defense" and not a "collective security" organization. See Hall Gardner, "NATO and the UN" in *NATO: The First Fifty Years*, ed. Gustav Schmidt (London: Macmillan, forthcoming).

42. See James Hooper, "Kosovo: America's Balkan Problem," *Current History* (April 1999), 162–64.

43. In addition to pressure from Madeleine Albright to engage NATO as soon as possible, Vice President Albert Gore is reputed to have "argued forcefully that the credibility of NATO was more important than paying attention to the sensitivities of the Russians," Jane Perlez, "Step by Step: How the U.S. Decided to Attack, and Why So Fast," *New York Times*, 26 March 1999. Secretary of Defense William Cohen and Chairman of the Joint Chiefs of Staff Henry H. Shelton put the issue bluntly: "Had NATO not responded to Milosevic's defiance and his campaign of ethnic cleansing, its credibility would have been called in question." *Report to Congress, Kosovo/Operation Allied Force After Action Report* (Washington, DC: DOD: 31 January 2000). http://www.fas.org/man/dod-101/ops/2000/b02072000_bt052-00.htm.

44. *International Herald Tribune*, 11 June 1999, 6.

45. *International Herald Tribune*, 26 March 1999, 1. See also *International*

Herald Tribune, 24 March 1999, 6. As an advisor to President Clinton put it, "the alliance itself is at risk because if it's unable to address a major threat within Europe, it really loses its reason for being."

46. *International Herald Tribune*, 21 July 1999, 1, 4.

47. Jacques Rupnik cited in "Stance on Kosovo may Jeopardize Further NATO Enlargement," FBIS–EEU–1999–0414 (14 April 1999).

48. It has subsequently been argued that had NATO continued to bomb targets in Serbia for a few more days, the Milosevic regime may have tumbled. If so, with what political-social-economic consequences? Which politicians would take his place? On the other hand, the subsequent victory of a pro-EU pro-NATO anti-corruption leadership of Ivica Racan in Croatia could indirectly influence Milosevic's downfall.

49. Accusations that NATO actions are based on "double standards," one for Serbia versus Albanians and the KLA, and another one for NATO-member Turkey versus the Kurds and the Kurdish Workers' Party (PKK), may have led the U.S., NATO, and EU to pressure Turkey to work toward a resolution of the Kurdish question. Interestingly, Islamic states tended to support NATO actions in Bosnia and Kosovo as the intervention indicated that the United States does not attack only Moslem states, as appeared to be the case in regard to Iraq in November 1998.

50. For a discussion of the "right" or "duty" to intervene, see Oleg Kobtzeff, this book. It is not entirely accidental that one of major advocates of the "right" to intervene, Bernard Kouchner, became head of the UN Mission in Kosovo, whose task is to coordinate the joint efforts of the UN, UNHCR, the OSCE, and the EU, in coordination with KFOR. See Bernard Kouchner, "The Challenge of Rebuilding Kosovo," *NATO Review* Autumn 1999.

51. In addition to the use of morally questionable weaponry such B-52s, cluster bombs, and depleted uranium ordnance, NATO attacks on dual-use military-civilian infrastructure (chemical factories, auto plants, oil refineries; electrical grids, bridges, water facilities) may have violated Article 14 of the 1977 Protocol to the 1949 Geneva convention which bars attacks on "objects indispensable to the survival of the population." See Michael Mandelbaum, "A Perfect Failure," *Foreign Affairs*, September–October 1999. The United States and United Kingdom claimed that Serbian actions caused up to 10,000 deaths; yet as of November 1999, only 2,108 bodies had actually been discovered. See "War in Kosovo Was Cruel, Bitter, Savage; Genocide It Wasn't," *Wall Street Journal* 4 January 2000, 1,7. In February 2000 the UNHCR reported that only 700–800 Serbs were now living in Pristina out of an estimated 20,000 in 1998. The war "over" Kosovo forced roughly 190,000 Serbs and 40,000 gypsies out of the region which once held between 200,000 and 250,000 Serbs. Roughly 700,000 Serbs are now "internal refugees" following wars in Bosnia and Kosovo. NATO actions may have directly or indirectly killed hundreds, perhaps thousands, of ethnic Serb and Albanian civilians.

52. On appeasement, see Hall Gardner, *Surviving the Millennium,* 51–54. Henry Kissinger proposed a *realpolitik* resolution, but one without Russian diplomatic involvement. See *Newsweek*, 31 May 1999; 21 June 1999.

53. According to *Newsweek* magazine, General Michael Jackson (UK) refused to obey NATO Supreme Commander General Wesley Clark's order to block Russian forces from entering Pristina airport, ahead of NATO forces, as the war came to an end. Jackson is reported to have said, "I'm not going to start World War III for you." See Reuters, 2 August 1999. Moscow appears to have learned that it needs to get "tough" with NATO if it is to get what it wants.

54. "Russia Acts to Toughen its Security Framework," *International Herald Tribune*, 15 January 2000. The revised national security doctrine also lowers the

threshold for the use of nuclear weapons, "In case of a threat to the existence of the Russian Federation as a sovereign state."

55. The latter conditions had been mandated by Presidential Directive 24 to justify U.S. military participation in UN peacekeeping actions; why do they not also appear to represent basic conditions for NATO actions?

56. Such a strategy has yet to succeed in Bosnia where sociopolitical divisions among Serbs, Croats, and Bosniaks are, to a large extent, based upon the *millet* system of the former Ottoman Empire. See Bernard Lory, this book. See also, Ivo H. Daalder and Michael B.G. Froman, "Dayton's Incomplete Peace," *Foreign Affairs* November/December 1999.

57. All parallel state structures in Kosovo were supposed to cease to exist on 31 January 2000, yet the shadow state parliament stated it would disband itself only once new elections are held. See *Radio Free Europe/ Radio Liberty Balkan Report* Vol. 4. No. 10, 4 February 2000.

58. Benn Steil; Susan L. Woodward, "A European 'New Deal' for the Balkans," *Foreign Affairs* November/ December 1999. "Whether one looks at the slow delivery and disappointing results of aid, at the costs of debt repayment, or at official corruption and aid dependency, the conclusion is the same: Financial aid will not bring about a self-sustained, self-governed peace. Indeed, aid can even hinder it. Peace requires fundamental political and economic reform. Western assistance can be instrumental in achieving this. What is required is nothing short of a European 'New deal'." The authors argue for bringing the region into the European Monetary Union (EMU); yet given the complexities now confronting European integration, it is not clear that any form of "New Deal" will soon be forthcoming.

59. In terms of loss of trade, the war cost Bulgaria between $700 million and $1 billion; Romania roughly $900 million; and Macedonia over $1.5 billion. Andrew J. Pierre, "De-Balkanizing the Balkans," *USIP Special Report* (Washington, DC: United States Institute of Peace, 20 September 1999. Damage to Serbia may be over $25 billion according to European estimates.

60. In February 2000, U.S. Senators threatened to pull U.S. troops out of Bosnia and Kosovo if the EU did not soon move to provide greater police enforcement and funding of $35 million. U.S. operations in Bosnia have cost at least $10 billion; the air war over Kosovo cost about $5 billion. The two missions will cost billions more in annual expenses.

61. See Hall Gardner, "NATO, Russia, and Eastern European Security," in Piotr Dutkiewicz and Robert J. Jackson, *NATO Looks East* (Westport, CT: Praeger, 1998).

62. See Robert E. Hunter, "NATO in the 21st Century: A Strategic Vision," *Parameters* (Summer 1998).

63. *International Herald Tribune*, 13 14 March 1999

64. The development of "separate but not separable" European and Euro-Atlantic defense and security identities may be one way to enlarge NATO's membership and include Russia without overextending NATO capabilities and breaking up its political consensus. See Hall Gardner, "Toward a Separate- but not Separable- European and Euro-Atlantic Commands" in *NATO's New Strategy and ESDI*, eds. Marcel van Herpen and Hall Gardner (Maastricht: Cicero Foundation Press, 1999). See also, an earlier version, "NATO Enlargement: Toward a Separate Euro-Atlantic Command," published by the Committee on Eastern Europe and Russia in NATO (CEERN): http//:www.fas.org/man nato/ceern/index.html.

Bibliography

GENERAL

Ash, Timothy Garton, *The Uses of Adversity*. New York: Vintage Books, 1990.

Barzany, Z.D. and I. Volgyes, *The Legacies of Communism in Eastern Europe*. Baltimore: Johns Hopkins University Press, 1995.

Carrere D'Encausse, Hélène, *Le Grand frère*. (Paperback edition). Paris: Le Livre de Poche, 1985.

Gélédan, A., *Transition à l'Est*. Paris: Le Monde Editions/Marabout, 1995.

Giblin, Béatrice and Yves Lacoste, *Géohistoire de l'Europe médiane: mutations d'hier et d'aujourd'hui*. Paris: Editions La Découverte, 1998.

Goldman, Minton F., *Revolution and Change in Central and Eastern Europe, Political and Social Changes*. London: M.E. Sharpe, 1997.

Grey, Robert D., *Democratic Theory and Post-Communist Change*. Englewood Cliffs, NJ: Prentice-Hall, 1997.

Lemarchand, Philippe, *L'Europe Centrale et Balkanique: Atlas d'histoire politique*. Paris: Editions Complexe, 1995.

Lhomel, Edith et Thomas Schreiber, *L'Europe centrale et orientale*. Paris: La Documentation Française, 1998 (annual).

Roskin, Michael G., *The Rebirth of East Europe*. (2nd edition). Englewood Cliffs, NJ: Prentice-Hall: 1994.

Sellier, André and Jean Sellier, *Atlas des peuples d'Europe Centrale*. Paris: Editions Découverte, 1991.

Sword, Keith, *The Times Guide to Eastern Europe: The Changing Face of the Warsaw Pact. A Comprehensive Handbook*. London: Times Books, 1990.

Wackermann, Gabriel, Violette Ray, and Christine Aquatias, *Mutations en Europe Médiane*. Paris: CNED, SEDES, 1997.

Who's Who in Central and Eastern Europe. Kingston-upon-Thames: Debrett's Peerage Ltd. 1994.

HISTORICAL BACKGROUND

Adams, A.E., I.M. Matley, and W.O. McCagg, *An Atlas of East European History*. London: Heinemann, 1967.

Aldcroft, D.H. and S. Morewood, *Economic Change in Eastern Europe since 1918*. Aldershot: Edward Elgar Publishing Ltd., 1995.
Allcock, J.B., *A Historical Sociology of the South Slavlands: Modernization in the 19th and 20th Centuries*. London: C. Hurst & Co., 1996.
Barkey, Karen and Mark von Hagen, *After Empire: Multiethnic Societies and Nation-building*. Boulder, CO: Westview Press, 1997.
Bogdan, Henry, *From Warsaw to Sofia: A History of Eastern Europe*. Santa Fe, NM: ProLibertate, 1989
Conte, Francis, *Les Slaves: aux origines des civilisations d'Europe centrale et orientale*. Paris: Albin Michel, 1986.
Delsol, Chantal and Michel Maslowski, *Histoire des ides politiques en Europe centrale*. Paris: Presses Universitaires de France, 1998.
Djordjevic, Dimitrije and Stephen Fischer-Galati, *The Balkan Revolutionary Tradition*. New York: Columbia University Press, 1981.
Djuric, Ivan, *Le crépuscule de Byzance*. Paris: Maisonneuve et Larose, 1995.
Fetjö, François, *Requiem pour un empire défunt: Histoire de la destruction de l'Autriche-Hongrie*. (3rd edition). Paris: Edima/Lieu Commun & Seuil, 1993.
———, *Histoire des démocraties populaires. Vol. 1: L'ére de Staline: 1945–1953*. Paris: Seuil, 1992.
———, *Histoire des démocraties populaires. Vol. 2: Aprés Staline: 1953–1979*. Paris: Seuil, 1992.
Hermet, Guy, *Histoire des nations et du nationalisme en Europe*. Paris: Seuil, 1996.
Inalcik, Halil, *The Ottoman Empire: The Classical Age 1300–1600*. New York: Praeger, 1994.
Jelavich, Barbara, *History of the Balkans: Eighteenth and Nineteenth Centuries*, Tome 1. Cambridge: Cambridge University Press, 1983.
———, *History of the Balkans: Twentieth Century*, Tome 2. Cambridge: Cambridge University Press, 1983.
King, Robert, *Minorities under Communism: Nationalities as Causes of Tension among Balkan Communist States*. Cambridge: Harvard University Press, 1973.
Lory, Bernard, *L'Europe Balkanique de 1945 à nos jours*. Paris: Ellipses, 1996.
Mantran, Robert, *Histoire de l'empire ottoman*. Paris: Fayard, 1989.
Rupnik, Jacques, *The Other Europe*. London: Weidenfeld & Nicolson, 1988.
Stokes, Gale (Ed.), *From Stalinism to Pluralism: A Documentary History of Eastern Europe Since 1945*. Oxford: Oxford University Press, 1991.
Sugar, Peter, *Southeastern Europe under Ottoman Rule 1354–1804*. Seattle: Washington University Press, 1977.

INSTITUTIONS AND POLITICAL DYNAMICS
Baldersheim, Harald, Michal Illner, Audun Offerdal, Lawrence Rose, and Pawel Swianiewicz, *Local Democracy and the Processes of Transformation in East-Central Europe*. Boulder, CO: Westview Press, 1996.
Berglund, Sten and Jan Ake Dellenbrandt, *The New Democracies in Eastern Europe: Party Systems and Political Cleavages*. (2nd edition). Aldershot: Elgar, 1994
Best, Heinrich and Ulrike Becker, *Elites in Transition: Elite Research in Central and Eastern Europe*. Opladen: Leske und Budrich, 1997.
Braun, Aurel and Stephen Scheinberg (Eds.), *The Extreme Right: Freedom and Security at Risk*. Boulder, CO: Westview Press, 1996.
Brodsky, Joseph and Vaclav Havel, "The 'Post-Communist Nightmare': An Exchange." *The New York Review of Books*, February 17, 1994: 28–30.

Bibliography

Crawford, Keith, *East Central European Politics Today*. Manchester: Manchester University Press, 1996.

Fetjö, François, *La Fin des démocraties populaires: les chemins du post-communisme*. Paris: Seuil, 1992

Fischer, Mary Ellen, *Establishing Democracies*. Boulder, CO: Westview Press, 1996.

Frydman, Roman, Kenneth Murphy, and Andrzej Rapaczynski, *Capitalism with a Comrade's Face*. Budapest: Central European University Press, 1998.

Gélédan, Alain, *Transitions à l'Est*. Paris: Le Monde Editions/Marabout, 1995.

Gibson, J. and P. Hanson, *Transformation from Below: Local Power and the Political Economy of Post-Communist Transitions*. Cheltenham: Elgar, 1996.

Glenny, Misha, "Why the Balkans Are so Violent." *The New York Review of Books*, September 19, 1996: 34, 36–39.

Gwertzman, Bernard and Michael T. Kaufman, *The Collapse of Communism*. New York: Times Books & Random House, 1990.

Havel, Vaclav, "The Hope for Europe." *The New York Review of Books*, June 20, 1996: 38–39.

———, "The Post-Communist Nightmare." *The New York Review of Books*, May 27, 1993: 8–10.

Hepper, Metin, Ali Kazanygil, and Bert A. Rockman, *Institutions and Democratic Statecraft*. Boulder, CO: Westview Press, 1997.

Hesse, Jens, *Administration Transformation in Central and Eastern Europe: Towards Public Sector Reform in Post-Communist Societies*. London: Blackwell Publishers, 1993.

International Institute for Democracy, *The Rebirth of Democracy: 12 Constitutions of Central and Eastern Europe*. Strasbourg: Council of Europe, 1995.

Kaldor, Mary and Ivan Vejvoda, "Democratization in Central and East European Countries." *International Affairs* 73.1 (1997): 59–82.

Kraus, Michael and Ronald D. Liebovitz, *Russia and Eastern Europe after Communism*. Boulder, CO: Westview Press, 1996.

Labrousse, Alain et Michel Coutouzis, *Géopolitique et Géostrategies des Drogues*. Paris: Economica, 1996.

Lewis, Paul G., *Party Structure and Organization in East-Central Europe*. Cheltenham: Elgar, 1996.

Lijphart, Arendt and Carlos S. Waisman, *Institutional Design in New Democracies: Eastern Europe and Latin America*. Boulder, CO: Westview Press, 1996.

Mason, David S., *Revolution and Transition in East-Central Europe*. Boulder, CO: Westview Press, 1996.

Mink, Georges and Jean-Charles Szurek, *Cet Etrange Post Communisme: Rupture et transitions en Europe centrale et orientale*. Paris: Presses du C.N.R.S. & Découverte, 1992.

Observatoire Geopolitique des Drogues/Geopolitical Drug Watch, *The Geopolitics of Drugs*. Boston: Northeastern University Press, 1996.

Observatoire Geopolitique des Drogues, *La Géopolitique mondial des drogues 1995–1996*. Paris: OGD, septembre 1997 (rapport annuel).

Offe, Claus, *Varieties of Transition: The East European and East German Experience*. Cambridge: MIT Press, 1997.

Remington, T.R., *Parliaments in Transition: The New Legislative Politics in Former USSR and Eastern Europe*. Boulder, CO: Westview Press, 1994.

ECONOMIC REFORM

Abrahams, R., *After Socialism: Land Reform and Social Change in Eastern Europe.* Providence/Oxford: Berghahn Books, 1996.

Blanchard, O., *The Economics of post-Communist Transition.* Oxford: Clarendon Press, 1997.

Centre d'Etudes et de documentation sur l'ex-URSS, la Chine et l'Europe de l'Est (CEDUCEE), *Transitions Economiques à l'Est (1989–1995).* Paris: La Documentation française, Les Etudes, décembre 1995.

Crawford, Beverly, *Markets, States and Democracy.* Boulder, CO: Westview Press, 1995.

Ernst, Maurice, Michael Alexeev, and Paul Marer, *Transforming the Core: Restructuring Industrial Enterprises in Russia and Central Europe.* Boulder, CO: Westview Press, 1995.

Estrin, Saul, Kirsty S. Hughes, and Sarah Todd, *Foreign Direct Investment in Central and Eastern Europe: Multinationals in Transition.* London: Pinter (Royal Institute of International Affairs), 1997.

European Bank for Reconstruction and Development (EBRD)/Banque européenne pour la reconstruction et le developpement (BERD), *Annual Report 1996*, 1997.

———, *Transition Report 1997: Infrastructure and Savings*, 1996.

———, *Transition Report Update*, 1997.

———, *Transition Report Update*, April 1997.

European Commission PHARE. Brussels: Phare Information Office, Directorate General for External Economic Relations.

———, *Agriculture*, by Etienne Claeyé, June 1994.

———, *Banking*, by Chris Clarke, June 1994.

———, *Energy*, by Jean-Luc Delpeuch, June 1994.

———, *Enterprise Restructuring and Privatization*, July 1994.

———, *Food Aid*, by Jean Pierre Peeters and Maya Dragonova, July 1994.

———, *Health*, by Hélène Bourgade, July 1994.

———, *Small and Medium-Sized Enterprises*, by Pierre Mirel and Stuart Thompson, August 1994.

Eurostat-Phare, *Enteprises en Europe central et Orientale.* Luxembourg: Office des publications officielles des Communautes européennes, 1996.

Evans, Geoffrey and Stephen Whitefield, "The Politics and Economics of Democratic Commitment: Support for Democracy in Transition Societies." *British Journal of Political Science,* 25 (1995): 485–514.

Goldman, Marshall I., "Can Democracy Take Root Where Tsars and Soviets Ruled?" *Theory and Practice of International Relations,* ed. William C. Olson. (9th ed.) Englewood Cliffs, N.J.: Prentice Hall, 1994.

Greskovits, Béla, *The Political Economy of Protest and Patience: East European and Latin American Transformations Compared.* Budapest: Central European University Press, 1998.

Gros, Daniel and Alfred Steinherr, *Winds of Change: Economic Transition in Central and Eastern Europe.* London: The Economics of Transition Series, 1995.

Herr, H., S. Tober and A. Westphal, *Macroeconomic Problems of Transformation: Stabilization Policy and Economic Restructuring.* Aldershot: Edward Elgar, 1994.

Jackson, M. and W. Blesbronck, *Marketization, Restructuring and Competition in Transition Industries of Central and Eastern Europe.* Aldershot: Avebury, 1995.

King, Neil, Jr., "Lost Commerce and Political Divisions Bedevil Central Europe's Great River." *Central European Economic Review,* Sept. 1996:14–17.

Bibliography

Lavigne, M., *The Economics of Transition from Socialist Economy to Market Economy*. London: Macmillan, 1995.
Meyer, Klaus E. and Saul Estrin, *Privatization, Acquisition and Direct Foreign Investment: Who Buys State-Owned Enterprises*. Bologna: Most, 1997.
Nelson, Mark M. and Lisa Trei, "A New Hanseatic League?" *Central European Economic Review*, Winter 1994: 10–11.
Redor, Dominique, *Les économies de l'Europe de l'Est depuis 1989*. Paris: Seuil, Mémo Economie, 1997.
Rey, V. (sous la coord.), *Les Nouvelles campagnes de l'Europe centrale et orientale*. Paris: CNRS Editions, Collection Espaces et Milieux, 1996.
Sgard, Jerome, *Europe de l'Est: la transition économiques*. Paris: Flammarion, Dominos, 1997.
Slay, Ben, *De-Monopolization and Competition Policy in Post-Communist Europe*. Boulder, CO: Westview Press, 1996.
Tiraspolsky, A. et G. Wild, *Economies de l'Est en transition: critéres de comparaison*. Paris: Masson, 1992.
UN/EEC, *Economic Bulletin for Europe (Bulletin Economique pour l'Europe)*. Volume 48, December 1996, New York, Geneva: United Nations, (annual). *Economic Survey of Europe in 1995–1996*, New York, Geneva: Commission économique pour l'Europe, 1996.
Economic Survey of Europe in 1996–1997. New York, Geneva: ECE, 1997.
Wiles, Peter, "Will Capitalism and Communism Converge?" *Talking to Eastern Europe*, ed. G.R. Urban. London: Eyre and Spottiswood, 1964: 223–240.
Winters, L.A. (Ed.), *Foundations of an Open Economy: Trade Laws and Institutions for Eastern Europe*. London: Center for Economic Policy Research, 1995.
World Bank, *From Plan to Market*. Oxford University Press: New York, 1996.
World Bank, Washington DC, *De l'économie planifiée à l'économie de Marché rapport sur le developpment dans le monde 1996*.
World Bank, Washington DC, *Privatization and Restructuring in Central and Eastern Europe: Evidence and Policy Options*. (Technical Paper 368, Finance, Private Sector, Infrastructure Network), 1997.
Zecchini, Salvatore, (Ed.), *Lessons from the Economic Transition: Central and Eastern Europe in the 1990s*. Norwell: Kluwer Academic Publishers & O.E.C.D., 1997.

SOCIAL ISSUES AND CHANGES

Ash, Timothy-Garton, *We the People: The Revolution of '89 Witnesses in Warsaw, Budapest, Berlin and Prague*. London: Granta Books, Penguin, 1990.
Barr, N. (Ed.), *Labor Markets and Social Policy in Central and Eastern Europe*. Oxford: Oxford University Press, 1994.
Brucan, Silviu, *Social Change in Russia and Eastern Europe: From Party Hacks to Nouveaux Riches*. Westport, CT: Praeger Publishers, 1998.
Coutouzis, Michel (sous la dir.) et Pascal Perez (cartes), *Atlas Mondial des Drogues*. Paris: Presses Universitaires de France (PUF), (Observatoire Géopolitique des Drogues), 1996.
Frybes, Marcin et Anne Nivat (Eds.), "Le nouveau paysage médiatique à l'Est." *L'autre Europe*, N° 32–33. Paris, 1996.
Hankis, Elemér, *East European Alternatives*. Oxford: Clarendon Press, 1990.
———, "European Paradigms: East and West, 1945–1994." *Daedalus* 123.3 (1994): 115–126.
———, "The Rope Dancers. European Civilization: Its Problems and Prospects." *World Futures* 47(1996): 263–276.

Liehm, Antonin, *Politics of Culture*. New York: Grove/Random House, 1972.
———, *Le cinema de l'Est*. Paris: Cerf, 1989.
Long, Kristie S., *We All Fought for Freedom: Women in Poland's Solidarity Movement*. Boulder, CO: Westview Press, 1996.
Maslowski, Michel (Ed.), *Cultures et Sociétes de l'Est*. Paris: Institut d'Etudes Slaves, 1995.
OECD Reviews of National Education Policies, *Czech Republic*, September 1996.
———, *Poland*, August 1996.
O'Neil, P.H., *Post-Communism and the Media in Eastern Europe*. London: Frank Cass, 1997.
Ramet, Sabrine Petra, *Social Currents in Eastern Europe: The Sources and Consequences of the Great Transformation*. Durham, NC: Duke University Press, 1995.
Renne, Tanya, *Ana's Land: Sisterhood in Eastern Europe*. Boulder, CO: Westview Press, 1996.
Rueschmeyer, M. (Ed.), *Women in the Politics of Post-Communist Eastern Europe*. London: M.E. Sharpe Inc., 1994.
Semelin, Jacques, *La liberté au bout des ondes: du coup de Prague à la chute du mur de Berlin*. Paris: Belfond, 1997.
Splichal, Slavko, *Media Beyond Socialism*. Boulder, CO: Westview Press, 1995.
UNICEF, *Children at Risk in Central and Eastern Europe: Perils and Promises*. New York, 1997.
World Bank, *Unemployment, Restructuring and the Labor Market in Eastern Europe and Russia*, Washington DC, 1995.
———, *Labor Markets in Transition in Central and Eastern Europe 1989–1995*, Washington DC, 1996.

FOREIGN POLICY

Bugajski, Janusz, *Nations in Turmoil: Conflict and Cooperation in Eastern Europe*. Boulder, CO: Westview Press, 1995.
Crampton, R.J., *Eastern Europe in the Twentieth Century—and After*. (2nd edition). London: Routledge, 1997.
Danner, Mark, "The U.S. and the Yugoslav Catastrophe." *The New York Review of Books*, November 20, 1997: 56–64.
Danopoulos, Constantine P. and Kostas G. Messas (Eds.), *Crises in the Balkans: Views from the Participants*. Boulder, CO: Westview Press, 1997.
Drew, S.N., *NATO from Berlin to Bosnia: Trans-Atlantic Security in Transition*. Washington DC: McNair Paper 35, National Defense University, 1995.
Dutkiewicz, Piotr and Robert J. Jackson, *NATO Looks East*. Westport, CT: Praeger, 1998.
Foucher, M., (ed.), *Les défis de sécurité en Europe médiane: Pologne, Hongrie, République tchéque, Slovakie, Slovénie*. Paris: Fondation pour les études de défense, Coll. Prespectives Strategique, 1996.
———, *Fragments d'Europe*. Paris: Fayard (2nd edition in progress).
Gardner, Hall, *Dangerous Crossroads: Europe, Russia, and the Future of NATO*. Westport, CT: Praeger, 1997.
———, *Surviving the Millennium: American Global Strategy, the Collapse of the Soviet Empire, and the Question of Peace*. Westport, CT: Praeger, 1997.
Ghebali, V.Y., *L'OSCE dans l'Europe post-communiste 1990–1996. Vers une identité paneuropéenne de sécurité*. Bruxelles: Bruylant, 1996.

Bibliography

Hassner, Pierre, *Violence and Peace*. Budapest: Central European University Press; Oxford University Press, 1997.
Havel, Vaclav, "The Charms of NATO," *The New York Review of Books*, June 20, 1997: 24.
Mandelbaum, Michael, *The Dawn of Peace in Europe*. New York: 20th Century Fund 1996.
Mastny, Voycheh and R. Craig Nation (Eds.), *Turkey Between East and West: New Challenges for a Rising Regional Power*. Boulder, CO: Westview Press, 1996.
Poulton, H., *The Balkans: Minorities and States in Conflict*. London: Minority Rights Publications, 1992.
Prévélakis, Georges, *Géopolitique de la Grèce*. Bruxelles: Editions Complexe, 1997.
Rupnick, Jacques (Ed.), *Unfinished Peace*. Washington DC: Carnegie Endowment, 1996.
Steel, Ronald, "Instead of NATO," *The New York Review of Books*, January 15 1998: 21–24.
Turander, Ola (Ed.), *Geopolitics in Post-Wall Europe*. London: Sage, 1996.
UN/EC, *Human Settlement under Transition: The Case of Eastern Europe and the CIS*. New York: UNDP, 1996.

EUROPEAN INTEGRATION

Conseil économique et social, Prate, A., *L'Elargissement de l'Union européenne et ses conséquences pour l'économie française*. Paris: Conseil économique et social, 1997.
Somai, M., *Agricultural Accession of Central and Eastern European Countries to the European Union*. Budapest: Hungarian Academy of Sciences, Institute of World Economics, 1996.
Van den Bempt, P. and G. Theelen, *From European Agreements to Accession: The Integration of Central and Eastern Countries into the European Union*. Brussels: European Inter-university Press, 1996.
Weidenfeld, W., *Central and Eastern Europe on the Way into the European Union: Problems and Prospects of Integration in 1996*. Gutersloh: Bertelsman Foundation Publishers, 1996.

NATIONALITIES, MINORITIES, AND RELIGIOUS GROUPS

Brass, P.R., *Ethnicity and Nationalism: Theory and Comparison*. London: Sage, 1991.
Kobtzeff, Oleg, "Orthodoxy Takes the Stage: Preventing Extremism in Eastern-Central Europe." *Scripta Politica et Economica*, 8.1: 10–11, 26–27.
Kupchan, Charles A., *Nationalism and Nationalities in the New Europe*. Ithaca: Cornell University Press (Council on Foreign Relations book), 1995.
Maslowski, Michel, (Ed.), *Identités de l'Europe Centrale*. Paris: Institut d'Etudes Slaves, 1995.
Mayer, Jean-François, *Religions et sécurité internationale*. Berne: Office Central de la Défense (Etudes relatives à la politique de sécurité) No. 2, 1995.
Norris, H.T., *Islam in the Balkans*. London: C. Hurst, 1994.
Ramet, Pedro (Ed.), *Religion and Nationalism in Soviet and East European Politics*. Durham, NC: Duke University Press, 1989.
Selier, A.J., *Atlas des peuples d'Europe Centrale*. Paris: La Découverte, 1991.
Stewart, Michael, *The Time of the Gypsies*. Boulder, CO: Westview Press, 1997.
Thual, François, *Les Conflits identitaires*. Paris: Ellipses, 1995.
———, *Géopolitique de l'Orthodoxie*. Paris: Dunod, 1994.

COUNTRIES

Albania
Glenny, Misha, "Heart of Darkness." *The New York Review of Books*, August 14, 1997: 32–45.
Vickers, M., *The Albanians: A Modern History*. London: C. Hurst, 1995.

Baltic States
Bilinsky, Yaroslav, *Endgame in NATO's Enlargement: The Baltic States and Ukraine*. Westport, CT: Praeger Publishers, 1999.
Fitzmaurice, John, *Estonia*. Boulder, CO: Westview Press, 1993.
Michaels, Daniel, "Scandanavia Sets Sights on Baltic 'Near Abroad.'" *Central European Economic Review*, Nov. 1995: 8–18.
Nelson, Mark M., "List Shows Baltics Have Far to Go." *Central European Economic Review*, Winter 1994: 13.
OECD, *Regional Integration and Transition Economies: The Case of the Baltic Rim*. Paris: OECD, 1996.
Vardys, Stanley V. and Judith B. Sedaitis, *Lithuania: The Rebel Nation*. Boulder, CO: Westview Press, 1996.

Bulgaria
Aramov, R. and V. Antonov, *Economic Transition in Bulgaria*. Sofia: Agency for Economic Coordination and Development, 1994.
Bell, John, *The Communist Party of Bulgaria: From Blagoev to Zhivkov*. Stanford, CA: Stanford University Press, 1986.
———, *Bulgaria in Transition*. Boulder, CO: Westview Press, 1998.
Crampton, Richard, *A Short History of Modern Bulgaria*. Cambridge: Cambridge University Press, 1987.
Dimitrov, A.G., *The Bulgarian Economy in Transition: Growth Factors and Specific Conditions*. Tokyo: Institute of Developing Countries, 1994.
Lampe, John, *The Bulgarian Economy in the Twentieth Century*. London: Croom-Helm, 1986.
OCDE/CCET, *Etudes Economiques de l'OCDE, Bulgarie 1997*. Paris: OCDE, 1997.
Todorov, Tzvetan, *Au nom du peuple, Témoignages sur les camps communistes*. Paris: La Tour d'Aigues, Ed. de l'aube, 1992.

Czech and Slovak Republics
Fogel, D.S. (Ed.), *Managing in Emerging Market Economies: Cases from the Czech and Slovak Republics*. Boulder, CO: Westview Press, 1994.
Goldman, Minton F., *Slovakia since Independence*. Westport, CT: Praeger Publishers, 1998.
Leff, Carol Skalnik, *The Czech and Slovak Republic: Nation versus State*. Boulder, CO: Westview Press, 1996.
Ministry of Foreign Affairs, *Czech Republic: Facts and Figures*. Prague: Arteria Info, 1994.
Musil, J., *The End of Czechoslovakia*. Budapest: Central European Press, 1995.
Svejnar, J., *The Czech Republic and Economic Transition in Eastern Europe*. San Diego: Academic Press, 1995.
Zrinscak, G., *Le Systéme agro-alimentaire tchéque: rupture et recompositions spatiales*. Univ. Paris I-Panthéon: ENS Fontenay/Saint-Cloud, 1997.

Bibliography

Germany

Hancock, Donald M. and Henry Krisch, *Germany*. Boulder, CO: Westview Press, 1998.

Judt, Tony, "New Germany, Old NATO." *The New York Review of Books*, May 29 1997: 21–24.

Koehler, John O., *Stasi: The Untold Story of East Germany's Secret Police*. Boulder, CO: Westview Press, 1998.

Le Gloannec, Anne-Marie, *La nation orpheline: les Allemagnes en Europe*. Paris: Fondation Saint-Simon, Calmann-Lévy, 1989.

Hungary

Horvath, M.T., *The Dissolution of Communist Power: The Case of Hungary*. London: Routledge, 1992.

OECD, *Economic Survey 1996–1997 Hungary*. Paris: OECD, 1997.

Romiscs, Ignac and Bela Kiraly, (Eds.), *Geopolitics in the Danube Region: Hungarian Efforts, 1848–1998*. Budapest: Central European University Press, 1998.

Tökés, Rudolf, L., *Hungary's Negotiated Revolution: Economic Reform, Social Change, and Political Succession, 1957–1990*. Cambridge, Russian, Soviet and Post-Soviet Studies no. CI, Cambridge: Cambridge University Press, 1996.

Poland

Ash, Timothy Garton, *The Polish Revolution*. London: Grantabooks, Penguin, 1991.

Beauvois, Daniel, *Histoire de la Pologne*. Paris: Hatier, 1995.

CRPCE (Center for Research into Post-Communist Economies), *Five Years after June: The Polish Transformation, 1989–1994*. London: CRPCE, 1996.

Dowall, David, Marta Sadowy, and Alojzy Zalewski, *The Warsaw Economy in Transition*. Aldershot: Avebury, 1966.

IMF, *Republic of Poland: Recent Economic Developments*. Washington, DC: IMF, 1997.

Roberts, K. and B. Jung, *Poland's First Post-Communist Generation*. Aldershot: Avebury, 1995.

Taras, Raymond, *Consolidating Democracy in Poland*. Boulder, CO: Westview Press, 1995.

Tworzecki, Hubert, *Parties and politics in Post-1989 Poland*. Boulder, CO: Westview Press, 1996.

Walicki, A., *Poland between East and West*. Cambridge: Harvard University Press, 1996.

Romania

Durandin, Catherine, *Histoire de la nation roumaine*. Paris: éditions Complexe, collection "Questions au XXe siécle," 1994.

———, *Ceausescu: vérités et mensonges d'un roi communiste*. Paris: Albin Michel, 1990.

Gallagher, T., *Romania after Ceausescu*. Edinburgh: Edinburgh University Press, 1995.

Kideckel, D.A., *The Solitude of Collectivism: Romanian Villagers to the Revolution and Beyond*. Ithaca: Cornell University Press, 1993.

Ratesh, N., *Romania: The Entangled Revolution*. (Center for Strategic and International Studies, The Washington Papers), Westport, CT: Praeger, 1991.

Shen, Raphael, *The Restructuring of Romania's Economy*. Westport, CT: Praeger, 1997.

Who's Who in Romania 1995. Kingston-upon-Thames: Debrett's, 1995.

Former Yugoslavia

Banac, Ivo, *The National Question in Yugoslavia: Origins, History, Politics*. Ithaca: Cornell University Press, 1993.

Bennet, Christopher, *Yugoslavia's Bloody Collapse: Causes, Course, Consequences*. London: C. Hurst, 1995.

Carlen, J. Y., S. Duchêne, and J. Ehrhart, *Ibrahim Rugova, le frêle colosse du Kosovo*. Paris: Desclée de Brouwer, 1999.

Carter, April, *Democratic Reform in Yugoslavia: The Changing Role of the Party 1967–1977*. London: Pinter, 1982.

Cohen, Lenard J., *Broken Bonds: Yugoslavia's Disintegration and Balkan Politics in Transition*. Bouder, CO: Westview Press, 1998.

Cot, Général Jean (sous la direction de), *Dernière guerre balkanique? Ex-Yougoslavie: témoignages, analyses, perspectives*. Paris: FED l'Harmattan, 1996.

Friedman, Francis, *The Bosnian Muslims: Denial of a Nation*. Boulder, CO: Westview Press, 1996.

Garde, Paul, *Vie et Mort de la Yougoslavie*. Paris: Fayard, 1994.

Glenny, Misha, "Yugoslavia: The Great Fall." *The New York Review of Books*, March 23, 1995: 56–65.

Gow, James, *Legitimacy and the Military: The Yugoslav Crisis*. London: Pinter, 1992.

———, *Triumph of the Lack of Will: International Diplomacy and the Yugoslav War*. New York: Columbia University Press, 1997.

Magas, Branka, *The Destruction of Yugoslavia: Tracking the Break-up 1980–1992*. London: Verso, 1993.

Malcolm, Noel, *Bosnia: A Short History*. London: Macmillan, 1994.

Poulton, H., *Who Are the Macedonians?* Bloomington: Indiana University Press/London: C. Hurst, 1995.

Ramet, Pedro, *Nationalism and Federalism in Yugoslavia 1963–1983*. Bloomington: Indiana University Press, 1984.

Ramet, Sabrina Petra, *Balkan Babel: The Disintegration of Yugoslavia from the Death of Tito to Ethnic War* (2nd edition). Boulder, CO: Westview Press, 1996.

Rogel, Carole, *The Breakup of Yugoslavia and the War in Bosnia*. Westport, CT: Greenwood Press, 1998.

Rugova, Ibrahim, *La Question du Kosovo*. Paris: Fayard, 1994.

Silber, Laura and Allan Little, *The Death of Yugoslavia*. London: BBC Books, 1995, New York: Penguin, 1997.

Sloan, Elinor C., *Bosnia and the New Collective Security*. Westport, CT: Praeger, 1998.

Thompson, Mark, *Forging War: The Media in Serbia, Croatia and Bosnia-Herzegovina*. London: Article 19, International Center Against Censorship, 1994.

———, *A Paper House: The Ending of Yugoslavia*. London: Vintage, 1992.

Wijnaendts, Henry, *Joegoslavische Kroniek: Juli 1991–Augustus 1992*. Amsterdam: Rap, 1996.

World Bank, *Bosnia and Herzegovina: From Recovery to Sustainable Growth*. Washington, DC: World Bank, 1997.

World Bank/EBRD, *Bosnia and Herzegovina: Toward Economic Recovery*. Washington, DC: World Bank, 1996.

Bibliography

PERIODICALS SPECIALIZED IN CONTEMPORARY CENTRAL/EAST-EUROPEAN STUDIES

Alternatives. Later renamed *Nouvelles Alternatives*. Published in French, in Paris. One of the most informative and influential periodicals on political conflicts in Central and Eastern Europe.

L'Altra Europa. Published bimonthly in Italian by the Centro Studi Russia Christiana, Milan (mostly religious and cultural affairs of the former USSR and all Central European countries).

L'Autre Europe. Published by L'Age d'Homme Publishing Company, Paris, France and Lausanne, Switzerland (closely linked to the community of Serbian exiles, this publisher's catalog of Slavic studies still includes titles with much wider interests than the recent pro-Serbian militant and polemic monographs).

Balkanistica. Occasional periodical published by a variety of academic groups—more recently by the South East European Studies Association, formerly known as the American Association for Southeast European Studies (AASES) and scholars of the University of Mississippi and the University of Washington.

Canadian Slavonic Papers. (*Revue Canadienne des Slavistes*). An Interdisciplinary Journal Devoted to Central and Eastern Europe Published for the Canadian Association of Slavists. The Canadian academic community's voice on Central and Eastern European affairs. A reflection of Canada's ethnically diverse society—with important Slavic minorities—it is a platform open to specialists worldwide.

Central Europe Online. Electronic newspaper published by the European Internet network along with several affiliated online periodicals accessible at http://www.einmedia.com/

The Insider. Bulgarian digest monthly.

Intermarum. A project of the Institute of Political Studies of the Polish Academy of Sciences and Columbia University's Institute on East Central Europe. "Provides an electronic medium for noteworthy scholarship and provocative thinking about the history and politics of Central and Eastern Europe following World War II. The journal is meant to broaden the discourse on aspects of national histories that are undergoing change thanks to the availability of new documentation from recently opened archives. Its name, Intermarum, reflects East Central Europe's geographic location between the seas: Baltic, Adriatic and Black." http://www.columbia.edu/cu/sipa/REGIONAL/ECE/intermar.html.

Kultura. One of the oldest-running independent Polish journals born in the expatriate community. (Published in Paris by a private association.)

The OMRI Daily Digest. Published on the Internet by the Open Media Research Institute, Prague and New York (successor to the Radio Free Europe/ Radio Liberty Research Institute). LISTSERV@UBVM.CC.BUFFALO.edu.

Östeuropa. The German academic review on many subjects Central and Eastern Europe, founded in Berlin in 1925. Published by a team of academics in Achen and at a variety of other sites.

Replika. Hungarian Social Science Quarterly.

The Slavic and East European Journal. Published quarterly by the American Association of Teachers of Slavic and East European Languages.

Revue des Etudes Slaves. One of France's oldest and richest academic journals, published in Paris by a team of academics from various French institutions. Some articles are in English.

The Slavic Review. Scholarly quarterly journal of the American Association for the Advancement of Slavic Studies, University of Illinois at Urbana-Champaign. One of the oldest and most reputed references in the field.

The Southeast European Yearbook. Published annually by the Hellenic Foundation for Defense and Foreign Policy.

Studia Slavica Finlandensia. SSF as it is known in abbreviation "is a yearbook published by the Institute for Russian and East European Studies (Helsinki) since 1984. SSF includes articles on culture, literature and history of Russia and Eastern Europe. Articles are published in Russian, English, German and French."

Transition. Events and Issues in the Former Soviet Union and East-Central and Southeastern Europe. Published by the Open Media Research Institute, Prague and New York (successor to the Radio Free Europe/Radio Liberty Research Institute).

The New York Review of Books. Highly literate book reviews or original articles, on Central/Eastern European contemporary subjects in at least one out of two issues, with bylines from George Soros, George Kennan, Czeslaw Milosz, Vaclav Havel, Timothy Garton Ash, or Michael Ignatieff are regular contributors.

Europ. A bilingual (English and French) independant quarterly published by an informal group of journalists from over two dozen different countries writing on European current issues and focusing on two or three common themes in every issue (poverty, the environment, Yugoslavia, etc.); as much as half of the features cover Central and Eastern Europe.

Readers with knowledge of French can also consult the catalog of the French government information service La Documentation Française for its numerous periodicals and occasional papers on Central and Eastern Europe. Many of the titles listed above were recommended by Dr. Edith Lhomel, whose selections constitute most of the Documentation Française bibliographic publications on Central and Eastern Europe.

Name Index

Agar, Mehmet 103
Ahtisaari, Marti 172
Albright, Madeleine 166, 169, 171, 172
Alexander I, King of Yugoslavia 178
Alia, Ramiz 106
Annan, Kofi 169
Antall, Jozef 55
Asmus, Ronald D. 164
Aspin, Les 164

Bachelet, Michel 138
Baker, James 155, 157, 158
Barthou, Louis 178
Berisha, Sali 61, 107, 162
Bettati, Mario 138, 139
Bismarck, Otto von 10, 22, 153
Bosevski, Valentin 135
Brandt, Willy 128
Brezhnev, Leonid 120
Brzezinski, Zbigniew 154, 166
Bush, George 156, 161

Calfa, Marian 160
Carson, Rachel 117
Ceaucescu, Nicolai 119, 126, 127
Chabrol, Claude 138
Chernomyrdin, Viktor 172

Christopher, Warren 162–166
Churchill, Winston 6
Ciller, Tansu 103
Cioran, Emil 26
Clark, Wesley 171, 172
Clinton, Bill 15, 152, 162, 163, 165, 168, 170, 172
Constant, Baron d'Estournelles de 14
Cousteau, Jacques 131
Custine, Marquis de 23

Debray, Regis 139
Delpal, Marie-Christine 139
Demirel, Suleyman 10
Dimitrov, Filip 135
Dole, Bob 165

Eagleburger, Lawrence 159, 162, 171
Eisenhower, Susan 168
Eisenstein, Serguei 49

Gaulle, Charles de 153
Gelbard, Richard 169
Genscher, Hans Dietrich 158, 159, 161
Georgescu, Vlad 22
Ghebali, Victor Yves 127
Girardin, Saint Marc 24
Gorbachev, Mikhail 127, 154–156,

158–160
Grachev, Pavel 166
Grass, Günter 153, 154
Grundmann, Reiner 115

Havel, Vaclav 11, 154, 159, 160, 163, 166
Hitler, Adolf 12
Hohenzollern, Charles 22
Holbrooke, Richard 166, 167, 170
Honecker, Erich 123, 157
Horn, Gyula 158
Hours, Bernard 139
Hoxha, Enver 39, 106, 119
Hunter, Robert E. 180
Huntington, Samuel P. 137, 140

Iliescu, Ion 66
Ilyés, Gyula 43, 49
Izetbegovic, Alija 63

Jancar-Webster, Barbara 121, 123, 136
Jaruzelski, Wojcheh 11, 46, 125
Jedlicki, Jerry 10
Jelavich, Barbara 22

Kafka, Franz 13, 45
Kaplan, Robert D. 21, 137, 140
Kennan, George 15, 168
Khrushchev, Nikita 153
Kinkel, Klaus 163
Kiseliov, Pavel 22
Klaus, Vaclav 18
Knabe, Hubertus 122, 123
Kohl, Helmut 155, 157, 158, 163
Kostov, Ivan 80
Kostov, Tchayko 128
Kouchner, Bernard 138, 139
Kosyrev, Andrey 164
Kugler, Richard L. 164
Kundera, Milan 20

Lake, Anthony 164, 165
Larrabee, Stephen F. 164
Liehm, Antonin 141
Lugar, Richard 165

Maiakovsky, Vladimir 45
Major, John 15, 158
Maurras, Charles 25
Mazowiecky, Tadeusz 11, 156

Meciar, Vladimir 54, 69, 73
Mesik, Juraj 122, 136
Michelet, Jules 23
Michnik, Adam 53
Milosevic, Slobodan 108, 167, 170–172, 175, 176
Mitterrand, François 11, 15, 16, 157
Modrow, Hans 158
Morrillon, Phillipe 138

Napoleon III 22
Nezmah, Bernard 66
Niksic, Miodrag 105
Nunn, Sam 167

Perry, William 166
Peter, the Great 21, 22
Pope Jean Paul II 103
Popov, Nikolai 128
Primakov, Yevgeny 171

Quinet, Edgar 23

Reed, John 24
Rugova, Ibrahim 162
Rühe, Volker 162, 163, 165, 166

Scowcroft, Brent 155
Serbes, Dragan 105
Stalin, Josef 12, 45, 157
Stoklasa, Jaroslav 118

Talbott, Strobe 164, 172
Thatcher, Margaret 157
Tito, Josip Broz 157, 178
Töpfer, Klaus 128
Tudjman, Franjo 7, 63, 65
Turcanu, Florin 25
Turkes, Alparslan 103

Vasilev, Valentin 135
Vershbow, Alexander 170
Vickery, Graham 131
Vucic, Borka 104
Vukovic, Goran 105

Wajda, Andrzej 49
Walesca, Lech 163
Weiner, Douglas R. 114
West, Rebecca 24
Wierzbicki, Zbigniew 127

Name Index

Wiesel, Elie 163
Wörner, Manfred 159, 164

Yeltsin, Boris 161, 163, 164, 167

Zapryanov, Anton 127
Zemunac, Ljubo 105
Zhirinovsky, Vladimir 165
Zhivkov, Todor 126, 127

Subject Index

Afghanistan 100, 102
Africa 13, 31, 139, 170
Albania 6, 9, 12, 13, 24, 26, 31, 32, 35, 38, 39, 41, 61, 62, 65, 67–72, 84, 104–107, 114, 125, 128, 133, 135, 157, 162, 171, 172, 177, 178
    Communist Party 126
    Ghegs 107
    "Greater Albania" 14, 174, 178
    journalism 61
    Kosovar Albanians 105, 106, 108, 170, 171, 176, 179
    media 61, 69, 71
    press legislation 68
    Sigurimi 106, 107
    Tosks 107
    Vlora 107
Algeria 32
Armenia 107, 125
Austria 12, 23, 106, 108, 117, 178
    Mürzteg Program 177
    Vienna 12, 24, 120
Austro-Hungarian/Habsburg Empire 8, 9, 13, 14, 22, 25, 31, 44, 177
Azerbaijan 100, 103

Balkans 5, 9, 10, 14–16, 17, 21, 22, 24, 25, 27, 31, 35, 40, 41, 62, 68, 174, 176

Balkan Wars (1912, 1913) 24, 31, 178
Black Sea 33, 117, 118
Congress of Berlin (1878) 24, 31
ethnic cleansing 173
intelligentsia 34
nationalism 15, 17, 23, 34, 47
Russo-Turkish Wars (1877–1878) 24
Baltic Countries 6, 9, 14, 18, 127, 152, 155, 169, 179
    Baltic Sea 18, 117
Belarus 113, 152, 177
Belgium 108, 120
    Belgian Constitution 8
Bosnia-Herzegovina 15, 31, 38, 40, 68, 71, 72, 139, 161, 162, 170, 174–178
    Bosnian War (1992–1995) 36, 107, 152, 157, 161, 163, 164, 166
    Dayton Peace Accords (1995) 26, 73, 104, 105, 167,
    Mostar 40
    Sarajevo 17, 32, 40
    Srebrenica 17, 163
Bulgaria 9, 12, 22, 23, 28, 31, 32, 35, 38, 41, 48, 53, 55, 71, 75, 78–83,

90, 91, 103–105, 116–118, 125, 127, 134–136, 176, 175, 178
    Communist Party 126
    currency crisis 86, 87
    economic crisis 80, 81
    Union of Democratic Forces 80, 135
    Sofia 12, 32, 120
Byzantine Empire 35

Canada 141
Caucasus 10, 100, 107
Central and Eastern Europe 5–11, 13, 14, 18, 32, 33, 47–50, 52, 62, 64, 70, 73, 75, 77, 81, 114, 116–118, 125, 128–130, 135, 141, 152, 179
    American model 48, 49, 67
    banking system 84
    Catholicism 40, 46, 47, 50
    Central East European Environmental Center 133
    Danube 114, 116, 117, 124,
    defamation laws 63–65
    foreign investments 82–83
    hate speech 70–71
    Jewish communities 14, 25, 39, 40, 100
    journalism 51–53
    Krakow Declaration 152, 161
    media and its privatization 56–58
    minority question 40
    press laws 63, 65, 67, 69
    privatization 77–82
    romanticism 23
Central Asia 10, 14, 100, 124, 152
China 154, 171, 179
    bombing of the Embassy 179
    Tibetan secessionism 179
"Clash of Civilizations" 7, 17, 137
Cold War 6, 10, 12, 17, 152, 153, 156, 157, 177, 178
Communism 26, 40, 41, 43, 44
Council of Europe 73
Croatia 7, 22, 23, 25, 31, 32, 38, 65, 156, 161, 177
    Dalmatia 140
    "Greater Croatia" 14
    press legislation 65, 73
    ustashe 178
    Vukovar 17

Cyprus 101, 104
    Nicosia 101
Czech Republic 6, 8, 11, 12, 14, 48, 62, 78, 82, 85, 88, 90–92, 108, 122, 134, 137, 152, 160, 163, 166, 168, 169, 172
    Bohemia 11, 49
    Prague 12, 45, 163
Czechoslovakia 6, 9–14, 18, 46, 53, 57, 67, 116–118, 122, 124–127, 135, 152, 154, 157, 161

Denmark 120

East Germany/German Democratic Republic 13, 123, 128, 152, 153, 157–159
    Communist Party (SED) 157, 158
    demilitarization of 155, 158
Eastern Orthodoxy 7, 9, 14, 18, 22
    Patriarch of Constantinople 36, 38
Egypt 101
Estonia 18, 62, 85, 125
European Bank for Reconstruction and Development (EBRD) 87, 88, 131, 133, 134
European Community/Union (EU) 11, 19, 40, 62, 83, 101, 104, 132, 152, 153, 155, 160, 163, 171, 172, 174, 176, 177
    enlargement 19
    European Convention on Money Laundering (Law 18–III) 101
    European Integration 7
    PHARE 131–133
    Stability Pact for Southeastern Europe 176
    Technical Assistance for the Commonwealth of Independent States (TACIS) 132
European Court for Human Rights (Strasbourg) 65, 66
European Parliament 129

Finland 117, 120
France 10, 14, 23, 25, 64, 113, 131,

Subject Index

138, 139, 157, 159, 161, 171, 178
French Revolution 23
Paris 25
Versailles Peace Treaty 10, 25

Georgia 107, 125
Abkhazia 98
Germany 6, 9–11, 13, 17–19, 23, 25, 117, 121, 123, 128, 129, 151, 152–155, 157, 162, 163, 165, 172, 177
Basic Law 155, 163
Berlin/Bonn 12, 24, 25, 151, 153, 157
Genscher Plan 159
German confederation 152–154
German-Czech Relations 157, 159, 160
germanization 10
German minorities 10, 39
German-Polish Relations 11, 157, 159, 160
German Social Democrats (SDP) 157
German Unification (1989) 152–155, 157–159
Kohl government 128, 154, 155
Mitteleuropa 11
Munich Agreement (1938) 10, 12
Oder-Neisse Line 11, 159
Ottawa Agreements on German Unification 158
Silesian Germans 160
Sudeten Germans 11, 160
Treaty on the Final Settlement of Germany ("two plus four" treaty) 11, 158, 159
Zentraleuropa 11
Greece 13, 17, 24, 28, 39–41, 71, 104, 117, 170–172, 178
Athens 25, 32
Greek War of Independence (1823) 31, 38
population exchange agreements 40

Hungary 6, 8, 12, 13, 18, 32, 44, 46, 50, 53, 68, 77–79, 82, 91, 104, 108, 116–118, 121, 135, 152, 156, 158, 160, 161, 163, 166, 168, 169, 172, 177
banking crisis 85, 88, 90
Budapest 12, 32
Budapest Stock Exchange 91
Horthy regime 9
Hungarian minorities 7, 39, 172

India 32, 162, 179
International Monetary Fund (IMF) 27, 28, 80, 86, 87, 105
International Union for the Conservation of Nature 132
International War Crimes Tribunal (the Hague) 71, 173

Iran 31, 102
Ireland 154
Islam 9, 22, 36
Israel 101
Italy 9, 25, 105, 107, 172, 178
Italian mafia 105, 107
Otranto 32

Japan 155, 162

Kazakhstan 6, 155
Korea 154
Korean War 178
Kosovo 13, 26, 32, 108, 139, 152, 161, 162, 167, 169–179
Kosovo Liberation Army (KLA) 108, 169–171, 173, 176
Kosovo Protection Force 176
Operation "Horseshoe" 170
partition of 174
Pristina Airport 175
Racak massacre 170
Rambouillet Peace Agreement 171, 172
Kuwait 161

Lebanon 101
Lithuania 6, 13, 160, 165

Macedonia (FYROM) 13, 14, 26, 31, 32, 38, 39, 68, 71, 103, 106–

108, 161, 162, 171, 172, 176, 177
    Greek embargo on (1992–1995) 108
    Macedonian Albanians 108
    Orthodox Church 39
    Skopje 32
Malta 32
Middle East 10, 31, 154
Moldova 69
Montenegro 65, 105, 106, 172, 177
Morocco 31

North Atlantic Treaty Organization (NATO) 26–28, 151–179
    1989 Brussels Summit 158
    enlargement of, 19, 152, 155, 158, 161, 164–166, 177, 178
    humanitarian intervention 173, 174, 179, 180
    Implementation Force (IFOR) 180
    Kosovo Force (KFOR) 173, 181
    London Declaration (1990) 159
    NATO-Russian Founding Act (1997) 168, 171
    NATO-Russian Permanent Joint Council 168, 171
    NATO-Soviet Relations 154, 155
    North Atlantic Assembly (NAA) 163, 170
    North Atlantic Cooperation Council (NACC) 161, 166
    North Atlantic Council (NAC) 159, 160, 169
    North Atlantic Treaty (1949) 169, 175
    Partnership for Peace (PfP) 164–168
    Stabilization Force (SFOR) 175, 180
Northern Ireland 41

Organization for Economic Cooperation and Economic Development (OECD) 118, 119, 130, 134

Organization (Conference) for Security and Cooperation in Europe (OSCE) 120, 159–162, 166, 174
    Helsinki Final Act (1975) 120
    Kosovo Verification Mission (KVM) 170
Ottoman Empire 5, 9, 10, 14, 15, 22–24, 27, 31–36, 39, 41, 177
    Battle of Kosovo (1389) 10
    Istanbul/Constantinople 22, 31, 41
    millet system 35–40

Pakistan 102, 107, 177
Pan-Slavism 12
    Slavic Congress of Prague (1848) 12
Poland 6, 9–11, 18, 43, 46–48, 52, 55, 57, 62, 68, 77–79, 82, 91, 92, 108, 116, 123, 124, 126, 127, 132, 135, 152, 156–161, 166, 168, 169, 172, 177
    Gdansk/Danzig 157
    partition of 12
    Polish-German Treaty (1990) 160
    restructuring the banking system 84, 85, 88, 90
    Silesia 18
    Solidarity movement 6, 53, 118, 121, 123, 124
Prussia 6, 10, 12, 44, 177

Romania 8, 9, 12, 13, 22, 23, 26–28, 39, 53, 55, 62, 65–67, 71, 82, 91, 92, 104, 116, 125, 127, 135, 172, 176, 178
    banking crisis 89, 90
    Bessarabia 23
    Bucharest 12, 25
    Orthodox Church 39
    privatization 80
Russia 5, 6, 9, 10, 12, 14, 15, 17, 19, 21–24, 28, 44, 69, 80, 101, 151–153, 161–163, 165, 167, 168, 171, 172, 175, 177–179
    Anglo Russian Entente (1907) 178
    Chechnya 152, 167, 179

Subject Index

devaluation of the ruble 84, 92
Duma 165
Kaliningrad/Königsberg 10, 18, 153, 180
KGB 100
Krasnodar 100
Moscow 26, 153, 156, 157, 158, 161, 174, 179
"near abroad" 14, 98
Russian Empire 14
Russian minorities 14
Russo-German Treaty on Good Neighborliness, Partnership and Cooperation (1990) 159, 164
Saint Petersburg 23, 24, 100, 120
Siberia 141

Saudia Arabia 161, 177
Serbia/Federal Republic of Yugoslavia 7, 9, 10, 13, 22, 25, 26–28, 31, 32, 38, 41, 67, 68, 72, 101, 104–106, 108, 152, 156, 161, 162, 169–172, 174–178
Belgrade 7, 25, 70, 105
"Greater Serbia" 14, 108
Patriarch 39
Vojvodina 172
Yugoslav Army (JNA) 104
Slovak Republic 6, 14, 52, 55, 65–71, 73, 74, 78, 82, 89, 90, 92, 113, 121, 125, 136, 163, 166, 168
Slovak union of defenders of nature and landscape (SZOPK) 121, 122, 126
Slovenia 6, 7, 27, 31, 32, 62, 66, 106, 123, 161, 177
Somalia 139
Soviet Union 5–7, 11, 13–16, 44, 83, 99, 109, 115, 117, 122, 124, 125, 127, 152, 153, 156, 158–161, 178
Brezhnev Doctrine 156
Chernobyl disaster 113–116, 120, 125–127
ComEcon 19
glasnost 113, 114, 125, 156
perestroika 125, 156

Soviet bloc 12, 113, 116, 118, 120, 128, 135
Sovietization 10
Spain 9
Sri Lankans 107
Switzerland 108
Syria 101

Tadjikistan 100
Taiwan 154, 179
Turkey 10, 17, 22, 23, 32, 41, 101, 102, 105, 106, 117, 157, 170, 171, 177
Edirne 103
Gray Wolves 101, 103
Kirklareli 103
Kurds 102, 103, 107, 138
PKK 102, 103
Turkish Intelligence Organization (MIT) 102, 103
Turkish minorities 9, 126, 127
Turkish Republic of Northern Cyprus 101

Ukraine 6, 13, 14, 31, 100, 113, 152, 155
L'vov 6
United Kingdom 68, 120, 157, 159, 172, 178
London 23
United Nations (UN) 119, 120, 131, 138, 152, 155, 161–163, 170, 173–176, 181
blue helmets 154
sanctions against Iraq 102
sanctions against Serbia-Montenegro 104, 105
Security Council 169, 174, 175
UN Charter 170
UN Conference on Environment and Development 131
UN Drug Control Program (UNDCP) 98
UN Economic Commission for Europe 119, 120
UNESCO 67, 72, 131
UN General Assembly 138
in Macedonia (UNPREDEP) 162

UN Program for the
    Environment 128
UNSC Resolutions 1160, 1203
    (Preventive Deployment
    Force 1998) 169, 173
United States of America 16, 21, 48,
    63, 64, 82, 99, 109, 120, 139,
    151–156, 158, 161, 162, 166–
    171, 173–177
    Bush administration 154–156,
        169
    Central Intelligence Agency
        (CIA) 172
    "Christmas Warning" 162, 171
    Clinton administration 137,
        166, 170
    Congress 121
    Department of Defense/
        Pentagon 162–164, 166
    Environmental Protection
        Agency 133
    Institute of Peace and Foreign
        Policy Research 137
    National Security Council 165
    Pentagon Defense Planning
        Guidance 161, 162
    RAND 164
    Resurgent Emergent Global
        Threat (REGT) 161
    Senate 169
    State Department 164–166,
        172
    U.S.-Russian Relations 162–
        169, 175
    Washington 152, 153, 155,
        157, 176

Vatican 39
Venetian Republic 31, 32
Vietnam 140

Warsaw Pact 8, 19, 151, 152, 156–160
Western Europe 21, 26, 41, 63, 64,
    102, 109
World Bank 28, 105
World War I 8, 9, 14, 17, 24, 25, 27,
    177
World War II 10–12, 14, 25, 34, 57,
    153, 177–178

Yugoslavia (former) 7, 12, 14, 17, 18,
    19, 44, 70, 71, 99, 102, 103, 105,
    114, 118, 121, 128, 135, 140,
    152, 154, 156, 157, 161 165, 169,
    178
    Contact Group 28, 169
    Kingdom of Slovenes,
        Croatians and Serbs 25
    press laws 63, 70

Contributors and Editors

HELEN DARBISHIRE is a Human Rights and Media Consultant and Europe Consultant for Article 19. She is presently concentrating on Albania.

CATHERINE DURANDIN: Historian, specialist in political thought and strategy in Central, South-Central and Eastern Europe. Professor of Romanian language and civilization, Professor of international Relations, INALCO (l'Institut National des Langues et Civilisations Orientales); European Studies department: "The Balkans of the XXth Century," University of Marne la Vallee; Chief managing editor, "Europe Today" series, l'Harmattan publishing house. Former Director of International Studies, INALCO. Courses, seminars, conferences in Amsterdam, Bucharest, Prague. Author: "Nations, Nationalisms: New Stakes and Crises in Europe of the 1990's," in *Nations, Nationalismes, Transitions, Terrains*, Paris: Editions Sociales, 1993. *Europe's Third World: Balkans Between the West and Russia* (to be published).

MARCIN FRYBES: Polish sociologist, specialized in the media, trade unions and Socialist issues in Central Europe. Researcher since 1990, Centre d'Analyse et d'Intervention Sociologiques (CADIS-EHESS). Project Director, "The New Mass Media Scene in Central Europe," (in progress). Co-directed "Le Nouveau Paysage Mediatique à l'Est," *L'Autre Europe* (no. 32–33), L'Age d'Homme, Winter 1996. Former correspondent in France, Polish daily, *Gazeta Wyborcza*.

HALL GARDNER: Professor and Chair of the International Affairs Department of the American University of Paris; Professor, University of Westminster, The Diplomatic Academy of London, Regent Campus Paris Programme; Visiting Professor, Johns Hopkins Paul H. Nitze School of Advanced International Studies (1989–90) and Johns Hopkins SAIS-Nanjing (1988–89). Author: *Surviving the Millennium: American Global Strategy, the*

Collapse of the Soviet Empire, and the Question of Peace (Praeger, 1994), and of *Dangerous Crossroads: Europe, Russia, and the Future of NATO* (Praeger, 1997). Member of the Advisory Board of the *Cicero Foundation* (Paris; Maastricht) and of the *Committee on Atlantic Studies*.

LEE W. HUEBNER: Professor of Communication Studies and Journalism at Northwestern University; former publisher of the International Herald Tribune (1979–1993); Special Assistant to the President and Deputy Director, White House Writing and Research Staff (1969–1974); member of the Board of Trustees and former President, American University of Paris; chairman, Center for the Study of International Communications.

OLEG KOBTZEFF: Researcher in comparative historic geography (Danube, Baltic Sea, Arctic, Pacific Rim). Assistant professor of political science, American University of Paris. Researcher, Collège de France, Center for Slavic History, University of Panthéon-Sorbonne (also post-graduate studies advisor, 1992–1995). Acting head curator, Gogol Library (now merged with National Library of Italy), Rome (1988–1991). Co-founding director, Veniaminov Institute (ethnographic museum and archives), Kodiak, Alaska (1985–1988). Member, Byzantine Society, University of Oxford, Oxford & Athens. Years of social work (education, relief and papers) with refugees from Central and Eastern Europe.

MICHEL KOUTOUZIS: Greek-born specialist in geopolitics and drugs. Senior researcher at l'Observatoire Geopolitique des Drogues. Advisor to the Greek Minister of Culture (1981–87). Director, *Atlas Mondial des Drogues*, PUF, 1996. Co-author: *Geopolitique et Geostrategies des Drogues*, Paris: Economica, 1996. Co-author: *Drogues à l'Est: Logique des Guerres et de Marche*, Politique Étrangere: Sécurité Européenne, Horizon 1996, Paris: l'Institut Français des Relations Internationales (IFRI), 1995.

ANTONIN LIEHM: Czech-born founder and editor of *Lettre Internationale* (1984), a sociological, political, philosophical, but essentially literary journal of cultural exchange published in four West and eight East European capitals, including Belgrade, Bucharest, Budapest, Sofia, Prague, Warsaw and Zagreb. Member of International PEN, American Association for the Advancement of Slavic Studies, Society for Cinema Studies, and Czech Society of Arts and Sciences. Professor, City University of New York (1970–76), University of Pennsylvania (1977–81), University of Paris (1982–87), École des Hauts Études en Sciences Sociales (EHESS) (1987–89)

BERNARD LORY: Historian, specialist on the Balkans. Professor of Balkan History and Civilization, l'Institut National des Langues et Civilisations Orientales (INALCO). Researcher in Novi Sad and Belgrade, Yugoslavia (1984–85), and in Bulgaria (1979–81). Author: *Balkan Europe (L'Europe Balkanique de 1945 à Nos Jours)* (Ellipses: Paris, 1996).

Contributors and Editors

NADÈGE RAGARU: Political scientist, specialized in East European politics and economics. Lecturer, Political Science, Faculty of Philosophy, Sofia University (Soros Foundation Civic Education Project); speaker, CERI conferences, Paris. PhD, l'Institut d'Études Politiques (ScPo). *Political Culture and Democratic Consolidation in Eastern Europe: The Case of Bulgaria* (in progress); MA., International Relations and East European Studies, University of South Carolina.

JACQUES RUPNIK: Political Scientist. Director of Research, Centre d'Études et de Recherches Internationales; Professor, l'Institut d'Études Politiques (ScPo) in Paris. Executive Director, International Commission for the Balkans, Carnegie Endowment for International Peace. Advisor to Vaclav Havel (1990–92); BBC World Service Central Europe specialist (1977–82); Harvard University Russian Research Center (1974–75), M.A., Harvard University.

ELINORE SCHAFFER: Her career has been in education. Having obtained her M.A. from Columbia University, she has conducted communication seminars and taught language at French universities, in industry, in China, and in Bosnia-Herzegovina. Returning to her original interest in political science—her major field at Cornell University where she received her B.A., she now organizes conferences on global issues.

DATE DUE

HIGHSMITH 45230